Dedication

I dedicate this book to the memory of Mrs. Searle. She faithfully folded thousands of bandages each month for the Red Cross, and produced innumerable quantities of carefully stamped and trimmed Communion wafers for the Church. She never complained, though she suffered much. She always had a kind word and a smile for everyone. She never condemned, but on her deathbed I heard her utter the bitter word. She poured out her soul unto the end.

Acknowledgment

I want to express special thanks to Willy Gommel, a fellow member of the Temple of the People at the Halcyon theosophical community, without whose interest and effort this manuscript would have continued to collect dust on a back shelf. He transformed my messy manuscript into a fully professional typeset and laser-printed copy and urged me to go forward on publication. I feel that Willy has a special connection with Mother even though he never met her.

Table of Contents

Preface

Who Was Mother Jennie?

Mother Jennie was an extremely talented psychic. She was also a pioneer feminist of the early twentieth century. But above all, she was a true and living saint.

Hers was a life which followed the classic pattern of all shamans, saints and mystics -- unusual psychism during childhood, a period of testing and shamanic illness, a "dark night of the soul," and inevitable appearance of tutorial spirits who would guide her into full expression and service.

It was my great privilege to know Mother Jennie intimately for six years. I brought many people to her, helped care for her during intermittent periods of illness, and served as friend and confidant. Everyone unburdened themselves upon her, and from time to time the need would arise for her to pour out her soul to me. But I remained her student.

As a professor of religions and an ordained man, I must say that she taught me more about these things than theological school and graduate school combined. She exemplified the highest standards of selfless service. She would have been a canonized saint in any religious tradition she had chosen, for her life was a chronicle of healings and "miracles." It was consecrated to the deepest and most sincere pursuit of spiritual living and service to humanity. Even her dreaming activity was centered upon helping those in need by working, as she said, "in the astral." It matters not whether one accepts the reality of this kind of service, for it demonstrates the depth of her commitment. It had totally permeated her unconscious mind.

She was led out of orthodox religious channels by her spirit Teachers and became one totally by herself. In the early part of the century the ordination of women was completely unacceptable, and Jennie received ordination in an obscure Spiritualist sect. During her life she refused payment for her services as an ordained minister and clairvoyant counselor. She preached and delivered inspired discourse, but would not accept students for "psychic development." She favored the "natural opening" which would come to each person at the proper time, rather than what she called "forced development."

There are many books on psychics and psychism, but the intention of this book is to go beyond the merely phenomenal aspect and glimpse the spiritual potential of mediumship. Although much of the subject matter deals with psychic phenomena, it has been my strategy to focus attention upon Mother Jennie's autobiography. This is the true value of the book, for it reveals the inner workings that cannot normally be found in later legends from which the lives of saints are written. Mother Jennie was an intensely human person, as I am certain all the saints were. Here we come face to face with the real-life and day-to-day developments which combine to produce a living saint.

As a scholar of the comparison and phenomenology of religions, and one familiar with saints' lives in many traditions, I have tried to interpret and illuminate Jennie's life-history as it unfolds for the reader. The hope is that each person who reads the book might be able to relate his or her own life-development to Jennie's motifs and patterns of discovery, for they are archetypal.

But Mother Jennie's story cannot be told without reference to me, for I am the narrator. It is important for me to indicate the ways I was affected and changed through my apprenticeship with her. There is no such thing as an unbiased, objective narration, and to present this material as such would be deceptive. It is too important to present without giving the reader a full perspective. For this reason I have included brief explanations of how I met her, certain interactions or experiences I had, and some of the events that occurred after her passing in February of 1976, two weeks after her ninety-seventh birthday.

I wrote most of this manuscript in the fall of 1973, but was held back from making a serious attempt to publish it. Jennie was too old to handle the hordes that would have descended upon her tiny Santa Cruz home in the wake of such publicity. At the time she was ninety-five years old, in fair health, and seeing over two hundred people a month! But now the time has come to make her known.

Mother Jennie consecrated her life to the service of God and mankind. May it serve as an inspiration and a guiding light for all who seek wisdom, truth and the inner rulership of God!

Lewis S. Keizer, M.Div., Ph.D.
Santa Cruz, California
October, 1976

Introduction

The most crucial thing to understand about spiritual awakening is its subjectivity. It is not that one type of religious experience is more valid than another, nor that an initiation into Sikhism is necessarily any more advanced than a conversion to Jesus religion. Religious formality, structure and language are cultural, and hopefully we are beginning to let go of the idea that some cultures (ours in particular, or perhaps the other fellow's in particular) are more "spiritually advanced" than others.

What we all have in common is our humanity and our personal subjectivity. It is through the complex medium of symbols, images and names associated with cultural and personal mythology that we experience what is called the Divine. That is why Black Elk sees the Six Grandfathers when he makes his shamanic ascent into the sky, but St. Stephen sees Jesus Christ sitting at the "right hand" of Yahweh.

The question of authenticity, then, is not one to be applied between various streams of human religious tradition. It is rather to be applied to each instance of religious experience -- to each occurrence within one person's development. Thus the ancient Christian imperative to try out the spirits to discern "whether they are of God" (I John 4.1) does not condone a process of exclusion against other religious traditions. If anything, it emphasizes the necessity to be circumspect about the quality and authenticity of one's own religious experience.

Is it possible to judge the authenticity of another person's spiritual life? On the whole I'd say no. One has enough to do just keeping himself straight. But by long-time and intimate contact with another, I find that it is possible to develop a general feeling for the quality of that person's inner life. After six years with Mother Jennie, I can say with deep certainty that this woman was truly a saint.

But before I recount my experiences with Jennie, I want to set forth the intellectual reservations I do have in telling the story.

For one thing, it is a "story." No one was there with a camera and tape recorder to verify what I remember. Others may have seen and interpreted things differently. No two witnesses really agree.

More important, anyone who has worked in literature, religions and oral history knows that memory is the stuff of which legends are born. With William James, I must confess that it is my very human tendency to exaggerate a story in order to communicate what I felt as the miraculous reality underlying a particular event. I've watched myself do it, and in telling some of my Mother Jennie stories I can't honestly say how much of what I now remember has been edited in through my own oral transmission.

I say this because I want the reader to know that I am aware of the process behind a good miracle story, and in this consciousness I will do my best to be as objective as possible. Since I understand the nuts and bolts of this process, I may be able to circumvent its power to some degree.

This, then, is not a book of miracles whose purpose is to amaze the reader with the same stupefaction that the writer has felt, like (for example) Castaneda's works on Don Juan. Again, I do not wish to poeticize Mother Jennie, as the Poet Laureate of Kansas did in his wonderful book, Black Elk Speaks. My purpose is to present the reader with as much of the same data, including doubts and attempts at analysis, as I myself had at my disposal while undergoing these experiences.

The reason for this concern is most important: I have come to find that it is not the mechanics of a "miracle" that is of first importance. Rather, it is the force, power, reason or "spirit" behind it. To put it another way, as Jennie was fond of saying, "It is not the messenger that is of first importance, but the message."

In John's Gospel, which represents one of the earliest mystic traditions in Christian thought, the "signs and wonders" of various magicians and thaumaturges are disdained. Rather, spiritual importance is attached to the semeia, the symbolic actions of a typological and allegorical nature which Jesus, like the ancient prophets, demonstrated sometimes in the most subtle ways. The editors of the Gospel make frequent reference to the connection between the activity of the Holy Spirit and the process of "remembrance" experienced by the followers of Jesus' Way: "When therefore he was risen from the dead, his disciples remembered that he had said this unto them, and they believed the scripture, and the word which Jesus had said" (John 2.22). It is said that after Jesus had been raised from the dead, the Holy Spirit will be given to help the disciples remember the words of Jesus (John 14.26).

It is this enlightened and spiritualized remembrance which will be the vehicle for the new divine truth (John 16.13). By meditating upon the life and symbolic works of the Master Jesus, the words of Jesus are "re-membered" and new words are received.

This is surely integral to the process of remembering my experiences with Mother Jennie. For me they were highly significant and meaningful experiences. But writing the book itself is a meaningful experience, and in writing down what I have known, new things become known to me. Not new facts, words or events, but clearer ways of seeing things in my memory.

What I have to say, then, is by no means a fiction. It is a thoroughly honest attempt to recount my personal historia with Mother Jennie. But it is a "history," that is, a narrative story. It is literary.

The same must be said for Jennie's remembrance of her own life. It is an "inspired remembrance, and therefore, like Jung's autobiography, it is a spiritual history. Being subjective, its veracity resides in the authenticity of Jennie's own religious experience.

Why did I see Mother Jennie with such special eyes? In retrospect I realize that old persons have always fascinated me. Furthermore, women have been instrumental to my growth in our patriarchal culture.

But most of all, I remember a strange parable or personal myth that I wrote down at the age of eighteen. It grew out of certain childhood fantasies which I later recognized as the psychological germs of Platonic thought. It went like this:

When I was a tiny infant, a beautiful old woman stood by my crib. She took me in her arms and with a tender smile whispered into my ear. In that moment she imparted all truth and knowledge to me -- all wisdom and science. But I was only a baby, and couldn't understand.

Now I am a man. Somewhere in the deep recesses of consciousness every gem of wisdom remains to be discovered. It is for me to uncover the treasures which were entrusted to me as an infant, and to share them.

So you see, Mother Jennie was a kind of archetypal figure for me. As it is said, "When the student is ready, the Teacher appears."

But she was not my personal "Teacher" alone. Hundreds of others sat at her feet. Every Tuesday night at 7:30 p.m., anywhere from twenty to fifty people would squeeze into her tiny living room. These were people of all ages and philosophies. A young flower-lady might be curled up on the floor breast-feeding her baby while a well-dressed matron from San Jose sat behind her supporting the young woman's back with her knees.

In 1973, several people contributed to buy Jennie a new rug for the living room. The old one had been worn out by countless visitors. When it had been installed, everyone took special care to avoid soiling it with muddy shoes during the winter. As the constituency of the Tuesday night meetings changed, the shoe-removing gesture became a kind of courteous ceremony. I suppose this is the way all liturgy develops. As time went on, very few of the people who came to hear Mother Jennie's discourses on God, Spirit and Christ remembered that removing their shoes had any purely mundane or practical significance. They did not come for mundane reasons.

They came to Mother Jennie to assuage a hunger for inner life which had gone begging in conventional churches, synagogues and temples. At the little house on Delaware Street they came into contact with reality rather than theory. Here they were sown with life-giving seeds like a plowed field.
This is a harsh judgment against institutional religion, but sainthood always is. It seems to flower when orthodoxy has made too many concessions to secularism. There has always been a Rumi or a Francis to point the way for earnest seekers, especially in the hardest times.

Institutional religion does not pretend to be "mystical" beyond a certain point. Its aims and goals are social. Community creeds take precedence over individual growth, and no one really expects much in the way of ecstatic experience. Even the charismatic churches are group-oriented with their glossolalia, which itself is the least of the charisms. "Tongues" is a kind of spiritual Tinkertoy, a "sign" for those without faith.

But public religion serves at least one useful purpose for the individual. It provides a man-made purgatory for persons in the first stages of spiritual awakening to test and try themselves; a place to stand naked and feel the flames of that which burns within, consuming itself; a place to discover the outer bars of the prison, and to learn the freedom of Spirit by experiencing what it is not.

Perhaps that is what this book is most about. It is a judgment against religious orthodoxy, which excluded a great preacher and saint from its pale because she was a woman who heard "voices."

For Mother Jennie, personal religious knowledge did not come through books, sermons, lectures or other vicarious means. It came directly to her through visions, dreams, auditions, psychic manifestations and especially the voices of her Teachers.

"One cannot know until one has experienced," she loved to say. "And one cannot teach what one does not know. Knowledge lies within. Seek within!"

Mother Jennie was a woman called to God by the Christian ministry in an age when women were not recognized by the churches in this role. The only Christian-oriented churches who recognized the authority of female ministry were the transcendental and New Thought movements of the late nineteenth century. Spiritualism was part of this movement. Since Jennie was gifted with powers of clairvoyance, clairaudience and mediumistic sensitivity by the time she had reached her early thirties, it was inevitable that she be ordained in a spiritualistic church. Her particular one was called the Church of Scientific Natural Law, which no longer exists. Jennie became an associate of Mother Clark, who founded the Orrilla Sisterhood and Brotherhood. Under her tutelage and with the help of Maud Lord Drake and two other gifted mediums, Jennie became a "Mother" along with her friend Francis Becker, who presided over the large spiritualist temple in San Francisco for many years.

But mediumship and psychism were just a phase for Mother Jennie -- a transition leading into a devoted inner life of prayer and meditation. She never allowed herself to go into trance. Instead, she would "listen" to the voices of her Teachers. They were not spirit-guides or "controls." Rather, they were sanctified and ascended Masters of Wisdom. They were not one, but many, who existed in the great communio sanctorum which comprehends all religions and human cultures. They included Omar, a Hindu of the Temple of Truth, and Savonarola, the martyred Florentine Christian monk. I have heard Jennie "greet" people in Sanskrit, Coptic, Greek, and other languages of which she had no personal knowledge, because she was speaking for her Teachers!

Jennie was an ardent feminist, and called upon God as both Mother and Father. The Orrilla Sisterhood, founded in the nineteenth century, surely ranks as the oldest spiritual arm of the contemporary women's movement. God was a Divine Mother as well as Father for Jennie, and for this revelation alone she stands as a theologian of some importance to Western religion.

She was a vital spirit, sharp as a whipcrack, and had achieved remarkable mastery over self and flesh. She spoke about things that were universal, yet no one who attended the discourses failed to abstract something of critical importance to his or her specific circumstances, especially when in need of counsel. Her examples and illustrations were near at hand, being drawn from the matrix of things familiar to each person. She was warm, natural, down to earth and practical. Her words carried a power to transform and work in human consciousness, like the words of Jesus. They stuck, like barbed seeds.

The main impression one had upon meeting her was of sincere warmth and kindness. But she had tremendous courage and shamanic physical endurance for her tiny ninety-pound frame. These had been developed during her homesteading years as a plains nurse in Canada. Once in a long while someone would try to show her up or compete with the discourse. In such a case she would hand out a stunning rebuke with the precision of a surgeon removing a diseased organ. One was abruptly brought to understand why age was held in respect and awe before the advent of America's youth culture!

Her spiritual power was rooted in the sensitive and poetic vocabulary that the Teachers brought and expressed through Jennie's vigorous humor. She was above all authentic. She treasured the things that nature and experience had proven for her. There was nothing hypocritical or theoretical about what she said. She taught what she knew to be true.

I saw Mother Jennie perform incredible feats of mediumship on countless occasions. She insisted that I remain during intimate sessions with persons bereaved or caught up in tragedy. I learned about the healing of the soul -- dynamic work that would seem more like magic or mumbo-jumbo to clinical psychologists. I watched her bring dead plants back to life by caressing them, and helped her bring one of my students, paralyzed in a swimming accident and given no hope, through to an amazing recovery. Neurologists held a special convention on Debbie K.'s remarkable progress. These and many other phenomena occurred regularly around Mother Jennie, but always as a sign for the beholder pointing beyond the phenomena themselves to the reality which sustained them.

Jennie's constant companion was a faithful black poodle named Cindy. The perfect communication between these two was reminiscent of the legendary ability of sages, saints and shamans to speak with animals. She maintained that all creatures, even plants and stones, have intelligence and can receive thoughts as "feelings."

She accepted the spiritualistic doctrine of reincarnation not because she had been ordained a Spiritualist, but because she had experienced first-hand glimpses of her own past lives. Many mystics of the West as well as the East, from Pythagoras and Plato through the early Church Fathers like Origen and certain European saints, have espoused the concept. The New Testament preserves strands of reincarnationist tradition (cf. John 9.2 et al). Whenever the mystic sets his sights upon ineffable heights and attempts to strive toward a far-distant goal, experience teaches that the path must be much longer than one brief lifetime. In any profound thought about God's justice and man's evolution, life must be recognized as continuous.

The critical thing for Jennie was not spiritualistic theory, but the inner experience and self-revelation of one who is a "sensitive." She often reminded her students that "We are the greatest mystery; therefore, look within." She had visions and memories of previous lives, and compared these experiences to the random dropping and lifting of a phonograph needle onto the surface of a record. Eventually she could put together the snatches of melody and understand the whole song.

Mother Jennie saw herself as a member of all religious traditions. Above her bed was an Islamic prayer for peace. In one corner of the bedroom a Hindu lesson was quaintly framed, and in another corner, a painting of the Buddha. Much of her wisdom had been influenced by American Indian religion, which she knew first-hand from her homesteading years. One of her first Teachers was a Cherokee girl who appeared in visions and auditions, speaking wise proverbs in childish rhyme. Jennie was also conversant with many of the world's Scriptures.

Her first love was mystic Christianity. She devoted many hours to "reading, not just skimming" her old leather Bible. She interpreted the Bible with the same freedom that Paul and the early Christians used -- not literalistically but allegorically, typologically and with profound spiritual insight. Like the ancient Kabbalists, she would correlate one verse to another and pull new meanings from them. She compared the process to opening a nut. The literal meaning was the hard outer shell. In order to find the real "meat," one needed to meditate and listen to the Spirit of God.

Christ was within each person, "entombed in the sepulcher of self." The story of Jesus' life was the key to all mysteries, and one which we must all act out, since the pattern of Christ exists within us. We are the Cross and the Crucified One together. The mind is like the serpent of Paradise, a deceiver. It is unstable like water, and is the source of prejudice, hatred, intolerance and self-destructive anxiety. It must be mastered by meditation and the exercise of Godly will in daily life so that it can become a "clear, pure channel through which Spirit can flow." In this sense, all persons must become "mediums" for God's Spirit.

She warned against "forced development" and refused to teach classes in psychic sensitivity. Mastery was "line upon line, precept upon precept." No temple could be built in a day, and the way to God was long and hard, with the ever-present danger of losing one's balance and "sliding down from the heights." When this happened, the whole distance would have to be traversed again.

Spiritual labor, she emphasized, was accomplished in unseen ways, masked in the myth and allegory of daily life. There was no need of rigorous asceticism, dietary restriction or prolonged meditation. Misuse of the "Serpent-Fire," she warned, could "burn the brain." Christ's way was easy and practical. It was to be trodden in the company of other human beings and in daily interaction with them. Forgiveness, peace and joy were natural things which lay in the grasp of anyone willing to take them. God was not harsh and punitive, nor was "hell" anything more than the condition each person created in his own soul. In the same way, joy could be created.

That is not to say the way to God is effortless. Indeed, as Mother Jennie often emphasized, it was fraught with testing and trial. But God's strength would be sufficient for each soul who opened to receive it. "There is no Devil," she said. "There is only the evil of our own nature," by which we test and try ourselves unknowingly. We cause much of our own suffering by neglecting responsibility for it and blaming someone else or other outer forces.

Not only are we our own Satan, but within us is the Christ. The key to this "greatest mystery" is to be found in silence. We carry in us the "seeds" of what we are to become, and suffer the results of what we have been. "It is just and equal for every soul," she often said.

Mother Jennie prescribed a brief meditation for those who asked. It was a single-pointed concentration upon the "holy white Light of Christ" within each person. She advised no more than five minutes each day at first. This could eventually be prolonged to a period of fifteen minutes, but thought and the "mind" had to be controlled. Otherwise one would simply "drift," and the image-making faculty of the mind would gain more, not less, power. Inner control was to be gained by commanding the mind in the name of Jesus Christ to be still. At this writing I have pursued the meditation faithfully for nearly seven years, and it has brought me much more than I can express.

The meditation is not the sum and substance of spiritual growth, but simply a helpful tool in preparing the soul for daily work. It is like the rudder of a ship -- a very small part, but extremely effective. It is not designed to repress, but to sublimate. It is through measured conscious sublimation that yogic self-mastery is attained in daily life, and this is exercised in the challenges of the day.

"Study Nature, and She will make an obeisance and reveal Her secrets unto you." This favorite maxim typified Jennie's love of flowers, landscapes and the lessons that all nature had brought to her. Like a medieval alchemist, she had undertaken the divine work of transmutation as nature teaches -- with simplicity, humility and in due season.

Her life was long and productive -- an epic of discovery, suffering and overcoming. She was constantly derided by Christian fundamentalists as a witch, and regarded by some of her neighbors as eccentric, to say the least. The traditional churches refused to accept her as a preacher and minister of God's Word, yet I'd never heard it so clearly as from her lips. She touched the lives of people in many lands during her ministry, and each month received mail from all over the world.

I like to think of myself as a rational man and a scholar. Perhaps writing this book is my way of integrating what Mother Jennie taught me. She was my Teacher, and I'm not hesitant to use the capital "T." She was also a dear friend. I believe that she is the first authentic saint that American Spiritualism has produced.

Because of my apprenticeship with her I can say, with Carl Jung, that for me God is no longer a matter of theory, philosophy or belief. I no longer need to believe.

I know.

Chapter 1

MY FIRST EXPERIENCES WITH MOTHER JENNIE

In the winter of 1970 I was teaching at the University of California in Santa Cruz while researching my dissertation. The whole tenor of student consciousness had changed. Radicalism, purged in the fires of its own psychological hell, had retreated to the cool waters of the green revolution. Whatever unorthodox tools were available for self-exploration and introspection found great demand. From Meher Baba to Urantia, Tarot and astrology to the mystical measurements of the Pyramids, Sufism, Spiritualism, Tantrism, Theosophy, Black Islam, esoteric Marxism, charismatic Hasidism or Jesus religion, Gestalt, TA or experimental communities, everyone was immersed in a withdrawal and renewal.

The whole situation turned me off, since I'd been an activist for several years. But in other ways it excited me. For the first time it seemed possible that the anti-war movement could measure up to the spiritual maturity of the civil rights years. Radicalism had concentrated on the material and external aspects of revolution, and rejected any form of inner or spiritual awareness. Perhaps now, in a mysterious and pluralistic way, young persons of conscience would learn to bring it all back home again.

Beginning with my period in theological seminary at the Episcopal Theological School in Cambridge, Massachusetts, I had worked in draft resistance and C. O. counseling, through B.D.R.G. in Boston and Clergy and Laymen Concerned About Vietnam in Washington, D.C. In the summer of 1968, when I returned to Oregon for ordination, I founded the Portland Draft Resistance Group. Under the umbrella of the Episcopal Peace Fellowship I trained both clergy and students in the legal skills of draft counseling, and helped set up centers in eight northwest colleges and universities.

In the fall we moved to Oakland, and I began work on my doctorate at the Graduate Theological Union in Berkeley. Demonstrations at San Francisco State and the mounting police violence which finally built up to the People's Park tragedy that spring pulled me back into activism, and I worked with Tom Hayden and the Black Panthers.

By this time my radical education was quite complete. Yet I seemed a paradox to most of my confederates. After all, I was associated with the Church which, as everyone knew, was the dispenser of the people's opiate. I also had the incomprehensible habit of reading right-wing literature from the John Birch Society bookstore and trying to show the common interests we shared with them. I didn't like the one-sidedness of the left. There was too much dogmatism, too extreme an exclusion of other segments of American consciousness. When I circulated my paper on Male Liberation (a term I'd coined in 1969), which I saw as a necessary corollary to the women's movement that was sweeping our ranks, only a few persons understood. Any concept of a spiritual or inner dimension to revolution seemed incomprehensible to my colleagues, and certainly not a priority.

But I knew too much to desert the movement. I saw the suffering of young boys, acne-faced and eighteen, called upon to make a more mature moral decision than their apathetic parents had ever exercised. I saw them disowned and condemned as cowards and traitors when they tried to follow the sacred promptings of conscience. Some lied their way out of induction, some ran like scared animals to Canada, a few who had peer support from a resistance group went to jail, and most of them broke down and were inducted. The conscience of young America was brutalized into exile.

Even bank robbers and murderers were treated with more compassion and understanding, and certainly never exiled from their own land. But these young men who dared to follow the highest that they knew were consigned to eternal damnation. Over and over again the draft boards and appeals boards held their kangaroo courts, their inquisition of inner motivation, and rendered their judgment: application denied.

Not only had we learned about "democracy" and "civil liberties" and "trying to work within the system," but we'd uncovered the whole ugly fabric of capitalism, the profit motive, American foreign policy and economic exploitation. As for me, I learned about the Ugly American not just from literature and media, but from brother clergy who had been expelled from Latin American countries for their work among the people. I learned about U.S. aid and involvement in fascist police systems, about counter-revolutionary projects by Green Berets to keep the dictators in power and American economic interests healthy. I saw the Reagans and Nixons on the ascendancy, and the burgeoning of American domestic police force.

When I saw my students retreating into astrology, Tarot and yoga, I was indeed disturbed. Social and conscientious movements were disappearing from the campus scene. The World Pig once again seemed to have triumphed. Yet I could not condemn these children for "copping out." Snowflakes do not survive long in Hades.

When the flower dies, life flows to the roots. Radicalism demands a new radix, or "root." It had no root, and could neither survive the heat of day nor bring forth fruit. The children had to go in search of a new root, and that root had to be within. They had to sink into themselves like a surrender unto death and strike deep roots. They had to find the inner nourishment that makes independence, as well as peer support, possible. I tried to respect this, but it was not easy.

It seemed all part of some monstrous adolescent puberty rite, the proliferation of these occult psychologies. Everyone was getting liberated or saved by some technique so quickly discovered, evangelistically obeyed, then dispassionately discarded. The strawberry fields of the drug culture brought forth stranger fruit than the thousand-petaled lotus.

But after all, God was dead and the universe absurd. The vacuum was too intense, the void too black. There was Vietnam, Cambodia, Latin America, Wall Street, the CIA, pollution. What a terrible time to suffer through a liberal university education!

My dissertation involved editing, translating and interpreting the newly-discovered Coptic initiation tractate of Hermes Trismegistus from the Nag Hammadi Gnostic Library, and learning whatever I could about Hermetic traditions of the Roman-Hellenistic period. I had already spent a year with scholars on the Corpus Hermeticum section of the international Corpus Hellenisticum Novi Testamentum project. Now I was trying to expand my perspective from the standpoint of the comparison and phenomenology of religions. The Hermetic mysteries formed the literary vehicle for the transmission of occult Tradition in the West. Why not teach a course which might reawaken student interest in Western religious history? A course in Occultism.

I developed such a course and offered it in the Religious Studies curriculum for the winter term of 1970. This was my first attempt at undergraduate teaching, and covered in a balanced and academic way such topics as Merkabah mysticism, Gnosticism, the schools of Hermes Trismegistus, and a cursory examination of magical, theurgical, astrological and alchemical practices revealed in monuments of the period.

After the course was a few weeks into the term, I was contacted by June Carrillo. She was then working as a staff person, and serving without pay as secretary to the fledgling Religious Studies Committee. June was interested in my course. She wanted me to meet a long-time Santa Cruz resident, 91 years old, whom she affectionately called "Mother Jennie." According to June, Mother Jennie was an expert on the occult.

Frankly, I wasn't interested. I'd had my fill of the various hybrid spiritualities which were making the rounds. For a few dollars I could walk into any bookstore and purchase all kinds of occult information about the lost continent of Mu, various recipes for enlightenment or other secrets from hoary antiquity. Most of this stuff was historically phony, pandered to anyone who could pay the price, and I'd studied too long and hard to spend time on tinkertoys. And I wasn't going to visit some little old lady who was an expert in this fantasy world.

I'm still not certain why I did call Mother Jennie. It probably came out of my interest in folk religion, oral history and funky things. But in spite of my disinterest I did visit her, and the rest is a remarkable story.

One part of the story must concern my personal experience with Mother Jennie. It must describe my own encounter with the numinous and awesome realities within and without. I will try to interpret these things not just as a simple man from planet earth, but as a scholar of religions attempting to grasp the mystic and the miraculous. Even though rational thought is inadequate, it is the only tool at my disposal.

But the story must center upon the stream of Mother Jennie's spiritual development. This I have gleaned from her in many hours of tape-recorded autobiography, and through six years of close association. This is a story of psychism and sainthood, a sanctified life of service, and a mystical education by spirit voices -- the Teachers.

I have included an appendix of poetry, lessons and photographs illustrating Mother Jennie's spiritual journey. Instead of collecting her best poetry, I have followed Jennie's wishes in making a selection of certain major rhymed lessons for Omar. They mark significant milestones in her progress, and should be read for their meaning rather than poetic beauty. A random collection of other minor poems is also included.

These monuments offer a unique glimpse into the inner discipline of prayer and meditation which sustained Jennie for well over half a century. They also lay bare the psychic process of the Muse phenomenon, since her poems came spontaneously and immediately without forethought -- already in meter and rhymed verse. Like the text of John's Gospel, Jennie's lessons make repetitive use of simple vocabulary and key ideas to propel her consciousness into mystic communion with the Divine. They flow in rolling, epic style, not unlike what one might have heard pouring forth from the lips of an ancient bard or scop.
For me, Jennie's inner life is as great a journey as what is chronicled in Jung's posthumous *Memories, Dreams and Reflections.*

But Mother Jennie's achievement transcends my poor words.
****** ****** ******

Early in February, 1970 I telephoned Mother Jennie and made an appointment to see her. For convenience I worked the visit in after class. Her address was difficult to find because the back yard, overgrown with weeds and vines, faced the street where the house should have been.

The small white cottage was separated from the side street which it faced by a brief patch of muddy grass. There were no walkway or porch -- only one cement step to the door.

The doorbell didn't work, so I knocked. This set off a sharp yapping sound from somewhere inside (Cindy always acted as Jennie's doorbell), and I heard footsteps. The door opened, and there stood a small but lively looking old woman, her wrinkled face wreathed in a welcoming smile. I immediately felt at ease, and introduced myself. She turned and led me through the kitchen into her small living room, hobbling slowly with the help of a dark oak cane. She offered me a comfortable overstuffed chair. Since it was apparent from our few words that she was hard of hearing, I cleared my throat and tried to project my voice.

Mother Jennie seated herself in a special carved chair opposite me. She seemed hardly formidable -- just another little old lady. Her snow white hair was done up in a fine transparent net. She was wearing an old-fashioned dress printed with large flowers. It seemed shapeless and almost too large on her tiny frame. The old woman radiated gentleness and humor with her soft blue eyes. She seemed very down-to-earth and friendly.

The living room was cluttered with innumerable articles of sentimental value: paintings, statuettes, post cards, crockery. Upon an overburdened bookcase was an old Seth Thomas clock whose ticking filled the atmosphere. It was partially buried under many knickknacks: a brass incense burner, a vial of water from the Ganges, another vial from the Jordan. On the wall above hung a colored chalk portrait of an Indian chief, and next to it an oil painting of an Indian maiden on a path.

To my right and directly in front of me were cases of occult literature, from books by Blavatsky to old copies of Fate magazine. Well, I thought, she probably knows a lot of theosophical stuff, but she's no scholar.

I asked her to tell me something about the occult, since June had recommended her in connection with the course I was teaching.

She began to speak. I was pleased to hear how eloquently, almost poetically, she used language. Clearly she was British, not so much in accent, but in her use of the Queen's English. She was not only lovely to hear, but the things she was saying made a lot of sense. Rather than going on about the lost continent of Mu or something of that nature, she was speaking about the inner meaning of alchemical transmutation and the progress of the soul. I was impressed and was content to sit back and listen.

Time went on, and suddenly I became aware that the late afternoon sun was reflecting off her pearly hair and shooting bright beams from the translucent white skin of her delicate hands and fingers, which she moved in a most sensitive way while speaking. It was late, and I should be getting home.

On an impulse I asked if she would be willing to lecture to my class. She was very flattered, and after a moment of silence assured me that her Teachers said yes.

Teachers?

She then closed her eyes and asked a blessing for my work at the University. Normally I dislike public prayer. It seems to be a forum for delivering long-winded opinions to an embarrassed and captive audience. But in this case my embarrassment was only momentary. Her brief prayer aloud seemed truly sacred. It reminded me of the words Uncle Johnnie's old Dad spoke when he said grace one Thanksgiving -- like an old Indian shaman praying to his Great Spirit in the setting sun.

I felt a growing warmth for the old woman, and sensed a depth of character that was rare in my experience and difficult to fathom. She had mentioned that her 91st birthday was coming up in a week on February 12, so I asked if there was anything she would like. She had (as always) refused any honorarium or gratuity, since her ministry has always been freely given.

In response to my question, she fixed me with her gentle eyes and said, "Professor Keizer, there is something you could do that would be of great assistance."

She explained that over the years her Teachers had given her volumes of spiritual poetry, lessons and prophecies which she, with failing eyesight, was not able to type into proper form. Would I be kind enough to take a few home and type them up for her?
I was happy to honor such a simple request, and she led me to her ancient chest of drawers. Removing one of several cardboard boxes, she fumbled with the ribbon and finally managed to extricate the yellowed top. Within were reams of paper bundled loosely together. Each paper was covered with faded type or penciled script. Typing paper, tablet paper, old envelopes and even paper napkins were painstakingly revealed as she shuffled through her treasures. On each page Jennie's name and a date were written, and the dates were generally between 1923 and 1925.

Finally she collected several of the untyped pages and handed them to me, evidently pleased by my interest.

"I hope you will be able to decipher them. They came to me as water from a spring, and I had to write with great haste." Even her eyes were smiling.

They certainly had been hastily scrawled, and I doubted that they could be of very high quality as poetry. I took the copies and promised to treat them carefully. She replaced everything in the box and saw me to the door. I promised to have the work done in time for her birthday next week, and said that I'd like another appointment to get some biographical information for my students when she came to speak. We had not yet set the date, so we agreed to meet when I brought in the typed copies next Wednesday, and we said goodbye.

I was able to get to her poems the next day, and as the verses and quatrains began to take form on the white typing paper I realized that Jennie's poetry was really exquisite for its genre. They were composed in a lyrical Elizabethan English, with flawless meter and rhyme. But more than this, the content of the poems was richly beautiful and revealed a deeply spiritual understanding of life and nature. What Jennie had said about spiritual alchemy came back to me as I read the poem entitled From the Heart of a Rose:

Breathe out, sweet rose,
The fragrance of a soul serene,
Within whose beauty lurks a thread
Of Life and Love Divine,
Radiating from each petal red
A Light -- like to a holy shrine.

Well hast thou been named
The Queen of Flowers,
For who beneath thy cool and shady bowers,
Sheltered, refreshed from sojourn there,
Hath not looked out, and seemed to see more fair
All things in life, freed from toil and care?

Thou liftest up thy proud and haughty head
In power and majesty, above thy lowly bed
Where thou, in darkness, take within thy stem
From mold of earth and refuse
And, in stillness, transmute them
Into beauty which attracts the eyes of men.

Then as the day declineth, and thy mission is fulfilled,
Thou droopest 'gain thy stately head,
And as thy life is stilled,
Thy petals flutter downward and to the earth return,
Giving Life new to all which is born,
Unmindful of the leaf and thorn.
Still breathing forth the fragrance sweet
As thou doth to dust return,
Each petal of the Queen of Flowers,
The sweetest of them all.
And so from you a lesson's learned,
A duty great and grand:
To lift again the fallen and transmute into men
The sinner and the outcast,
The lame, the halt and blind,
The fettered and the lonely ones,
All, heaven on earth shall find
Thru' Christ, Eternal Spirit, Eternal Life and Love,
And sons of men shall see the Light,
And be 'gain Sons of God.

Clearly this and the others had been scrawled every which way on these yellowed sheets in great haste, and yet they exhibited the sort of excellence that would require much forethought and a good deal of careful craftsmanship.

What did she mean by her "Teachers?" My impression was that she claimed to have received her writings in dictation from spirit controls, or something of this sort. I was not totally dubious about mediumship and spiritualist phenomena. My mind was open to these things, but I did not accept the explanations that are usually offered for them -- simple reincarnation and other spiritualistic doctrines.

Yet history and literature do provide other references to such phenomena which fall under the Muse and theories of divine inspiration for poets and writers. Certainly the classical epic poets gave deference to the Muse, whether Greek or Latin, by prefacing their works with a plea and invocation to their inspiring spirits. Was there really some form of phenomenal experience which underlay this literary convention?

I thought about the problem of jazz and improvised music. I am a jazz musician, and have always been a little curious at how impossible jazz improvisation is for most trained symphonic musicians. It is not just that they have been trained to feel music as a visual thing through performing other people's compositions from written pages. I and many other good jazz musicians have undergone a classical musical education. No, it is something else, some other factor that enables some musicians to play jazz and not others.

I considered my experiences as a professional jazz musician. There were times when I could sing on my horn like an Orpheus, and other times when inspiration just didn't seem to come. Drugs, in fact, are often substituted for inspiration by jazz musicians who go dry in their playing -- giving a feeling of euphoric inspiration at times. But the real experience of inspiration is independent of drugs, and many of the jazz musicians of the recent period have taken to meditative and other inner techniques to stay in touch with their Muse.

Could there be some process, some psychic or spiritual phenomenon, at the root of various mythologies about a Muse? The prospect excited me, and I decided to ask Jennie more about her Teachers. It was the integrity of the phenomenon, not various explanations offered for it, that intrigued me. Was it real?

The next Wednesday I arrived fully prepared by recent research into Muse traditions. In the meantime it had occurred to me that the old pages I had copied may have been her own second, hurriedly written versions, and not represent the speed and apparent ease with which her poems were written. Since she had no idea what intellectual processes I was following, I asked her casually if the pages she had given me were the original composition papers. She confirmed that they were. Perhaps I'm too naive, but I believed her. As far as I can tell, she had no reason to be dishonest, and my succeeding years with Mother Jennie have proven to me that she is absolutely scrupulous about the truth.

Here again is the problem of subjectivity. I am confronted with a few poems that an elderly women has written fifty years ago. In my esthetic judgment they are not only beautifully crafted, but carry a precious message. To write this sort of thing, using my mind and critical faculties, would require quite a bit of time, with rewriting and editing. Jennie's poems, however, appear to have been written down as fast as she could move the pencil over the paper, as though she were taking dictation. She claims to have received them from spirit Teachers.

Well, this is a strange combination of evidence and potentiality. But I made the subjective decision that the evidence merited further investigation. Someone else might not even have bothered.

Jennie was telling me the story of her first encounter with the Teachers. It was about fifty years ago in Santa Cruz. She and her husband Louis Peterson were living in a tar shack they had erected on a piece of land over on Seventh Avenue, and it was mid-winter. All they had was a kerosene lamp and a little wood-burning stove to keep out the biting cold, and it was storming.

Sometime early in the morning Jennie was awakened by a voice. The voice, she said, spoke in tender and sweet tones, and she had an urge to get up and write down what was being said. It seemed so logical and beautiful that she was sure she could go back to sleep and remember it in the morning. She turned over and went back to sleep. The next morning all she could remember was "Come Thou, great Light" and something about a tomb. She felt very distressed that she had let something that seemed very wonderful and important slip by. It was not until much later that she again heard that voice speaking. She took up pencil and paper, but this time the voice delivered a poetic rebuke for failing to "respond to the Higher Intellect." Meekly she wrote it down. After many more days the voice returned and delivered the full version of the first poem:

Come Thou, great Light,
Dispel the shadows and the gloom.

Teach us of Life,
Not beyond the tomb,
But here and now,
While we are sore oppressed,
That we may lift Life's shadows,
Ere we seek our rest.

The night is dark,
And we are far from home.
Teach us the Way,
That we may ne'er need roam.

Teach us to love,
That we may e'en dispel
The shadows
That do e'er around us dwell.

Give us knowledge,
Strength and power,
That we may through Life's storms
Smile through all the showers.

Give us patience
To await thy love's fulfillment
Power and might
To erect a living monument.

Thy Word unto our feetA Light shall be,

That all who look within
Shall brightness see.

Where unto others
All is dark as night,
We may be guided
In thy love's strong Light.

So unto Thee
Our thanks are given,
For by sweet love
Our clouds are riven.
By endurance, truth and might,
Wrong shall fall in face of right.

This and many other poems she recited to me by memory, her eyes elevated as though seeing beyond the immediate surroundings into a place of timelessness. I was impressed with the acuity of her mind and the dramatic feeling with which she spoke at times. Her speech was poetic and spellbinding, but not inauthentic. Certainly this encounter with the voice was very real to her, and had deep meaning in her life. For her, this was the beginning of a spiritual Odyssey which she had experienced for more than fifty years.

Clearly she had the personality of a medium: psychically sensitive, dramatic, poetic and with a flair for the sort of receptive impressionability that would be appropriate to theater or the mime. I wasn't quite sure what to think, but she was most interesting to hear.

She went on to tell me about her Teachers: an Indian girl, a Hindu master, and in the last 25 years the martyred Christian prophet of Florence, Savonarola.

"How appropriate," I thought, "to be instructed by a Christian saint who was denied sainthood by his own tradition." Jennie was certainly a woman denied any validity by church traditions. Could this be why in her fantasy-life she had chosen to be taught by Savonarola?

Mother Jennie described her ten-year discipleship with the Hindu. He came every morning at ten o'clock. She sat before her organ, sang a hymn, and took "lessons" in dictation.

I was more interested in her first experience with the voice. Some of the words of the major poem, "Come Thou, great Light," which seemed to synopsize the direction that all her ensuing revelations were to take, appealed to me personally. I liked the concept of learning about life, "not beyond the tomb, but here and now, while we are sore oppressed." This seemed to be a more unitative, psychologically whole approach to religion than the old mind-body dualism which has persisted so long in Western religion. This pleased me, and I decided to analyze the poem as a kind of synthema which might contain the germs of Jennie's development.

Having collected some biographical details, I arranged to pick her up the following Wednesday for her lecture to my class. On the way out I noticed what a jungle her back yard had become in the last year, most of which she had spent in a hospital convalescing from a serious heart attack. She had been back home only since Christmas. According to her, she had "passed out of the body," and was flying with joy and happiness "above the earth-sphere" with the doctors trying to revive her body. Her heart had stopped. A voice told her, "You must return to Santa Cruz." She paid no attention, and the voice repeated its injunction. She did not want to return to the physical life. She was free and ecstatic with joy. But again the voice with great force confronted her with the imperative: "You must go back to Santa Cruz." She felt a dizzy whirling and blackness, awakening several days later in her hospital room. She wondered why she was brought back to Santa Cruz, and in fact puzzled over that question for at least a year after I first met her.

I looked again at her overgrown lawn and back yard, and resolved that I'd do some gardening for her. I had no place to garden myself, and I recalled the wonderful hours I'd spent as a gardener, contemplating the parables of Jesus, thinking of the seed which must die before it can bring forth fruit.

The following Wednesday I came for Jennie. To my surprise she was dressed in a white robe with blue and gold trim. This, she told me, was what she wore when she did "the Work."

I had many reservations in my mind about this. It had been enough to compose an introduction to Mother Jennie for my hip students, who were all caught in the generation gap and many of them fascinated with various Eastern gurus or occult ideas like alchemy. Now she would be appearing in a really corny get-up. I'd hoped to give the students a glimpse of Western mysticism in some "live" form. Now I feared they would be snickering too hard to appreciate old Jennie's religious life, seeing how "camp" she was.

I had, in fact, devoted one entire lecture to preparing them for Mother Jennie. There were some 150 registered for the course, but daily the attendance ranged upwards of 300. I had to speak through a microphone and use a projection screen and opaque projector instead of a blackboard.

In the lecture I had brought out some of the interesting aspects of Jennie's first experience with the "voice." I had drawn a comparison to Joan of Arc and heterodox "faerie religion" of 15th-century Lorraine. More striking, I had discovered some parallels to the sort of Platonic cosmological spirituality found in the Timaeus and the later Kore Kosmou of Hermetic tradition: light versus darkness, unity and the Way of Right versus diversity and error, the "brightness" of the sun (as in the Allegory of the Cave) versus the "shadows" of phenomenal perception, the concept of contemplation or meditation ("all who look within shall brightness see") as an inner quest leading to illumination, enlightenment or whatever other terms might refer to the experience of "light" spoken of in so many traditions. All these things were to be found in Mother Jennie's first major revelation, the poem on the great Light. Like Muse traditions, it was in the form of an epiklesis or invocation, a "calling down" of divine light. In its negative interpretation it could be seen as a Thessalonian witch "drawing down" the moon's light. In its positive form, a classically feminine mystery -- the Beloved in search of the Lover. In this way I had carefully drawn attention to the enduring themes of religious mysticism inherent in Jennie's "Come Though, great Light," thus preparing my students to listen intelligently and analytically to her lecture.

As we arrived at the large cafeteria where my students were still gathering noisily for class, my fears seemed to be realized. People were staring incredulously at the strange old woman in the white gown, as though she were Amy Sempel McPherson resurrected from the thirties. I seated her on a wooden chair on the platform, and she asked for some water. She had brought along her own glass, which I filled. She then covered it with a brass lid from a jar, as though afraid some pollution might enter the water if it were left exposed.

"Now that," I thought, "is real animistic spiritism."

I asked for everyone's attention, and noticed that the class was larger than usual. After my brief introduction, Mother Jennie, with my assistance, stood and came to the microphone. Suddenly it was very quiet. She looked intensely at the crowd, very much in control of the situation.

"Sure glad she's an actress," I thought to myself.

She then proceeded to deliver one of the most beautiful discourses I had ever heard in my life!

For over an hour you could have heard a stomach growl, if anyone had been overly hungry. I had never seen three-hundred-plus students listen to anyone so intently. She told us that there is consciousness in everything, and that life cannot die. She illustrated her points with simple and familiar examples from observable phenomena. She spoke of God as Spirit, and of the myriad spiritual encounters we experience every day without recognizing them. She spoke of the tomb of personal existence and the mental prisons which we erect around us. But the one thing which came through most clearly was the beauty and enlightenment which Mother Jennie had attained within her own tradition and understanding.

When she was through with the lecture, students crowded in to speak with her like hungry orphans begging a meal. The response amazed me, and I was very pleased with the whole affair. She had succeeded in communicating something far more profound than popular occultism. As the little conclave around Jennie began to break up, one of the students told me that she had agreed to meet with a group of them on the following Tuesday night. I checked with Jennie, and she confirmed the date and time. With her permission I wrote down the address and the time, 7:30 p.m., and projected it onto the large screen which served as my blackboard. With this final announcement, the class was over.

That is how the Tuesday evening meetings began. We started with eight or ten people, and within a month the meetings were jammed. Jennie always insisted that I sit in a special chair across the room from her. The old armchair was held for me even when I could not attend, and she rarely allowed anyone else to use it. Later I found that it helped her to have a trusted man across the room, for the sake of "polarity" and the "lines" which sustained her during the discourse.

The tiny living room had seating space for ten persons when all other chairs had been brought in from the kitchen. Most people sat on the floor, with some using spare cushions from the couch. People overflowed into the kitchen and closet-like dining room, and everyone signed his name on a sheet for Mother's prayer list. It was not unusual for over 50 people to attend.

They were of all sorts -- hippies, straights, radicals, conservatives. The central core of regular hearers changed slowly. The Lynch family commuted from Monterey and others came from as far away as Davis. Everyone kissed Jennie as they arrived and before leaving. The feeling was warm and affectionate.

After I had attended regularly for a few weeks, I offered to come once or twice a week and work in her garden: it had become a vigorous jungle of grass and weeds since she had been incapacitated by last year's heart attack. The first real problem was her lawn, which was three feet high. After this I planned to begin work in her garden when spring came. I also dropped in to visit her from time to time, to chat and see how she was getting along. I discovered that she had some old-time friends who were in touch, and a woman coming in as a "student" one day a week, so I asked if she would take me on as a student. I wanted to learn more about her, and found myself growing internally through contact with this loving old woman. She agreed, and I'd come to visit on a regular schedule, sitting quietly in the overstuffed chair while she spoke of many things.

From time to time I'd ask her about problems of religion and philosophy, and her answers would amaze me. They could have been made by Anaxagoras or Plotinus in their logic, terminology and profundity. I began to develop more respect for the tradition which had produced such a beautiful metaphysic, and for the woman who had made such excellent use of what was at hand.

That year there were several faculty members who were or had been ordained men. Glen Martin, a campus minister who had taken his Ph.D. with Tillich at Columbia and whose selfless concern had led to my coming to UCSC, was a Methodist minister. Noel King, my dear friend, Chairman of the Religious Studies Committee and a scholar who had headed universities in third-world areas, was a fellow Anglican clergyman. Stu Schlegel was still an Episcopal priest, though he'd managed to hide this fact from the academic world and was making an excellent career in Anthropology after returning from the Philippines and taking a doctorate at the University of Chicago.
None of us could stand to go to a church, so we began meeting with our families once a month in each other's homes for our own Eucharist. We baked our own bread and said our own words, prayed together and really enjoyed this form of "public" worship.

One afternoon Mother Jennie mentioned to me that she hadn't been able to get to a Sunday Communion service for many years, since it was so difficult for her to go anywhere. I asked if she'd like to come to our home service, and she gratefully accepted. That next week we picked her up and took her to the Martins' home.

After the gathering was over, Ann, the children and I returned Jennie to her house. We went through the scuffle with her keys, finally getting the door open with Cindy jumping excitedly to see us back, and were just getting the front door closed when Jennie began to cough and wheeze. Large tears rolled from her eyes; her tiny frame shuddered in discomfort.

I quickly sat her down in the living room and asked if I could help.

"Lewis," she said in a choked voice, "someone from the spirit world wants to talk to you." More coughing.

I don't know how to tell you what I felt at that moment. Perhaps the word "insult" would carry the most accuracy.

"God," I whispered to myself in disbelief. "It's been so nice up to now, Mother Jennie. Why do you have to pull this sort of phony deal?" I was smarting inside with a feeling of betrayal. I had thought she was wise. Now she was trying to mess with my mind, to demand some kind of belief that I simply wasn't willing to share.
"Oh, really?" I said to her, trying to hide my feelings. She must be more of an actress than I'd thought. The tears were streaming down her wrinkled cheeks, and she was off into another paroxysm of coughing. Ann had brought a glass of water. Jennie sipped a little of it, still in discomfort.

"It is someone in your profession. He went out with a terrible coughing and wheezing about five years ago. Can you tell me his name?"

She turned her head toward her right shoulder and command, "Take your condition off me, please." No one was standing there. She sneezed again, nearly dropping the glass.

Still smarting, but making an embarrassed attempt to humor the woman, I said, "Well, it must be my Grandma May." My favorite grandmother had died some six years before. I thought that by providing Jennie with a name I'd appease her, she'd probably accept it and go on to say whatever she wanted.

"No!" she said firmly. "It is not a woman. It comes from the heart-side, and it is a man. He says that you knew him for only two months, but you were very fond of him. He died of a terrible lung condition, and when he died you were grief-stricken and wept over his casket."

It came like a shock of light: Father Geiser.

How could she know all that? How could she know about a man who was very important to me, but whose memory had not been revived in my mind for at least three years?

Father Geiser was an Episcopal priest at St. Mark's in Portland, Oregon. When I had been accepted by the Bishop of Oregon as a postulant for Holy Orders, I met old Father Geiser. For some reason I felt very drawn to him, and it was easy to tell him my innermost thoughts.

He was still attached to St. Mark's, but was bedridden with emphysema. I used to look at the oxygen respirator that stood next to his bed, and as he wheezed his kindly words to me he'd puff on a Salem cigarette. In horror I'd ask him why in the world a man with emphysema would puff a cigarette. He'd smile and tell me that since his wife left this earth a year ago he'd been looking forward to joining her, and besides, smoking was one of his vices. He had access to so few vices these days that he had to exercise at least one a day to say humble. Father Geiser did not far death. In fact, he looked forward to it, as to a great and mysterious experience.

Sometimes he'd get out of bed and walk with me to his garden. Other times he'd lead me to the basement, where he kept his paintings. He was an artist, even more than a priest, and had taught at the University of Colorado. It was he who had done the marvelous religious paintings which cover the sanctuary of both the Lady Chapel and main altar at St. Mark's. Often when I dropped in I found a group of art students from Portland State University talking with him about details of sketching or whatever.

I especially remembered his basement, where we'd sit for an afternoon listening to the music of Bizet or Berlioz, sometimes Bruckner or Mahler. The walls were covered with his mystic paintings -- mountains, mist, vast clouded sunrises and verdant hills. He never talked about them, but we sat contemplating them.

It had been two brief but meaningful months during the summer of 1965 that I'd known Father Geiser. I had planned to visit him that Monday morning, but other things came up. Tuesday morning I dropped by St. Mark's. Lying in state before the altar was a thin black casket. Something recoiled deep in my solar plexus, and I had to see who had died. I came forward in the silence of the empty church, my footsteps echoing from the old brick walls. There was the thin frame of Father Geiser, his eyes closed, his skin so white, and the strands of long white hair combed carefully back over his head. So thin, so empty. No one was there.

I threw myself onto the rail of the nearest pew and wept. Why hadn't I taken the time to see him a day or two earlier? Now he was gone. I grieved for a long time in the darkened church.

All these memories came to me in a flash, like a light bulb suddenly switched on in my head. In an instant my whole attitude was changed. I felt awake and very alert. My mouth must have dropped. Ann hadn't heard what Jennie said, and was looking at me strangely.

How could Jennie know that? A man, died five years ago of a lung disease, in my profession (clergy), I'd known him for two months and been grief-stricken when he died. She must have been reading my mind. Not my conscious mind, for I hadn't thought of Father Geiser for many years, but my unconscious mind. Or something.

"He wishes to tell you this," Jennie went on. "One time in the recent past he has come to help you by soothing your mind and guiding your fingers to paint. Now he will help you to learn spiritual truth by teaching your fingers to paint. He wants you to know of his continued love and presence." She stared unblinking, with her eyebrows arched.

As if one mind-blower hadn't been enough, number two was beginning to sink in. I'd never taken any interest in painting before in my life, except on one occasion two summers ago in Cambridge, Massachusetts. I was undergoing an intensive twelve-week training course for clergy in clinical pastoral training at Boston State Mental Hospital. The first week had been spent in daily psychological testing to determine personality strengths and weaknesses. It was found that I am an "over-achiever," one who likes to see the results of his labor. For this reason I was assigned to the geriatrics mental ward, so I could learn patience and "under-achievement." These wards were considered to be places of hopelessness. We spent half the day in the ward with patients, and half the day in various rip-em-up encounter groups with fellow seminarians. It was the hot summer of 1967, and the black ghettos were burning.

Over the shrill objections of an officious head nurse I had managed to convince the chief psychiatrist that six of his old patients (whom he was able to see once a year) did not belong in this hell-hole nut-house, to shrivel up and die before their time. With the aid of our social services woman, we had moved them out into nursing homes. But the interpersonal conflict had been so intense, along with the daily hours of encounter groups, that my anxiety level had risen to the point that I was in a constant nervous exhaustion.

One afternoon, on impulse, I walked down to the Harvard Co-op and bought a water color painting set. I produced several paintings of flowers and trees. They were intense and lifelike, and my newly-discovered talent gave me much pleasure and escape from nervous pressure. I then bought some oil paints and produced some very good work. My parents had come for a visit, and were surprised at my paintings. This was only a brief interlude in my life, but a very pleasant one. The soothing, carefree periods that painting brought to me are high points in my memory.

Again, a battery of thoughts passed through my mind. How did Jennie know that the name Father Geiser was in any way associated with painting, let alone that he would "guide" my fingers when I painted? How did she know that I had painted once before to soothe my mind?

Mother Jennie took a deep breath, held it for a moment and expelled it with force through her mouth. It occurred to me that her coughing and tears had ceased suddenly when I'd blurted out the name, Father Geiser. She'd said, "That's right," waved her left hand over her right shoulder as though urging someone to move away, taken a deep breath and seemed totally restored in composure as she gave me the message. Now everything was back to normal. Her face was soft and smiling.

I was dumbfounded, and didn't know what to say except to thank her and ask if there was anything I could do before we left. She said no, but that I should remember what Father Geiser had said. We thanked her and left.

Clearly there was no way Jennie could have discovered, even by sophisticated research, any of the highly personal things she had told me. I decided that I'd better start rearranging my epistemology and looking for some answers to questions I'd never thought of posing before.

Was there more reality to psychism than I'd previously thought? How would this tie into religious thought and phenomena?

Like a blossom in the morning sun, my mind began to open to a greater reality than I'd ever known.

As the year progressed and Jennie's discourses began to make more sense, I asked if she would be willing to sit for several tape-recorded interviews and tell me the entire story of her life. She agreed. I was overjoyed, not only because it would be a privilege to write her autobiography, but because as a scholar of religions I had a living example of some of the most puzzling aspects of mysticism. How did Mother Jennie's life relate to shamanic spontaneous vocation, the lives of other mediums, the lives of saints?

Starting from the beginning, she narrated to me all that she could remember of her personal life-history.

Chapter 2

JENNIE'S CHILDHOOD AND EARLY YEARS

My mother was alone. Dad hadn't come home yet from work. He heard St. Mary's bells chime twelve, and it took him just about fifteen minutes to get home. He found me on the concrete floor, and my mother struggling to get up.

A little girl had been born.

It was the twelfth of February, 1879, in the Court Building district of Nottingham, England. The winter was severely cold in this lace works tenement, and the people, back to back in their two-story structures, were poor. The thin exterior of the tenements was surfaced with faded blue brick. There was no running water or plumbing except for the sinks and toilets added for public use to the house of each supervisor. These provided for the inhabitants of the surrounding several blocks, and were in constant use. Heat was furnished by coal stoves, and light for the upper stories came through the bleak skylights which punctuated every sooty roof.

The painful birth of another child, especially a female, was hardly noticed. The chances of her surviving to adulthood, through illness and accident, were slim. If she did survive, she was destined to marry a lace worker and live in poverty, tending the next generation of luckless children and perhaps taking in sewing for shoe-money.

A tired man helped his exhausted wife wash herself in the cold water which had been carefully measured into the large tin tub next to the fireplace. He tied the little baby's umbilical cord with lacer's thread, and prepared to bundle her into bed with her mother. He stole quietly past the beds of the three other girls, and thought of all his dead sons. The first two had been stillborn. The third lived to be almost talking age before dying of encephalitis. The fourth died in his crib at seven months.

Looking intently into the baby's face, he said, "This child is the spitting image of my Aunt Jane. Her name will be Jane." He called her Jane from that time forward, although the nickname Jennie was more popular with the family.

Jennie's father was shop foreman of the Lace Dressing Rooms. He worked until midnight during peak periods, earning about 18 shillings a week. He had been born the illegitimate child of Ann Hopkins, a woman of upper-class family. When it was found that she was pregnant, she was ostracized from polite society. Aunt Jane and Uncle William had taken pity on her and helped her with the child.

Jennie remembers Grandma Ann, who never married and lived in poverty, supported by monthly sums from Jennie's father, and by her own meager earnings.

"I saw her every little while. She was in desperate circumstances. She was earning a living, and she used to appear, when conditions were bad, and would meet Dad as he came home on Saturday, because Saturday was the payday, and Dad would give her something to help out."

Jennie treasures a little sampler made by Grandma Ann when she was a girl of 13. It portrayed a white cottage with picket fence, trees and fruit, a gate open into the garden and a man with silk hat dangling his legs over the fence. Beneath it was written: "Jesus, permit thy gracious name to stand / as the first effort of a female's hand, / and as her fingers o'er this sampler move, / permit her grateful heart to seek thy love. / With thy dear children may she have a part, / and write thy name, thus sewn, upon her heart."

Jennie's mother had been born in the lace country of Nottingham, Nottinghamshire. Her father had been a master craftsman with five sons and Emma Watterson, the only daughter. Emma's parents had come from somewhere in Staffordshire. The only "nobility" in Jennie's family, then, had come through her father's side. Since she had been named after Aunt Jane, she was often the butt of jokes: "You were born a lady but the money short," her sisters used to tease.

Little Jane walked and talked at nine months, and was an excellent student when she became of age for school. She went to school at less than three years of age, and won prizes for punctuality and scholarship. At the age of five, in 1884, she was reading facilely. She still possesses the Sunday School awards of a little Bible and other certificates from this period, commending her for punctuality, good conduct and scholarship. Her mother used to call her a "bookworm."

Jennie passed through all the grades or "standards" of the British Infant School System by the time she was ten years old, and at 12 years had earned a scholarship and was teaching a class of 72 students. Every Friday there had been spelling bees, and usually Jennie had been the victor. She had passed "standard seven," the highest standard, with honors, and at this time the central district in London had created a special classification for Jennie and a few other bright students, known as "standard eight." Jennie's mother was very proud of her daughter, and worked late every night doing special lacework by lamplight to make the extra money to keep Jennie in books for school. To this day, Mother Jennie has maintained a deep love and respect for her mother and the sacrifices she made on her behalf. There is no generation gap, or adolescent need to express "hatred" toward her mother, and never was. Clearly Jennie has always loved her mother, and she has written many poems over the years demonstrating this strong love.

But Jennie could be stubborn as a child, and her mother was capable of exercising a firm discipline. Jennie recalls one occasion when she refused to do something her teacher had asked. She was assisting the teacher with a classroom of students in preparation to become a student teacher herself. Jennie was told to sit in the corner with her face to the wall. Shortly her mother came in, upset and angry. She asked what Jennie had done, and when she had decided that the young girl was acting badly, she turned her over her knee before all the watching children and gave her a spanking.

"So anyway, it was more of a shaming before the classes, than of the hurt itself. But I never forgot it, and they never had to send for my mother again!"

Jennie's stubbornness was a trial to her mother, but she often philosophized about it: "It's no use trying to change her. If she makes up her mind, ten thousand mules wouldn't move her. But if you lead her with a string of kindness or a word of praise, there's no limit to what she will do for you."

Undoubtedly it was Jennie's mother who planted the seeds of wisdom in her. By teaching her obedience, she gave her the resources to develop self-discipline. In setting the example of loving self-sacrifice with no strings attached, she instilled a deep appreciation for service to others. Perhaps most important, she provided a sense of support and security, even in relation to social authorities that she herself had been trained to obey -- most notably the Church of England. Emma Hopkins never allowed her children to be bullied by anyone.
Probably the earliest indications of Jennie's spiritual sensitivity were to be found in her "stubbornness." She loved Sunday school, and especially Miss Mason, her teacher.

"Miss Mason was one of the most serene, loving women I've ever met. I've always remembered her."

In spite of her prizes for punctuality and attendance in 1887 at the Albion Sunday School of Sneinton, troubles began to brew for Jennie in her religious education.

She had wanted to be a missionary, and loved the hymns and the general feeling of church religion. Her mother always stressed moral living, the value of truth and the high calling of service to others. She took in extra work to be able to provide the children with a farthing for the missionary boxes.

"One Sunday Mother didn't have any farthings. On Saturdays Dad always bought four ounces of bits-of-twist, and we each were given one piece of that broken candy as we went off to Sunday school. This Sunday we had the usual piece of candy, but we did not have a farthing to put in the missionary box. And during the prayer at the opening of the afternoon Sunday school, I had to take a bite of a hidden apple, and the blessed thing slipped out of my fingers and rolled on the floor. So I went after it. Was I given it by my mother? Yes, they made it their business on Monday morning to go see my mother, and to tell her of my misbehavior in Sunday school, that in the midst of prayer I dropped an apple and that I went to pick it up. Since I did not have a farthing to put in the missionary box, I must have spent it on candy, because I was also chewing candy!

"All right. And I've always remembered her name -- Miss Mosely. She was a real old woman, an old maid: well, not such an old woman, but an old maid. And I can just remember my mother giving her one piercing look, and she said, `You say that my child must have spent her farthing for candy?'

" `Most decidedly,' she said. `She had the candy, but she did not have the farthing.'

"Mother said, `Let me tell you, I train my children to be honest, and I did not have any farthings yesterday, and they were sent off without them.' "

With that she showed Miss Mosely to the door, while the gleeful Jennie, hiding at the top of the stairs unknown to her mother, glowed with gratitude.

At the age of eight Jennie had become quite a tomboy. She was considered to be mischievous but brilliant. Her favorite activity was climbing trees. Something seemed to sing in her as she made her careful way up the branches, one by one, until at last she reached the topmost part and could reach out for the sweetest fruit which grew in the heights, beyond normal access. She remembers these ventures as the bright times of youth, and speaks of the peacefulness she felt while squatting amidst the upper branches.

For her there was no contradiction between church worship and the mystery of climbing a tree. Her stubborn habit was to climb for an apple before afternoon Sunday school, and hide it in her skirts, rolling it between her palms as the prayers were said. Somehow the wholeness of the apple, the ripeness of its meat, inspired in her a wonder which was appropriate to worship.

Miss Mosely did not like Jane Hopkins. She was not feminine and soft, like the other little girls. She may have been bright in school and the top student in Sunday school last year, but this year she had obviously become a mischievous tomboy who showed no proper respect for the Church. Something funny was going on with that Hopkins girl, and she was going to get to the bottom of the situation at the first opportunity.

The opportunity came quickly. One Sunday afternoon Jennie had hidden an apple in her skirt and refused to turn it over to Miss Mosely.

"You must give me the apple, child, or I'll have to go calling upon your mother again," she venomously whispered as the priest dismissed the children for school. Jennie tore it away from the surprised woman and ran out of the chapel. She was not crying, and she did not feel weak or guilty. She simply realized that she did not want to attend Sunday school any more.

"But Darling," said her mother, "you must go to Sunday school to learn about the Bible."

"I will read the Bible myself, Mama. Please don't make me go back," Jennie begged.

Miss Mosely never came to Emma Hopkins. She knew that the Hopkins family had been disgraced by Jennie's headstrong behavior, which was the topic of general conversation that Monday. She had no desire to confront Emma Hopkins face to face, and hoped that instead Jennie would return meekly to class the next week. Emma was not certain how to handle the situation, so Jennie settled it for her by absolutely refusing.

"That was where I began to show the stubbornness of my nature," Mother Jennie recalls. "I stamped my foot and cried, `I am not going back!' "

Since she was too old for Miss Mason's class and too young for the adult class, she was finally put into the Pleasant Sunday Afternoon gathering. This was chaired by a sweet old woman who was practically illiterate and, as Jennie remembers, was highlighted by her painful readings from scripture.

"Since she had no idea how to interpret anything but a literal meaning, she spent the time reading verses from the Bible. She would read a verse to us first one way, with stress upon one word or phrase, then reread it another way with different stress."

Needless to say, this experience effectively showed Jennie the limits that public religion had attained, and she lost interest in the Church.

About this time, however, she began to experience out-of-the-body phenomena which assumed critical importance for her. They came in the wake of several debilitating illnesses which were to culminate in a severe bout with the Spanish flu and eventually force her out of school.

Jennie had assumed the role of teacher at the age of 12 in the Infant School system, and was indentured for a teaching scholarship to the Nottingham school board for four years, until she would be 16. But a strange form of illness, which the doctors diagnosed as "dyspepsia," was beginning to interfere with her health. In fact, Jennie was experiencing ecstasies known as "astral traveling." They came just as she entered into menstruation and puberty.

"This was more prevalent in those days of the change in my physical life, that when I went to bed and relaxed, then I could sense the foot of the bed going down. And it started to go around until I was catapulted out, and went flying off all over the city. Then I'd come back to bed, and when I hit the bed it would revolve in the opposite direction, and then I lay flat on the bed. My body hadn't gone out, but what we didn't know -- my spirit had. Well, the doctors were quite concerned about it -- we'd never heard any talk of mysticism or occultism at that time, or Spiritualism. And I used to get up and go work my lessons out while I was asleep, and I sang. Everyone was warned not to touch me or to speak roughly to me if they found me sleepwalking, because I had to get down two flights of stairs to get to my books."

Jennie says that she could see various events happening in the city of Nottingham during her night-flights, and the next morning would tell her mother things that had occurred the night before. Many of these things were confirmed.

She remembers the gay events of childhood. She excelled at swimming and won prizes for it. Her parents had been able to move to better quarters, out of the tenement, and on the Bank Holiday, the first Monday of August, her father reserved rail passage for an excursion to the seaside. They would awaken at three in the morning to catch the train.

"I can remember Dad saying, `We're drawing closer.' He'd put his head out the window and say, `I can smell the salt air,' and then he'd say, `Here's the Lincoln Cathedral in the distance.'

"Sometimes we got off the train at Grimsby, and we walked through the fish-docks where the trawlers were unloading fish. Then we walked along the shore where the real excitement began. They had a donkey that you could hitch up and pull them out to where the surf was. Once I was running across the sand and got into quicksand. Well, they brought up a plank and said to keep treading, and they laid it to me and someone helped to get on it."

Other vacations were usually spent up at her father's garden. He was a great gardener, and eventually had access to several greenhouses. Jennie used to enjoy helping him water the plants, and from him she developed a love of plant life.

"Of course in the winter season there were the home affairs. Christmas, my mother being the only woman in a family of brothers, had all the other families to our house where we spent Christmas Eve together. We always had this wonderful English pork pie, and we had roast goose for Christmas dinner. We knew nothing about turkey, and there were no Christmas trees in that central part of England. But we did have a Christmas bush hanging from the ceiling, which was composed of green boughs and holly. It was decorated with things hanging. We also had the little mistletoe bough hung over each doorway in the little house. And we used to have a lot of fun dodging in and out. But the stockings were hung, and to make room for the youngsters, all the cousins and everything, we were put to bed with three at the head and three at the feet, with our feet to feet.

"As we got a little older, we wanted to know who was Santa Claus. So we made it up amongst ourselves that one was to keep the other one awake. But they got wise to it -- they saw a movement under the bed-blankets, and they went back. They explained it to us when we asked, Didn't we hear somebody come up the stairs? They said they thought Santa had been, and they had come to look."

Jennie was not deceived for long, however. One Christmas Eve she awakened and sneaked downstairs to wait for Santa. As she rounded the last turn, she could see her father and mother busily loading the stockings.

"I've got it, I've got it!" she cried aloud for the other children to hear. "Come and see who Santa is!"

Her father was so startled by the noise that he dropped everything in his hand. Jennie was ecstatic to confirm the suspicions which had lingered in her mind, and would rather it had been Dad and Mother than some fat man from the North Pole.

Her memories of the Christmas morning stocking:

"And what did we have in the stocking? Ah, yes. You had to start at the top, and you probably had a little toy. Then you had perhaps a pair of new stockings. You may have had a pair of gloves, if you were in need of them. You may have had some other little toy, and you had an apple and an orange. But oh, down in the toe you got a thre'penny piece, and that was wealth!"

Easter was a major event in the Court Building tenements. Choir practice was held for many weeks preceding Holy Week itself, and the children faithfully attended. Jennie always loved singing and had a fine voice. Spring cleaning was combined with decoration of the chapel, and there was a great bustle of activity. Easter clothes were made each year by Jennie's mother, but were usually unfinished until Whitsuntide.

"Mother made everything we wore from the skin out, and I can remember the big leghorn hats with the daisies around, and the ribbons here and tide under the chin, and weren't we proud!"

Other fetes and festivals marked the yearly round. In spring and fall the children put on a bazaar to raise money for the Church. Each child would be asked to portray a famous person in the "moving waxworks," as they called their rowdy show.

"They placed me as Joan of Arc, tied to the stake. One of our counselors had to wind me up with a key, you see, and I had to die. And he came up and said, `If I hadn't seen them loosen you from that stake, I would have thought you were waxen. How could a mischievous girl like you stay still for so long?' "

Jennie always retained her love of drama and costume, and her posture as Saint Joan, the woman who refused to wear women's clothes and scandalized the Church with her "faerie voices," was more than caricatured in this tomboy of the tenements who loved to climb trees.

There was also the annual farmer's fair, which had begun many years before with a flea market and week-long celebration of summer, and now was observed from Thursday noon to Saturday night.

"As the great clock in the marketplace began to chime twelve, the Lord Mayor would ride on a white horse through what we called the Shambles, which were the central meat districts. When the clock stopped striking he would say, `I, the Lord Mayor of Nottingham, declare this fair open for three days only,' and up would start the shouting and singing, and it was all Bedlam!"

One Christmas Jennie came face to face with the sort of ghostly phenomena for which England is famous. She and her elder sister Emily had been invited to spend the season with Aunt Jane, since Uncle William had passed away. When the two girls arrived, there was no one to meet them. They walked.

"Jesse Watson, a second cousin, had missed us because she'd had difficulties with the dog-cart in the blowing snow and she was late getting there. You know, we never had left Mother before. And oh, the tears that we shed!"

It was during this visit that Jennie's sister Emily experienced hearing ghostly footsteps.

"It turned out that she must have had some inner sense or power, because you couldn't hide anything from her. She'd find it no matter where you put it."

Her father used to play cards, to the great chagrin of his wife, who would hide the deck. Little Emily would please her father by tracking down the cards, no matter how carefully her mother had hidden them.

"And I remember, while we were staying in the country, we had gone upstairs to our room, and all at once she grabbed me by the arm and said, `Listen! Don't you hear those footsteps?'

"You see, at the side of the house there was a well which was all bricked in, and that's how they got the water for the house. But anyway, she could hear the click of the latch, because there was the gate here, and it came through out the other side through another gate and into a wonderful kitchen garden. And in it was a hothouse with all kinds of plants there. At the front of that hothouse, at the door entrance, there was a stone slab, and that came in as part of this experience. "And she listened, and she listened. Then she heard a gate latch like it dropped a heavy iron bar, and so we asked Aunt Jane about it. So that was after Uncle William had passed away, and she said, `So you heard it, did you?' She said yes, she had heard it, but she couldn't see anybody.

"Aunt Jane said, `Well, it's said that Uncle William walks because there was no will found, and there was a substitute made. He always comes to that slab and stops.'

"And then later I heard my father speak about it, and he said they can go digging after it if they want, but he says, he'd had enough of the disorderliness in the family. And Uncle was supposed to be restless in the spirit because that will was not destroyed. It was buried under that slab. But Dad would never submit to be drawn into it."

Jennie remembers the bitterly cold winters of her childhood.

"It was a wet snow that would be very disagreeable, and that's how we were taught to walk when the snow was thawing out -- to walk at the edge of the sidewalk, because when it got so wet, it would drop straight down. It could kill you with the weight of it.

"But when a wind was blowing, keep close to the houses. Because, the chimney-pots would go flying across and drop in the street, you see? And the slates also. We had slate roofs.

"We had fireplaces in every house, and in the bedroom on the first floor. But in the top rooms, the skylight rooms, as we called them, we had to have a kerosene heater. There was gas, and we used to have gas light, and kerosene lamps, most of them, up in the other parts of the house. "In the kitchen there was a fireplace that had an open grate at the front. There was what we call a drop-bar at the top -- had about three bars, so that you could rest a larger pan on that, 'cause you had to cook on it, and you had some bars that went across that could be removed. On one side was the water heater, and on the other side the oven. And that warmed the house.

"But in the living room we had more of an open fireplace that was backed up with a sheet, like this. It had a door that would drop down and close it when it was not in use. When it was in use, it had a dust-preventer underneath, because, as the coals would burn they settled down, and the ashes would drop into this ash-pan. And of course in your living room you had something a little more ornate, because it was made of brass. The heat going up the chimney would also heat the upper floor, but my little skylight bedroom was so cold, since it was above that second floor, that we'd put warm bricks into bed with us. But we never had the heater going all night. Now, we never had this, but when I got out among the gentry and took a job as nursemaid to the wealthy people's children, I used to bank up the coals by raking out the ashes and getting the coals together and clean. That would hold some heat all through the night. In extremely cold weather, you would put a little more on it about the middle of the night. But that was how you heated the rooms. But upstairs you got dressed, and no fooling about it!"

Jennie, then, experienced a happy childhood and a close family relationship. Her father was able to gain enough during his life to eventually bring the living standard up, and Jennie was brilliantly successful in school.

The hardships of the period were met with courage and humor, and Mother Jennie gained a foundational optimism which was to carry her through the tests and trials that marked the next phase of her life.

England has been a spawning ground of mediums and spiritualists because of the cultural credence for ghostly phenomena which characterizes it. Jennie was certainly exposed to such ideas through her sister Emily. But Jennie's private experiences with out-of-the-body sensations were not well enough known to be easily categorizable. As time progressed, her "illnesses" became worse, and the idyllic childhood drew to a close.

Chapter 3

THE PERIOD OF STRUGGLE

Raw ore must be fired to produce pure gold, and the precious stone cut carefully before it sparkles with light. The same is true of our lives. Any path to human excellence must, at some time, follow the desert dust and the dry stream beds. For the Christian mystic, there is a fiery baptism into the service, suffering and death of the Christ. The Death of God must come as a soul's dark night, until the faint glimmerings of the Eighth Day arise in a heart purified for the dawn.

It has been difficult for me to get much detail for this stage in Jennie's life because she doesn't like to recall it. That surely must speak eloquently for the period. She is a woman who has been able to reconcile so many of the opposites of human nature and feel true love for all -- yet still unable to find much joy in personal events that occurred more than fifty and sixty years ago. This, I believe, is not because she has failed to make a complete reconciliation with them in every psychological sense: she has no bitterness or condemnation. Rather, it is because there are aspects of human reality that simply and plainly are horrible, and no amount of adjusting can alter that fact.

I shall sketch the outlines of the period, much as I have the childhood. This will bring the reader up to the part of Mother Jennie's life that is of most interest, namely her spiritual awakening and the coming of the Teachers. But I caution the reader to look seriously at all that has preceded. As Mother Jennie says, "There are no little things. It's the `little things' that trip us up." And it is the mundane reality of a life spent in the vicissitudes of poverty, loss and struggle that lays the groundwork for a lasting victory. Perhaps the meaning of seemingly fruitless, absurd labors drawn out over more than a decade is best grasped in the following revelation which Jennie received many years later from one of her first Teachers. She was a beautiful Indian maiden called Rosa Lee. Jennie saw her sitting cross-legged in a birch-bark canoe paddling vigorously upstream.

"Why do you struggle upstream against the force of the current?" she asked.

"Because it makes the muscles strong and the face to shine," was the gay answer, as energy and light seemed to burst forth from the vision.

It is significant that Mother Jennie's period of struggle began with her experience of abnormal perception as a young girl entering puberty. This is the awkward "change of life" when the most intimate parts of oneself seem so blatantly exposed. Moodiness and the onset of genital sexuality flow in like an oncoming tide. One kind of self-knowledge flees, and a more social form takes its place. It is a critical period during which the subtle balance of yet unknown bodily and psychic forces is in continual upset. In Jennie the natural imbalance led her for a time into psychic experiences in a raw form which manifested as casually as a frightened fawn, momentarily wandering out of its forest camouflage. Still new and vulnerable, yet showing the promise of a fine stag.

Jennie's psychic sensitivity opened the doors to ill effects and a liability for disease which began to afflict her from this time for several years. Yet the very sensitivity which made her vulnerable would one day return in positive form. This could occur only because Jennie became the master of her "illness." Like the shaman, who must experience death and disease, the perils of the underworld journey, and be victorious before he could return as the healer of his tribe, Jennie had to know the depths of incarnate suffering before she could emerge as the mystical shamaness of Christ.

Shamans of a certain type characteristically undergo what Eliade has called a "shamanic illness." These are periods of nervous disorder and neurotic syndromes, like Black Elk's adolescent "compelling fear" or Saul of Tarsus' divine blindness. They either grip and hold the person, perhaps even unto death, or are mastered by him. If he fails to achieve self-mastery, the person becomes a simple neurotic -- possibly a psychotic. If he succeeds, he has found a divine vocation.

Details of werewolfism, vampirism and witch-cultism are preserved in the annals of medieval grimoires. Modern cases of cannibalism, infanticide, necrophilia are recorded in textbooks of abnormal psychology. Instances of persons afflicted by poltergeists or engaging in congress with incubi and succubi, and many other strange epiphenomena, are chronicled in contemporary occult and supernatural magazines. All these represent cases in which supersensitive persons have been swallowed up in the uncharted waters of their own unconscious powers.

Unfortunately the only charts and maps that exist for the consciousness that comes with many of these abnormal perceptions are in the ill-defined notions of demonism. If the prevailing notion is that the person who experiences strange phenomena is being attacked by demons, he will experience himself in that light.

The one important factor beyond the person's own strength of character that determines whether he can deal with abnormal psychic experience is the "chart." If he can be introduced or initiated into a system of interpretation by which he can "make sense" out of what happens to him, he can grasp the experience with tools of language and thought. He can discover the necessary steps to control and self-mastery. Otherwise it is like trying to get hold of a greased pig, or a bar of wet soap -- there is nothing which can be firmly grasped.

In other words, the great paradox in mystical experience is this: in order to live with the Mystery, we must de-mystify it. This is the point of departure for the varieties of religious experience, and the origin of religious diversity among mankind. Jennie's Mystery was too great to be comprehended by public church religion. Spiritualism offered a better "chart."

What if Jennie had fallen into the hands of a psychiatrist during these critical years? Psychology no longer recognizes the validity of that of which it was supposed to be the science -- namely the soul, the psyche. It prefers to speak of "personality," and to interpret abnormal perception as a "disorder." It labels what it doesn't understand with words like "paranoia" and "schizophrenia." Surely psychology could have offered a "chart" for the murky waters of Jennie's experience.

In the hands of a psychiatrist Jennie might have been encouraged to "express" all her feelings -- hostile, erotic or whatever -- to rid her of the "disorders." Psychology still operates on the model of demon-exorcism, with the belief that by expressing a feeling one magically rids himself of it. But what happens? The hater expresses hatred, until hatred becomes a habit he cannot control.

Jennie lived with feelings and sensibilities that neither she nor those around her understood. Instead of losing her mind, however, she sublimed the raw sensitivities which made themselves known at puberty. I did not say "repressed," but "sublimed." Being fully aware of her feelings, she tilled them into the earth of human encounter, to re-emerge many years later laden with the fruit of service. Through disappointment she was to gain hope; through despair, faith. In the terrible struggle with recurrent fear she became courageous, and by failure after failure she was to emerge victorious.

Psychology could have provided a chart for Jennie's journey, but it would have taken her to a much different port. It would have attempted to "liberate" her from the suffering which made her strong and holy. It would have exorcised her demon.

True catharsis does not come about by the expression or acting out of feelings of which the feeler himself does not consciously approve. Rather, it comes in the felt recognition of feelings hitherto unfelt -- that is, hitherto repressed, and thus given a mystical power to run rampant in that person's inner realm.

It has been standard for modern psychology to "liberate" people from the pangs of guilt by changing their minds about the various intimate areas of conflict which they experience. Thus we rid ourselves of sexual hangups by talking freely about sex, and advertising through sex, and entertaining with sex, and holding the image of manhood and womanhood in sexist roles -- "I'm Barbara. Fly me to Miami."

We rid ourselves of violence by experiencing it vicariously in movies, television, sports and newspaper reports. But is it really gone? Or is it happening in unthought-of ways hidden from public view in Vietnam and Cambodia, in dark alleys of New York City, or in the drug-hazed lives of high school children who have become virtual strangers to their parents?

Thank God Jennie did not get into the hands of a psychiatrist! Instead of the mental dogmas of orthodox intellectual culture, she had to go it alone.

In the crucible of her own hard-won experience she forged a pure vessel for God's service. She learned the alchemist's mystery of transmutation in her own body. She practiced nature's mystery of metamorphosis, transformation and the divine secret of transfiguration in the elements of her personal existence.

Psychology has only the first half of the process, the surgeon's part. It can cut people open and make them bleed. It may even be able to remove the infection that has long festered within. But it cannot make the person heal. Only the shaman knows the mystery of healing.

He knows that the unstopping of repressed energy is only stage one. Now transformation must begin. As the energy flows, it must be sublimed and channeled into a higher purpose. Desire must be transmuted into aspiration, and hate must be analyzed until the original love that brought it forth comes clear. Anxiety must be elevated into euphoria, and boredom or depression energized into slow, arduous gain. The key to forgiveness is self-love. Not self-indulgence, but devoted love to the reality of one's being, which is the common denominator of all beings.

It is a great accomplishment for anyone of abnormal perception, sometimes politically as well as psychologically, to stay out of a mental institution. It is a greater accomplishment to somehow master oneself and harness abnormal perception. But it is the greatest and most laudable accomplishment to make right and spiritual use of the faculties thus gained, rather than to exploit them for fame, money or other selfish illusions. This is Mother Jennie's achievement.

Jennie's supersensitivity made her vulnerable to much trial and confusion during her younger years. Yet this woman, who was affectionately known as the "creaking gate" because of her ill health, far outlived anyone else in her family. Her students became her family, and she their spiritual mother.

Young Jennie lived for several years with illness until a mechanism of inner control had established itself at a necessary level. After this stage came years of labor leading finally into nurse's training.

For many years she tended the flesh of the sick and midwifed the newborn children which cruel circumstances had dictated that she herself could never have. How little anyone suspected that she was one day to nurse human souls and serve as midwife to spiritual rebirth! The trials of this period made little sense to Jennie as she struggled through poverty, hard physical labor and a bad marriage which finally ended in divorce. But later she would be able to look back and find meaning in even the smallest details. These had been her years of preparation.

*******   *******   *******

Jane Hopkins was just entering her teens when she was indentured to the Nottingham School Board as a student teacher in the British Infant School system. The term was to be four years but, though she enjoyed her work and education very much, her health was on the wane. Dr. Mullholland had begun by prescribing milk for her strange "spells" which he had diagnosed as dyspepsia. But Jennie's behavior became less understandable. Her sleepwalking had become a serious problem, and she seemed to pick up every disease germ in the area. Her physical stamina was severely taxed by repeated episodes of illness.

Her father was very worried. Jennie could not simply quit her job and education, since the terms of the indenture were binding yet another 2□«" years. It would cost him half a year's pay to break the indenture, and Jennie cried at the idea of quitting. Yet Dr. Mullholland was becoming more insistent that Jennie be given complete rest.

At that point the worst possible thing happened. Just as Jennie was experiencing her first menstruation, she was hit hard with the Spanish flu.

"Everything went up to my head, and with it developed eczema. They had to cut my hair and shave my head. The general upset was terrible. You see, we were not educated or prepared for those changes in life, and when they took place it almost scared me to death. I'm talking about the female change. And at the same time it went up and caused a terrible confusion in my head, with terrible headaches. All things taken together, it almost laid me out."

There was no longer any choice in the matter. Jennie's father borrowed the necessary money and broke the indenture. It nearly broke Jennie's heart. She had successfully passed the Pupil Teacher's Exam and taught classes at the Harcourt Street Pupil Teacher's Center for nearly two years. This provided her with scholarship aid in furthering her own education. Now all the dreams of education and perhaps a better lot in life were ruined. How could God allow such a thing? Jennie broke all ties with church religion for many years.

Most of the winter was spent in recuperation: for three months she lay flat on her back. When she was finally declared well again, it was her duty to find work for the support of the family. Dad's loan to break the indenture had been a crushing blow for everyone.

She took her first job in a local laceware house and progressed through various phases of the business. Work was scarce and pay was pitifully small. When laceware went into a slump and she was laid off, she found a job in hosiery. She had learned the whole lace business, operating the jennying machines and various sewing machines, then on to finishing and facing. Because of this experience she was able to help Mother work late at night with special lace orders.

Soon however there was another economic slump, and Jennie was laid off. She found a part-time job selling clothes for a while until that job also vanished. The economy was on a downturn as events led up to the Boer War with its turbulent years.

There was time for boyfriends, and the discovery of herself as a woman nearly made up for her disappointment about school. Jennie spent chaperoned afternoons at the beach with various beaus while Mother looked discreetly on.

After a long search for work, Jennie took on the lowest-paid and perhaps most difficult option available: nursemaid to the local gentry. At times she received room but not board. Children liked her, however, and this made things easier.

Finally she made her way to the C. E. Bastow dress coat and cape makers of Nottingham. There was little chance of getting employment with anyone, let alone the best coat maker in England at the time. They wanted experienced people, and preferably of the gentry. Jennie was neither.

"I walked up those winding stairs five stories. When I got to the door I knocked. `Yes?' they asked. Had I made any before? Was I familiar with it? I said, `No.' They asked me several questions, and finally I said, `I can run a machine.' They said, Oh, could I? What kind of machine? Well, they were sorry but they wanted experienced hands.

"Well, I think my heart went down to my toes, but I put my foot in the door and I said, `Please give me a try. I'll work for nothing, if you'll only let me have a try. I need work badly.'

"The man there turned and spoke to somebody inside, and he turned back and said, `Well, when can you start?' I said, `Right now.' He opened the door and said, `All right. Come in.' "

She began without pay, but soon was fully employed. The skills she had learned on the lace machines were easily applied to the new Singer sewing machines used by Bastow, and she quickly learned what was needed. The early Singer machines were gas-run, like those of the lacework house, and Jennie made herself indispensable as a mechanic.

At the age of 18 Jennie had met a man while visiting the beach with her mother, and she fell very much in love with him. He was chief engineer on a fishing boat from Grimsby. The two of them were engaged to be married.

"His name was John Edward Collier. He was a big, swarthy fellow. Mother took my younger sister to the seaside for a holiday every year, but one year she took me. It was there we met."

Jennie's work kept her away from John too much, and eventually the two of them drifted apart. The responsibility which she had incurred to the support of the family as a result of Dad's loan weighed heavily on her mind. From the time she had taken her first job at a candy store, she had vowed to put personal concerns behind family concerns. Jennie was also beginning to feel uncertain about marriage. She continued at Bastow's after the breakup with John.

What went through her mind in this period? Was the burden she had undertaken for the family finally taking its toll? Was the poverty she experienced closing in on her, with the specter of spinsterhood? She was twenty years old and still unmarried. Her sisters had married, and all her childhood friends.

It is difficult to get details of Jennie's first marriage. All she is willing to say is that her first husband worked with the telephone company. It was in the first few years of this marriage that Jennie suffered the loss of two children who were stillborn, and through the pain of this decided to go into nursing. Possibly it was her experience of the Spanish flu while beginning menstruation which caused her problems in childbirth.

"The first child I carried full term. They didn't have Caesarean operations then, and I had too small a passage. They had to turn the baby, and they put a tie around its feet. I had been in agonizing labor for a week, and was finally put under chloroform. They got the baby, but I was torn badly. The baby was dead. But the day before, I had felt that baby kick. It died in childbirth. The next day I reverted with a dreadful hemorrhage. I remember drifting, and I remember my jaw dropping. My sister grabbed me and screamed, `My God, she's dying. Fred, Fred, get the doctor!'"

"And I saw my dead grandmother up in the corner of the room, and she extended her arms saying, `Come, come.' And all at once the doctor came, and I saw her put her arms up and heard her say, `Not yet, not yet.' I'll never forget that experience."

The loss was terrible for Jennie, since she loved children. They put the dead little child in her arms after the delivery, and she wanted so much just to feel the little hand squeezing her thumb -- but no response.

"2□«" years after that I was pregnant again, and we went to stay with my husband's people. We had a mattress on the floor and his sister slept with me. During the night she tossed and slung her arms right across me. I gasped and I thought, `Oh my God.' Well, we went back home, and my husband left for work on the Monday morning. He worked for the Midland Railway. I got up -- it was the 15th of July, St. Swithin's Day -- and he was gone for the week, and I had an awful stomach ache. I thought, `Well, if I get up and make a hot cup of tea, I'll feel better.' I stirred up a fire, made a cup of hot tea and went back upstairs. Suddenly I lost everything, just like that. The houses were built in rows, so I hammered on the floor for help. The neighbor came and got the doctor. I hadn't cleared, so he had to correct me, and I had to bite the pillow while he did it. But again, I'd lost my baby, and it took quite some time to get over that."

As a result of this trauma, Jennie was scheduled for surgery -- a hysterectomy. The date was May, 1901, but on the third day of that month her beloved mother died. Jennie refused to leave Nottingham until her mother's body had been properly buried, and as a result was forced to give up the hospital bed that had taken so long to become vacant. She had to wait until October before there was another vacancy. During these and other crises her husband, because of the nature of his work, was not present. He was gone for weeks at a time all during the marriage, which lasted 15 years, and then for nearly a year when he went ahead to Canada to homestead.

Jennie had spent a great deal of time taking care of children, and Dr. Druitt, who performed her operation, was very fond of this brave young woman. He was quite elderly, and wanted to be of help to her. One afternoon he came calling.

"Jennie, I feel that you are naturally born to be a nurse. If you would like to undertake nurse's training, I will pay your tuition and fees. Now please don't object! I want to do something nice for you before I pass away. Just consider this to be a kind of scholarship."

The offer came as a Godsend. No longer able to bear children, Jennie had begun to think again about some sort of work beyond simple manual labor. She had watched the nurses at work in the hospital and talked to them. What sort of training was necessary to become registered? What did it cost? Old Dr. Druitt had heard of her interest and was moved to help her. Jennie had developed quite a reputation as a local midwife already. Dr. Druitt pointed out that a new law had been passed making special training mandatory, so why not just go ahead into nurse's training?

"Well, he arranged it. So I went down to the offices of the Royal Derbian Nursing and Sanitary Association, and there began to be instructed."

Jennie was a bright student. She had gained plenty of experience in midwifing local women. Her own pregnancies and misery had taught her great compassion for women undergoing similar experiences, and she wanted to help other women avoid the suffering she had felt. The school soon had her out working on her own. After the first year Dr. Druitt died, and to make up her tuition Jennie had to forfeit three quarters of her wages as a practical nurse.

During the many years that Jennie worked to gain status as a registered nurse, two incidents stand out in her seemingly all but dormant spiritual life. The first involved a return to church life, and the second her meeting Florence Nightingale.

"One time I was sent to nurse the Methodist minister's wife in Langley Mill. The parsonage was next door to the church, and when I had time off I went to the Christian Endeavor meetings. I always sat at the aisle end of the pew toward the back. That night it had been dreadfully stormy, and they finally had word that the speaker could not come. So Mr. Governor, who was the Superintendent, said, `I feel that God has sent someone to us tonight to give us a message, and will that one please come forward.' Nobody moved. We sat as still as mice. He waited a little while and again made his statement. No one responded, so he looked down the aisle and said, `Nurse, won't you please come forward?' And I said, `Me?' He said yes, that he felt God had sent me with a message for them. So I walked down this aisle to the chancel, and I looked at him and said, `Then, if God has sent me with a message, let us pray,' because I had no idea of being called upon. So we went into prayer.

"Soon I began to speak, and I spoke on conscience. I've always remembered it -- it was so definite. But I gave them such a talk, you could have heard a pin drop, and that was a large church.

"The next day three of the ladies from the Ladies' Society came to see if I would give that sermon next week at a Pleasant Sunday Afternoon meeting. I looked at them and said, `I can't do it.' They said, `Well, couldn't you give us what you said last night?' I said, `My dears, it was not written. That was a message from God through me.' "

The ladies refused to take no for an answer, so Jennie agreed to speak but warned that God might not give her words to say for them. The next Sunday, however, she was able to deliver another sermon on conscience, this one different from the first. Jennie was amazed that she could speak before a religious group without notes or written preparation.

Soon she was called to serve in another nursing situation and moved away. From time to time she wondered about what had happened at Langley Mill, but passed it off as an unusual incident. Nothing like it was to occur again for many years. In retrospect, however, she sees it as the first sign of her ministry.

Jennie has always remembered her encounter with Florence Nightingale as the highlight of her nursing career. She had been put in charge of the newly-built isolation hospital in Ralston.

"Florence Nightingale was coming to dedicate it, and it was to be named for her. I'd just come out of the delivery room, and I ran upstairs to put on a clean apron. While I was still busy the photographer set up the camera and took the picture. I was sick about that!

"And she was a very sweet appearing old lady. She was dressed in black. She had a sailor hat on -- a crown about this high, with a pin gathered up here and a few roses set in. I can remember it as distinctly as I remember your face."

The visit with Florence Nightingale injected something into Jennie's work as a nurse which always served to lift her up in difficult circumstances. Jennie saw in Florence a vision of true service with inner peace, and through few words were spoken between them, the impression was deep and permanent. Surely this attests to the power of a life sanctified in service to others -- not in a strained or self-consciously martyred selflessness, but in sincere compassion for the suffering of others. The real-life "feeling" of the "very sweet appearing old lady" stayed with Jennie. It enabled her to find meaning in the most mundane and even repulsive aspects of nursing. Florence Nightingale had earned her peace and inner sweetness in the same daily tasks that Jennie performed -- in the environment of pain, bedpans and excremental fluids. For Jennie the memory of Florence Nightingale was enough to make it all worthwhile.

In 1908 Jennie's husband decided to join relatives who were homesteading in Canada, and went ahead to prepare a land site. Jennie remained at her work in England, economically independent as she had been for several years, for ten more months. When the time came to make the voyage, the husband of her last patient, who was an auctioneer, volunteered to sell the surplus goods she could not take along. Finally, on the 15th of January, 1909, Jennie set sail from Liverpool.

Chapter 4

AGONY AND INDEPENDENCE: THE DARK NIGHT OF THE SOUL

In many religious lives there is a period of despair, a sickness unto death which either conquers or is conquered. It is a period when Job would damn the day he was born, and the Psalmist would cry out but Yahweh would not seem to hear. It is a foundational experience of the absence of God, the death of the sacred.

It cannot be spoken about.

*******   *******   *******

The Empress of Britain was one of England's largest ships. It was supposed to make the Atlantic crossing in four days. Ominously, however, it ran into a violent storm midway which smashed half of the ship's rigging and left everyone, including the Captain, quite ill. Jennie arrived at North Brunswick several days late. She was to meet her family in western Canada by rail, but when she finally was able to get into Montreal the train for southern Alberta had been put out of service by a terrific continental blizzard which had accompanied the storm at sea. There was no way to send a message to her sister, since all the telegraph lines were down. It was now January 23, three days beyond the date she had been expected.

During the storm at sea, Jennie had dreamed vividly about a strange world called Atlantis. It seemed that the ship had sunk, or perhaps she had been sleeping in her old room in the tenements of Nottingham and found herself whirled out of bed. In any case, she was with several persons dressed in robes and strange golden headwear. They were crawling through deep underground caverns which narrowed down like the passage of a womb, until finally they could barely squeeze along. It seemed that they were beneath the ocean floor. Almost imperceptibly a tiny light began to grow in the pitch blackness. She inched her way forward. An opening was beginning to appear. Joy welled up inside her, and she strained forward with her friends. Finally they pulled her up through the bright opening, and she saw a vast and beautiful expanse of unspoiled ocean. Her strange friends then narrated to her that she was a priestess of Atlantis who as a child had been left at the foot of the Temple, and was raised by priests.

At this time in her life, Jennie knew nothing of Spiritualism and its myths, or so she says. It is interesting to note the comparison of the experience narrated by Plato in his Allegory of the Cave to the images of Jennie's dream, and to further note that it is Plato who transmits the legend of Atlantis in his Timaeus. Possibly Jennie had been exposed to some of the writings or ideas of Plato in her childhood, which served as input for the imagery of the dream. This could explain her unconscious knowledge of the word Atlantis, and the association with caverns and sea.

In any case, Jennie returned in thought to the dream many times in her first few days on the new American continent, and finally she spoke with the ticket agent at the Montreal station, asking if he knew of any place in America called Atlantis. He puzzled for some time, then told her no, but that there was a place in the United States called Atlantic City, and that must be what she had in mind. No, said Jennie. The name was most distinct, and it was "Atlantis."

Jennie was able to board the train for southern Alberta in another day. She brought blankets for the cold, food for the trip and a little alcohol lamp to make her tea -- as her sister had suggested. The journey was rough, but she joined with a group of the passengers in singing most of the way.

The journey was four days by rail. At McLeod Jennie transferred to the Calgary line, which took her to a small town called Brannon.

"When I got off the train, there was nothing but the vast wide prairie with sun shining on the snow. And not another soul in sight. So I went into the little depot, and a man came from across the street. I said, `Is there a train that goes back this other way?'

" `Not until tomorrow, Madame. We only have one train a day.'

"I said, `I expected someone here to meet me.'

"He says, `Are you looking for the Whittles?'

"I said, `Yes, I most decidedly am.'

"He says, `They were all in yesterday expecting you. You've come from the Old Country.'

"I said, `Yes, and my passage was delayed by storm.'

" `Well,' he says, `you'd best wait here and see if they come in again for you today.'

"I asked him what the temperature was, with all this blinding white snow. He said it was 54 below zero, and they'd had a blizzard yesterday. I said, `I'm glad there wasn't a train going the other way, or I'd have gotten on it!' "

This was Jennie's introduction to the most difficult and painful part of her life, which she was to spend as a homesteader, midwife and plains nurse, and which was to end in divorce, serious loss of health and total bankruptcy.

Things started rough and got rougher. The work was backbreaking and thankless, and the only goal was survival through a subzero winter to another parched summer on the endless prairie. Tragic accidents and human loss were encountered at every turn, as the inexperienced homesteaders tried to work the stony land of what seemed a God-forsaken territory. There could be no time or leisure for "spiritual things." There were not even churches. There was only vast isolation, with people, struggle and pain. There were only the cruel earth, the bitter cold, the mammoth hailstones which indiscriminately flattened crops, livestock, homes and hopes.

For Jennie all this came in the context of a marriage which should never have been -- a life without love and a struggle without reward. Divorce was absolutely unthinkable and would represent an irrevocable failure to this young nurse, a death blow to any future self esteem for the young lady who had preached on conscience to the congregation of Langley Mill. Life on the plains was not only a struggle for biological survival, but a losing battle for spiritual survival. In her own eyes, what little faith she had died a cruel death in southern Alberta. But in retrospect, it simply went underground -- invisible to her, but manifest to all others in her selfless mission of midwifery and nursing which she never abandoned, even though her husband finally forbade it. That was the issue which was finally to divide them.

Sister Gert and her husband finally came into town later that afternoon, and on January 26 Jennie began ranch life.

"What could I do? I couldn't sit there and twiddle my thumbs. My sister was going to town to do some shopping. She says, `What about making the butter while I'm gone?'

" `Oh, yes,' I said, I could do that. So she had all this churned cream and everything (she'd just been churning when I'd got there), and she gave me the paddles and board. I got to work, and she got me to work the salt well into it. Well, when she came back I had it set up, and she looked at me and said, `Do you mean to say you got all that out of that cream?'

"I said, `Yes, isn't that wonderful?'

"She said, `It is? You wait until I get at it and you'll find out!' She took it all out of the bowl, put it on the board and started to work it, and she had half the quantity of butter when she got through. She sais, `You have to wash butter well and work it well to get all that fluid out, or in a week it will be rancid.'

"So anyhow, I learned to make butter, and then I learned how to make bread. I had to set the yeast the night before. Then I had to work it into some flour. We had a big tin pan with a lid which we lined with heated flour, and put this in the middle. You had to wrap it around with blankets to keep it warm, then it was kneaded in, and you covered it again and put it as close to the stove as you dared, but wrapped in blankets overnight. The next morning you kneaded it again, and when it grew you'd make it into loaves and put it in your bread pans and let it rise again, and by the second night you had bread.

"Well, I noticed a funny odor, and I said, `If that's what they have for bread, I don't think I want any.' Then I noticed all this fluid that was around the dough, and suddenly it struck me through: `I bet that cat sat on the ledge to keep warm, and she wet!' And that wet went into the dough, and into the nice warm bread I'd baked after all that work!

"I had a .22 (and this was a few weeks after I got there) and I picked it up and went after that little yellow cat. He jumped over a root cellar that had caved in, and he sat across there looking at me. I popped him and he just went over -- I hit him right between the eyes.

"I had to start that bread process all over again, and did they ever ha-ha-ha me! The next batch I made, I wasn't quite so particular about kneading, and when it was baked, you could have built a house with it, because you couldn't chop it, only with a hatchet! So it went out too. And honestly, the chickens pecked at it for over a week. It did feed the chickens, but that was all. But on the next batch I was more particular, and I did get the first nice batch of bread."

Life never became too difficult while Jennie was living with the Whittles, but in June of the following summer they set out for the plot of land her husband had claimed for their homestead. They had sent machinery and dry goods overland by rail, but had to drive their wagon for several days over waterless desert to reach the site. They took sixteen head of stock with chickens and poults in cages. The hay rack, which was set over the running gear, was loaded with bags of oats for the stock, and Jennie and her husband slept on the hard sacks at night. When the oats ran out, they slept on the buckboard. Soon the water failed.

"We got down as far as Purple Springs, where there was supposed to be a well. When we opened the top, the gophers had got into it and rotted it, and you had to shut it down fast. Now, we had eight days trekking over the prairie to get down there, and we went 36 hours without a drop of water. One day we took a wrong road and got into a steep ravine without room to turn around. Gert's husband found a shallow ford, and he said, `You keep to the wagons and I will direct you. Don't stir one foot from where I point.' We sat behind with bated breath, but we went."

They found their way over rocky ravines and traveled quietly through fields of skittish buffalo until they found themselves again without water. Now it was hot and dusty, and they had entered the flatlands. Finally they saw a wind-pump and stopped, asking the people there if they could get a cup of water. They were refused. The man said they had none to spare, and had barely enough for themselves. Jennie asked if they could at least have a cup for Gert's children, but was told that a few miles further there was another well. Ask there, and they might have a better well from which they could share.

"They wouldn't give us one drop of water for those children, so we went on. It was getting toward evening, and at one of the big mile-squares we saw another pump going. Our horses had their heads down, barely pulling the rig, and we were choked and could hardly speak for faintness. And these people came running out from their house, and they looked up at us, and we said, `Water.' And they brought us water. They started to unhitch our horses and said, `You'd better come into the house.' So we went in, and they fed and watered the horses, and turned their horses out of the barn and put ours in.

"They said, `You look pretty tired out. Are you hither bound to the homestead?'

"We said, `Yes.'
" `Well,' they said, `you'd better stay overnight. A fire went through there yesterday. There won't be any grazing for your stock.' "

The little Mormon family cooked them a delicious meal and gave them the best beds for rest, and in the morning and hitched and harnessed the homesteaders' wagon and fed the stock before Jennie's people had awakened.

In several more hours they arrived at their site. It was totally blackened by fire. They set up the tent and gave thanks for the water which had been provided them, settling in for the night. They lived in the tent for five months. There was a spring several hundred feet downhill in a low gully, and the daily supply had to be hauled up on a shoulder balance by Jennie. The stock had to be watered one at a time with a pail.

Since there would be no grazing for several months, it was necessary to buy bundled hay from the railroad, which had a tiny station 35 miles away, or one day's journey. Machinery and goods were also brought in from the rail station. With the help of neighbors, a roof was finally raised before winter had become too bitter.

The ground had to be prepared for crops, but it was embedded with stones. Jennie's job was to guide the "stoneboat," or sliding platform rigged to a horse, while she loaded loose rocks and small boulders onto it. These were stacked in long rows around the fields as walls. Then the deeper stones had to be dug out by hand -- a process resulting in broken fingernails and strained muscles. She had to stretch barbed wire for fencing in stock, another duty which left her nurse's hands so sore and punctured that she could hardly knead dough for the week's supply of bread. Sod shacks were built after the main cabin, then a barn to keep the stock alive during the harsh winter. While all this was going on, the neighbors had discovered that Jennie was an experienced nurse and midwife. She was in constant demand.

"One day I had three cases of pneumonia, a case of typhoid fever, and seventy miles in the other direction a baby was to be born. When I got through I just crawled up a ladder and flopped on the floor. I told my sister, `I just can't stand it.' But there was no other help to call but me, and I had to respond."

Jennie became known as a veterinarian as well. One afternoon she saw a mule wandering and braying outside the wire fence. The animal had been gashed the full length of its left side, and the red flesh was exposed in a large flap of bloody hide. Jennie approached the animal and began to sing softly to it. After some time the mule allowed her to lead him into the barn. He lay down, and she washed and bound his wound. Suddenly the door opened with Gert and one of the neighbor men looking on in amazement.

"You're lucky to be alive, Jennie. That poor animal wouldn't let anyone come near, and broke my foreman's ribs when he tried to help him. We thought we'd have to shoot him. But come on, now, if you will and bandage some broken ribs for us."

Despite her love for animals, Jennie found herself becoming increasingly irritable toward them. Life was so hard, and her heavy nursing load seemed to draw the very life from her. Jennie's husband, as always, was absent most of the time. While she cared for everyone else, who would care for her?
Specifically, the little Angus cow had become Jennie's nemesis. She gave rich milk, but was the breachiest animal in stock, always breaking over the barbed-wire fence into the ten-acre crop. One day in particular Gert's husband had been quite angry about the cow. Jennie was chasing her, feeling lower than ever, frustrated and tired enough to die.

"I took a board and whacked her on the rump into the little sod barn. As I got her whacking through the door I stood there, and I did swear. Then I heard a voice say, `What goes wrong here?' I looked up, and on this little cayuse was a man."

The man was Hugh Speak, an Anglican priest sent from Alaska to minister to the homesteaders of the area. He spoke soothingly to Jennie, and offered to run down the Angus for her on his cayuse from then on. She'd never have to do that dreaded task again. He was living in a little shack just over the rise with his partner.

This was an important contact for Jennie during her homesteading years. The last period of her life had become spiritually barren, and somehow religion regained personal importance for her as she sat on the dry grass for Hugh Speak's open-prairie services. She began to turn inward, to examine herself and to find inner moorings that would bolster her for the worst period of all, which was yet to come.

"Although I called it God-forsaken country, I came more and more to know that of myself I could do nothing -- that I must ask for guidance and help to do whatever was necessary. And you know, I midwifed many babies, but I never lost one, and I learned to give thanks."

The only doctor in the area lived two days' journey away. After witnessing her work several times, he drew her aside and begged her to take all but the most serious cases.

"Jennie, there isn't anything I can do short of major surgery that you can't do as well. It doesn't make sense for me to come way out here for most of these things. Here is a large bottle of chloroform, scalpels, syringes -- everything you need. Please take them. I'll stand behind whatever you find it necessary to do. It's either this or no doctor at all. I'm getting too old to make this trip. Please do this for me."

She couldn't refuse the old man's request, and from that time forward Jennie's workload almost doubled.

Late one afternoon Mr. Thompson was bringing Jennie back home from a delivery up north. They were traveling the new North-South road, which had many treacherous dips that often tended to sink and throw unwary rigs. Suddenly the horse started and, lurching sideways, threw off one of the traces. The horse was about to bolt when she saw an Indian form appear. He made a grab for the horse's nose and held it, gently stroking and speaking softly to the frightened animal.

Thompson jumped down to reconnect the traces. He had seen the Indian too. As he turned to thank him, the Indian had disappeared. There was no place into which anyone could have disappeared, since the land was flat as a pancake. That experience gave both Jennie and Thompson something to talk about as they made their way south, and Jennie something to ponder in the coming weeks.

Jennie's husband was growing more and more discontented with her medical work. After a hard summer's work they had finally been able to build a separate dwelling, to live apart from Gert's family. The new homestead required a great deal more work from Jennie than she had previously given at Gert's, and the nursing would simply have to end.

Jennie refused to quit nursing. She had been trapped into the terrific case load by the circumstances of plains life, it seemed, but she was not going to refuse a call when it came, no matter how desperate her own schedule. If it came to a choice between setting a bone or sweeping the floor, there was no question in Jennie's mind what the priority would have to be.

The issue, I think, was one that is common today among husbands and wives: the basic issue of liberation and sexual equality. Jennie's husband just couldn't comprehend her subversiveness, her unwillingness to yield to his demand. Jennie herself simply refused to turn her back on what she felt to be a clearly sacred duty of service.

One afternoon an urgent call came. A baby was to be delivered prematurely. Jennie prepared to go, then felt her husband's strong hand gripping her wrist.

"You will stay here."

"I will not."

He slapped her face. She threw a kettle at him and ran out to the waiting rig.

When she returned, her husband of 15 years had left to seek summer work in Montreal. Jennie spent the three worst months of winter alone, eking out a survival and tending the sick. When her husband finally returned, she had made up her mind to leave him.

Neighbors who had relatives in Minot, North Dakota, offered to take her south, but the morning of departure Jennie was seriously hurt by the Angus, who accidentally stepped on her stomach during a fall. Jennie was adamant about leaving, and they began the buckboard trip.
Midway Jennie began experiencing violent intestinal pains, and by the time they crossed the border into the States she was in a semi-coma. Her neighbors rushed her to the hospital in Northfield for emergency surgery. Most of her liver had been crushed and had to be sewn together, and the gall bladder, which had to be removed, was hanging by a thin thread of tissue. Doctors Sayer and Peterson told her that it would be a miracle if she could ever walk again, but in a month she was on her two feet and checking out of the hospital. Her husband didn't even bother to write.

After a short rest with friends she had met in the hospital, Jennie returned to Gert's house in Alberta. She received a lukewarm greeting. Most of the neighbors whom Jennie had nursed shunned her. The plainsmen eyed her suggestively, and she received a proposition of marriage from an elderly cattleman who wrote to her mail-order style.

The divorce process was totally demoralizing. She realized that Gert and her husband secretly condemned her decision, and didn't want her to stay with them. In sorrow and blackest, guiltiest defeat, Jennie turned all her financial interest in the homestead over to her husband.

With failing health, having lost everything for which she had labored all her adult life, Jennie departed for North Dakota. She carried with her only one suitcase and a worn medical bag.

Chapter 5

A NEW LIFE

What is life, and what remains when hope itself has temporarily dissolved?
I am told that if a person were to attempt suicide by holding his breath, soon after he had fallen unconscious the natural respiratory process would begin anew. Even the most advanced yogin cannot circumvent this inevitability.

This suggests to me that what remains when human will has fled is the basic pulse of life itself. This life-pulse is eternal. Like the Will of God, it is compelling and takes ultimate precedence. Given enough time, all things are molded to its way. Since it is the root of aeons and the Mother of Eternity, there is always enough time.

I can close my eyes to the river, or stop my ears against its gentle chuckling, but still it carries me along. I can even drown myself in the river, but still I am buoyed upward and on my way.

Life is like light. It is a real energy that cannot be created nor destroyed. Rather it must be brought to birth. Omnia celluli cellulae. It is a high form of reality that varies only in density. A tiny match will illuminate a dark room, but held against the disc of the sun it appears as a shadow. In the same way, one form of life appears "dead" to a more live or conscious form.

The hills and stones have their lives, and death is not an enemy. Death is a reaper. What it seems to destroy in life-density it restores in life-breadth and perspective. What it seems to require in captivity it restores in undreamed-of freedom. There are many dimensions to every continuum, but how narrowly we see with these eyes of flesh!

I am told that there are stars in the astronomer's universe that are so dense that their brilliant light collapses continually back into itself, unable to break away from the dense gravity. No light is perceived, but rather a conspicuous intense blackness. The great star is seen as an absolute hole in the sky, like a tunnel to some other universe beyond man's conception.

Who knows that energy, far more potent and sublime than what man calls "light," emanates from that mysterious star?

I cannot see God. Therefore (I reasoned in my mind) God is dead, or absent. I cannot find meaning in my life. Therefore, life has no meaning. It is absurd.

But life inexorably continues. It pulses forward, and no matter how I try to squelch it, to divide, trap and end it, life continues. I cut away my arm, and it feeds the grass. I give my flesh to the fire, and it nourishes the earth.

I snuff out the flame of a candle. Surely this is death. Where does the flame go? It disperses itself back into the cold, solid elements in which it had been rooted. Still it burns, but much more slowly. My eyes of flesh do not see a flame, but the scientist knows that oxidation never ceases. I have not killed the flame. I have only transformed it, bound it into a longer continuum.

It is by a breath that a soul's flame is kindled, and by a breath that it is blown out. It is the same breath, and the same breather.

Surely life must be continually lost in order to be gained. The images of hope often dissolve, only to re-crystallize in far greater beauty than the mind of flesh had conceived.

******* ******* *******

The period of the divorce was made easier by the Olsens. They had insisted that Jennie stay with them when she returned to North Dakota for her final decree. They owned a small but carefully tended hog ranch near Minot. It was clean and always in repair.

The Olsens had been very fond of Jennie ever since their daughter had shared a hospital room with her. They understood more than was ever expressed how great Jennie's need was for warmth, rest and peace. After so many years of physical and psychic agony, Jennie no longer resembled the cherub-faced nurse of Nottingham. She had become muscular and sinewy. Her complexion was flinty and wind-worn, with her eyes sunk deeply into their delicately-formed setting.

Jennie had lost her porcelain-like gentle beauty. Yet something more striking had grown up in its place. There was an attractive depth to her features. Her hands and fingers had become lean and bony, but infinitely more expressive. As she settled into a long period of recuperation and synthesis, Jennie reflected upon herself and her life. What was the purpose of all this? What did she now want to do?

She changed her name back to Hopkins and slowly eased into work as a nurse. The time had come when she could no longer accept the Olsens' hospitality without making a contribution to the household. She tutored their daughter, who had become Jennie's fast friend and admirer, and tended the younger children as well.
A winter passed, then a summer. Jennie had heard little from Gert and nothing from her ex-husband. Occasionally people from up north would pass through town with news of the homesteads, but Jennie was beginning to look to her own future. She had decided to remain in the United States and apply for citizenship. She wanted to work as a nurse.

On a Sunday afternoon after church, as Jennie walked the dirt path to the ranch, a man approached from behind in his buckboard. Jennie stepped to the side and looked up. It was Louis Peterson.

Jennie was swept with amazement and pleasure at seeing her old friend. He, on the other hand, didn't seem the least bit surprised to find her on this deserted road in North Dakota. He leaned down toward her with a softness in his eyes and said, "Hello, Jennie Hopkins."

They rode the buckboard in a flood of conversation until long after the sun had set. As they reminisced about life on the homesteads, Jennie felt the stirrings of new and exciting possibilities. Waves of long-forgotten joy seemed to break gaily against the lump in her throat, which felt like a sea rock too long widowed from its wet spray.

"Why were you not surprised to see me here?"

"Well, I was quite surprised." Louis tried to avert his eyes. Jennie fixed him with a compelling stare.

"Well, you see," he began painfully, then with a twinkle of humor, "I knew you were here. Gert told me. And there was no one I wanted to see more than the wonderful nurse who saved my hand!"

"Now, now," laughed Jennie. "It wasn't your hand, but your thumb. If you hadn't been so stubborn, I wouldn't have been able to do anything. Besides, it was God's healing, not mine."

While plowing his stony field, Louis had received a bad puncture to his thumb. It refused to heal. When the red streaks began to run down his wrist, he came to Jennie for help. She feared blood poisoning and possible gangrene, and sent him south to see the old doctor.

The old man had referred Louis on to doctors who wanted to amputate, since the whole hand was infected and looked hopeless. It was either amputate or die. Louis returned to southern Alberta and again approached Jennie. He told her that he was absolutely certain she could heal him if she'd just try. Faced with this, Jennie had prayed, and decided to make a plaster of fresh cow dung as a last resort. In a few days the whole character of the infection had changed. The red streaks shortened up and disappeared. When the plaster was removed, it was found that a quantity of deep pus had formed into a head, which Jennie drained and cauterized. By late that evening, Louis' fever had vanished, and in a week the hand was good as new. It had seemed like a real miracle.

The fact is that Louis had developed a deep love for Jennie while she nursed him. When he'd heard about the divorce he decided to sell his homestead and follow Jennie to the United States. This took quite a while, but finally he was able to make his way to Minot, where he knew she was staying. He had asked all around town for her, learned that she had reclaimed her maiden name of Hopkins, and eventually tracked down the Olsens' ranch. They had told him how to find her on the road from church.

There were many more buckboard rides. Jennie and Louis talked for long hours about their individual plans for the future. It wasn't long before Jennie began to realize that she enjoyed simply being with Louis and talking more than any hypothetical future plans could offer. She had been fond of him even while married, but never allowed herself to indulge this feeling. Now, however, heaven seemed to have settled on earth.

Louis was a fine and honorable man, and offered his sincere attention and heartfelt love. He respected her professional calling, her personal individuality. To him she was an attractively independent person, not just a potential wife, cook, homemaker, and breeder. He was aware that she could bear him no children, but this did not even enter into the relationship.

It was not romance -- at least, not the sort that is idolized in movies and pulp novels. There was no obsession, no compelling need for some sort of psychic completion. Without any psychological props or illusions, Jennie and Louis discovered a deep-running affection for each other based in mutual affinities and mysteries which, when explored, revealed an exquisite happiness unlike anything either had previously experienced.

Their union transcended romantic love. Mutual sensibilities seemed to extend into each other's inner lives like sensitive capillaries, communicating more than was ever spoken. The hollow voids of deep emotional suffering, which had once seemed fathomless, now bubbled over with the sweet fullness of life.

Not as a flash flood, nor as the bursting of a dam, but gently as rain, softly as a hidden spring ran the life-giving course of love. It was a sacred love, and each knew that it would not die with death.
Jennie thinks of Louis as her "twin soul." Her life with him was the pinnacle of human happiness, and comprehended the loveliest years of her time on earth. Their mutual love was not only physical and emotional, but profoundly spiritual. Not "spiritual" in the sense of churches, but in the sense of an Easter sunrise, or the flight of an eagle.

Jennie's health was still fragile, and she had lost all that she owned. But in finding the kind of love she had with Louis, the past became insignificant. It seemed more like a void, and nature always fills a void. By creating the void, one creates the fulfillment. By posing the problem, one defines the solution. Jennie had to suffer in order to reach any higher, to grow any more sensitive.

She began to find that suffering and its fulfillment create compassion in a person's heart for the suffering of others. As she continued her nursing career, Jennie discovered that she was able to minister not only to the physical, but the emotional wounds of her patients. She learned that real help is extended not by simple sympathy, which pulls the hearer down to the level of the sufferer, but by compassion, which lifts up the fallen spirit and reveals hope. Like the primitive shaman, having experienced the descent to the underworld and the victorious return, Jennie carried the living light of fulfilled hope in her very presence. It didn't matter what she said or did to help the sick at heart. It mattered simply that she was, and that she was present.

Louis was not like any man Jennie had ever known. He was strong with great integrity, yet gentle like a tender mother. He didn't want Jennie to wash his dishes or cook his meals, or even to do the housework. He simply wanted to be near her, to spend his life with her. Yet he was not dependent upon her. There was no compulsive emotional need to possess or dominate her. Even his ideas were strange. He was a spiritually-minded man, yet without church ties. He sometimes spoke of unusual and seemingly un-Christian ideas of which Jennie had never heard, like "reincarnation."

They were married in a simple civil ceremony in North Dakota. Louis was very concerned about Jennie's health, and with the advice of doctors the two of them traveled west to Spokane, Washington.

"Louis had a brother who met us, and we went to the Spokane Hotel. Later we found an apartment, and then we decided to buy a grain and fruit ranch."

Louis was as much a carpenter as he was a homesteader. During the day in Minot, he had contracted and built the new public schoolhouse. With the money he had saved from the sale of his homestead and what he made in Minot, the Petersons were able to purchase a sizable piece of land with fruit trees and arable fields near Asti in northern California.

At least, the land was supposed to have fruit trees and clear fields -- so the land company had said when they bought it sight unseen from Spokane.

"Well, when we got down there we were advised to see the company surveyor in Cloverdale, which was the nearest town. He was a cheerful old fellow. His wife was much younger than he was, and she was quite pleasant.

"So he said, `You bought land up there, did you?'

"He didn't say a word, but took us out in his surrey. We crossed dry stream beds to the end of a road leading up the mountains. Finally he pointed up to a silver spruce hanging from a crag high up in the cliffs.
" `Do you see that white patch? That marks the corner of your land. Only a mountain goat could get up there. I'd advise you to file a complaint.' "

While awaiting legal action on the complaint against the land company, they rented a small cottage from an elderly woman named Mary Shaw.

Mrs. Shaw became very fond of the young couple and urged them to stay. Louis, however, was anxious to settle the claim, which had by now been the subject of delay after delay. The old woman introduced them to a Mr. Smith, who was willing to lease his silver prune orchard to Louis, but after much consideration Jennie and he decided to return to Spokane.

It was wartime, and the government was encouraging farmers to plant Navy beans. With the money which the land company finally returned, Jennie and Louis bought a farm south of Spokane near Rockford. They worked night and day to get the bean crop planted and keep it watered. Ten acres were in orchard, two in stock grazing, and the rest in the small white Nay beans.

"By the time of harvest there was a glut on the market, and the government didn't want the Navy beans any more. All we got out of that crop was a suit for Louis, who had ruined most of his clothes working all summer! We lived on what we got from the chickens and the cow. But Louis had to get a job in the shipyards of Vancouver, and we had to close down. We relinquished the farm and lost the $700 we had put down on it, and I went also to Vancouver, Washington, where the housing was worse then than it is now."

Louis worked ten hours each day for 60 cents an hour. Life was hard, but still the two of them were happy. Then disaster struck.

The year was 1918, and a large part of the world's population was shortly to die in one of the worst of modern plagues -- the Spanish Flu. Jennie was needed in nursing service again.

"Soldiers were dropping right and left at the barracks. The doctor I worked under was a wonderful man. He took ill, and so did I, and in five days he was passed out. I didn't, but one morning I was coughing, and all at once out comes a ball -- dark-looking mass as big as a walnut -- and the water started to run. That's what made me, in later years, determine that what killed the soldiers was the amount of mucus that got into the lungs and choked them to death. And I think that's what killed the doctor."

It was in Vancouver that Jennie had her first contact with Spiritualism. One evening a bag of groceries had been delivered to her doorstep by mistake. She checked the address and walked over a few blocks to a nicely painted old house. The door was answered by a lovely old woman who was apparently suffering a great deal of arthritic pain. She spoke gratefully to Jennie.

" `I was just getting ready to try and go downtown, because I have nothing to eat in the house.'

"She looked me up and down and said, `My, but you've got a lot of etherealization around you.'

"I looked at her in amazement. What was she talking about?"
The old woman invited Jennie to come in, but Jennie was on her way to the hospital. It was several weeks before she could find time for a visit, but finally one sunny and bright day nearing the end of the long siege of disease, she was able to get over.

The old woman said that her husband had been dead for 20 years, but that she had a recent photograph of him. Jennie asked how this was possible. She replied that she didn't know, but that several months ago she had been sitting for a photograph which her daughter had requested, when the photographer came out of the darkroom visibly disturbed.

"It has happened again," he blurted.

"What has happened again?" she asked.

"I keep getting another image, like a double exposure, yet I know these plates are brand new."

She looked at the plate and stood up in disbelief. There next to her in the photograph was a transparent image of her husband. It was distinct and clear -- no mistake. He was posing for the picture, standing just behind and over her as she sat in the chair.

"Oh, I want this one! Do you realize that this is a photograph of my dead husband?"

The photographer relaxed. "Oh, yes. Very interesting. Well, you are the third, then."

This was not the first time such a phenomenon had occurred for the photographer.

This incident had started the old woman (Jennie does not remember her name) to change many of her ideas, and she had subscribed to a New-Thought magazine being published in Chicago called the Progressive Thinker. It was primarily Spiritualist in orientation, and it was through this instrument that the old woman had gained her knowledge.

Jennie asked to borrow a few issues, which she took home. Louis was very intrigued since his own ideas were unorthodox, and the two of them subscribed to the magazine. Thus began Jennie's initiation into Spiritualism and her contact with a framework and language of self-interpretation which was to serve her well in the coming years.

The First World War had ended, and work at the shipyard slackened. Jennie and Louis invested money through another land company, but this time with a legal gimmick allowing them to recover the money quickly if necessary. The land was supposed to be ideal for farming and have an orchard on it, and be located less than a mile from the little town of Orland in northern California. They had both loved California, even though the first visit had been an irritation.

When they arrived the land was much as it had been advertised, but nothing had been said to indicate that it had served as a hog farm for at least a generation. That meant much of the rooted growth had been snouted out of the ground, and could pose a farming or fertilizing problem.

Something in Jennie -- not yet a "voice," but certainly a strong impulse with intelligent direction -- began to constantly warn her that something was amiss. She tried to overcome the premonition, but remembered what had been said in certain issues of the Progressive Thinker. Perhaps she should take heed and tell Louis.

He listened attentively to her feelings, then the two of them decided to reclaim their money and move on south to the San Francisco area. He too felt vague intuitions of warning.
Before they could pack up, however, Jennie came down with a bad case of chills and fever, shaking so badly that the entire bed was vibrating. The condition was diagnosed as malaria. For several weeks Louis stayed by her side caring for her. Finally they were able to leave, and Louis insisted upon returning to city life until Jennie was more fully recovered. He would work in the shipyards of Oakland.

In the last week of their stay in Orland, however, a significant event occurred which established clairvoyance as a conscious fact of Jennie's life.

Doctor Young had been taking care of Jennie. From time to time he and his wife would join the Petersons for dinner. The conversation often turned to Spiritualism, which by then had become an international movement. Before her bout with malaria Jennie had written a rebuttal of blistering attack upon Sir Oliver Lodge which had been sponsored by a local church. The local newspaper editor had been so impressed with what she'd written that he asked permission to publish it, and Jennie had gained something of a local reputation through this event.

It wasn't that Jennie knew much about Spiritualism, or Sir Oliver Lodge, for that matter. Rather, when she had gone to the public lecture, which had been advertised on the topic of Sir Oliver Lodge and Spiritualism, she had expected something exciting. Instead it was a parochial and embittered personal attack upon the man by local church people apparently threatened by his new ideas. Jennie had felt deeply insulted by the whole show, and left with a burning desire to refute what was said. She wrote down her ideas; then, as though impelled by something more than herself, she wandered through the small town. She found herself standing in front of the local newspaper office, and on an urge went in. Upon seeing it, the editor offered to publish it with her permission.

The Youngs had a friend named Mrs. Saidler. She was somewhat mysterious and held much in awe by them. One afternoon they introduced the Petersons to her.

"We were all seated at her library table, chatting around about the country and so forth, and Mrs. Saidler turned to me. Handing me her wedding ring, she said, `See what you can see in that.'

"Well, I made fun of it. I looked and said, `I see a ring, and it's a wedding ring,' and I laughed.

"She says, `We know it's a wedding ring. What do you see inside it?'

"So I looked and I said, `Well, I look through it and I can see you.'

"She says, `I don't mean that. Why don't you get serious? Now tell me -- look in that ring. Tell me what you can see.'

"I looked in it, and that was where I saw this steam engine -- a train -- come chuffing along with smoke coming from the stack, and the bell hanging there. All at once it put on the brakes, and the train came to a stop. At the end of the carriage a man came down in a light, snuff-colored suit, and he carried a suitcase and had on a sailor hat with a band around it and a little tiny bow at the side. He got down off that train and stepped to the ground.

"Mrs. Saidler said, `I knew you were clairvoyant.'

"I said, `What do you mean?'

" `Well,' she says, `you can see further than these eyes give.' "

The conversation went on, and Jennie dismissed the whole thing. But at the end of the week the train from Oakland came into the Orland station with Mrs. Saidler's brother from the East. He was wearing a snuff-colored suit and a sailor hat with a bow. Mrs. Saidler had asked Jennie down to the small station to witness the event, since that afternoon she had received her brother's telegram.

"Is this what you saw?" she asked slyly. Jennie was dumbfounded.

Mrs. Saidler was very well read on Spiritualism. As Louis and Jennie prepared to depart for Oakland, she strongly advised them to avoid the San Francisco mediums and fortunetellers.

"They'll mislead you and strip your pocketbook as well," she said. "Spiritualism is knowledge of God, not the undependable exercise of human psychic power. Stay clear of those who read you for profit."

The stay in Oakland was fairly brief. Mrs. Saidler had recommended a medium in San Francisco who lived on 17th and Mission Streets, who had a good reputation. Louis felt somewhat lost and decided to see the woman with Jennie.

"We went in at the door. There was a little room and a table set up. A little woman sat there. She looked up and said, `Yes?' She stood up and came toward us. `Anything I can do for you?'

"Louis walked forward and said, `Yes. We were recommended to come and see if you could give us any help or advice.'

"She had him sit down, though I still stayed at this end of the hall. She was talking to him when all at once she says, `Excuse me, but there's a gentleman here with a little boy at his side, and he keeps asking to see his daughter. He says he must talk to her, and that he's never had the chance before.'

"And my father came, and I barely saw him. He had on his decorations from the Odd Fellows, and the little boy on the side. And the lady asked, `What's his name?' looking at the child. And I said, `He never was known by a name -- only the name I had intended to give him, J. H. C.'

"To me this experience was a conviction of life beyond what we call death, because nobody in America knew. I'd never talked about my marriage and my baby's loss."

The medium saw Louis getting a job in the Oakland shipyard. After the meeting he went directly to the yards and was able to get a job.

The Petersons took a small apartment near Lake Merritt. In the meantime they had found Trinity Church, the Spiritualist organization which Mrs. Saidler had mentioned. Sunday night they went to the service, and Louis was seen by a medium carrying his tools. She saw Jennie and Louis in a small coastal town called Santa Cruz. They pondered this reading for several months.

They had made the acquaintance of a Dr. and Mrs. Moon, who held Spiritualist meetings at their home which from time to time they attended. One night an interesting reading came out.

"It was there that my nephew in spirit came and made himself known. The medium had to break through a message that she was delivering to someone else.

" `There's someone here named Arthur, and he says to please tell his Aunt Jennie to go to Mother and tell her not to sit over my picture and cry. I am not dead. I am with her in spirit!' "

Gert's son Arthur had been blown to pieces with shrapnel in the war so that only his identification disc remained. Jennie wrote to her sister and transmitted the message. It was this letter that brought the two back together, so that Gert and Jennie could reconcile the unspoken feelings left over from the divorce. Somehow things had come full circle since the divorce, and all was well once again.

Chapter 6

THE ADVENT OF THE TEACHERS

Mother Jennie's spiritual life developed over the last half century through her contact with the Teachers of Wisdom. These, she said, are enlightened beings who have attained self-mastery after many aeons of incarnate experience. Some are more advanced than others, and have achieved the ability to dwell in high levels of reality far beyond the sphere of earthly existence. Yet these, with others who have earned a long rest between incarnations, selflessly choose to renounce their high estate. They humble themselves and draw near unto persons of the lower planes who are able to receive their influence and guidance.

We might sense their wisdom only as an urge prompting us to a better way of life or more enlightened kind of activity. Some may hear a voice speaking from the heart of silence or find guidance in a dream. A deeply sensitive person who, like Jennie, has devoted herself to the service of others may actually see their forms, since the level of reality which she has carefully prepared within herself extends beyond normal human perception.

Without discussing the epistemology or "reality" of the Teachers, it is well to note the comparison with other psychic guides in the history of spiritual consciousness.

Perhaps the best known was the daimon of Socrates. According to Plato's Apology, at his trial Socrates claimed that his wisdom came from a "voice" he heard which always warned him what to avoid. Scholars have generally understood the "voice" to be a kind of personification of conscience, and Socrates has been honored as one of the earliest conscientious persons.

Jennie's first inspired discourses at Langley Mill were on the subject of conscience. The phenomenology of Jennie's Teachers clearly transcends what is known of human conscience, however, which is not usually associated with psychism. While the normal experience of conscience is internal, in the case of "voices" like those of Jennie and Socrates the perception ix external. It should also be said that while the hearer, like Jennie, might respond to the wisdom of a guide through the psychic instrumentality of her conscience, the wisdom itself transcends the personal dimension.

Human conscience seems to be greatly conditioned by particular and prevailing moral climates. Conscientious persons have disagreed and even gone to war against each other on the basis of "conscience," each certain that God was on his side. Yet, as the comparison of religions shows, wisdom that has been transmitted through divine revelation, psychic guides or other transcendental origins has a unity of meaning, regardless of its cultural vehicle.

For example, Lao Tsu has learned from the great Tao to be good to those who seem good and those who seem bad alike, since strength resides in goodness. He has learned to have faith in those who seem faithful and those who seem faithless alike, since strength resides in faith (Tao Te Ching, 49).

In an entirely different culture which had no connection with classical Chinese philosophy, in a wholly different mythological frame of discourse, Jesus of Nazareth urged his disciples to become children of his great Father, Who had taught him all he knew. They were to imitate the Father, "Who makes His sun to rise on the evildoer as well as the well-doer, and sends forth rain on the just person as well as the unjust person" (Matthew 5.45). Clearly Jesus means the same thing as Lao Tsu.

A bit further on in both literatures, Lao Tsu and Jesus advise that the Sage must become as a little child. The wise person, says Lao Tsu, "walks the way of a little child" (49). Unless one becomes as humble, teachable and free of mental domination as a little child, he cannot enter into the Kingdom of Tao.

Of the many traditions in spiritual history which have been founded upon the revelations of psychic guides, there are two main sorts: philosophies and mysteries. The distinction is often blurred, but hinges upon whether the great teacher has appeared in flesh or only in a vision. In the case of Lao Tsu we speak of a philosophy, since he was a human being who left written records. Yet his Teacher was the Tao, the Great Spirit of the Universe. To Lao Tsu, it was a matter of revelation. To his followers it became a philosophy.

In the case of Jesus we usually speak of a mystery. Jesus received Christhood through obedience. According to tradition, his teachers were not only the Father, but his Mother, the Holy Spirit, and great beings like Moses and Elijah, with whom his disciples saw him conferring. In this vision, Jesus the man appeared to the eyes of men in transfigured glory. Jesus, like Moses and Elijah, spoke directly with God.

The Gentile mysteries of the Christian Church were established in revelatory visions of St. Paul and St. Peter. It was St. Stephen who saw Jesus the Christ sitting at the right hand of God's power in a vision as he was martyred, with the unconverted Saul of Tarsus looking on.

Like the mysteries of Eleusis or Dionysus, the Church was seen as a mystery house established on earth by a god. Just as Demeter, the Great Mother of the Universe, had established her mysteries of immortality with the Eumolpidae of Eleusis, so Christ had come down from Heaven to establish His Church for the salvation of all mankind.

I am stressing this now because integral to Jennie's development is the Orrilla Sisterhood and Brotherhood which, like all mysteries, was established on earth through an epiphany of divine beings. The same is true of the Holy Grail Foundation and other Spiritualist organizations.

Shrines in the Christian tradition, such as that at Lourdes, were established by an epiphany of the Holy Mother or other high saint, just as cults of heroes were defined in ancient Greece by miraculous or divine demonstration. The temples of Asclepius functioned as centers of healing in the ancient world much as Christian shrines do in the modern world. Like the holy places of worship in primitive Hebrew religion, they have sprung up wherever God has "made His Name to be remembered."

Such holy places are patronized by resident angels or saints, who can be called upon in prayer for help in the particular realm of service to which they have been assigned. This includes not only healing, but such diverse services as help in finding things that are lost (St. Anthony), protection on a journey (Hermes Trismegistus) or aid on child-conception (one of the kama devas).

Some of these beings are guides, such as the Hindu Ganesha, who removes obstacles to understanding. There are greater and lesser guides, and perhaps one of the greatest was Hermes Trismegistus, the Third Hermes of Isian tradition. In his mysteries the seeker was gradually lifted up from mundane consciousness to be spiritually reborn in the Ogdoad. Through inspired discourse, the student was elevated through the seven psychic planes to attain the eighth nature, or apotheosis in a divine brotherhood. In so doing he became clairvoyant, clairaudient and the possessor of all magical arts.

In early Christian tradition, especially as illuminated by the Alexandrian Fathers, Christ was the Master, Guide and Psychopomp. He was both Mystagogue and Hierophant of divine mysteries, and communicated his teaching to earthly followers through the Holy Spirit.

Like the "spirit" of Delphi, the Holy Spirit could possess her devotees and deliver prophecy through them. She could admonish, like the Hellenistic Jewish Spirit of Truth, or teach like hypostatized Sophia. Like the Chaldean Teacher of the Sacrifice she could specify sacramental procedure. But above all, like Iamblichus' tutor-spirits, the Paredros of Greco-Oriental magical papyri, the Genius of Roman traditions, like Agathos Daemon, Hermes Trismegistus and the "voices" of Socrates, Joan of Arc and many other charismatics such as Elijah and Moses -- above all, she was the psychic guide of Christians as they followed the Way. She was the Teacher, dwelling in her obedient servants as in a holy temple. If the temple were profaned from within (for desecration came from within, not from without), she departed until it might be made holy again.

The desert saint might have his ministering angels. The tribal shaman of Asia or the Americas might have his tutelary spirits who teach him his craft. A little child might have his "invisible playmate." Throughout history there has been perception of spirit teachers or associates, whether for good or for ill, angelic or demonic.

In understanding Mother Jennie's Teachers, parallels might be drawn with those of Carl Jung. The great psychologist underwent what might be termed a "shamanic illness" during one period of his life in which he was visited by tutelary dreams and visions. Through this education he gained the substance of his psychological thought. Although he took instruction from male teachers like Philemon, or the archetype of the Wise Old Man, Jung points out that his great Teacher was the Anima, which he variously understands as his own personal or collective unconscious mind, or the repressed opposite-sexed nature within himself. She would be the face of an archetype, like the Magna Mater, Isis, the Mother of Christ.

The shamanic pattern is best expressed among the Goldi of Siberia. The shaman is chosen by an ayami, or opposite-sexed (female) tutelary spirit who demands his affection and total commitment. If the subject is lax in obedience and in terminating sexual relations with his wife, the ayami may threaten his life. Like hypostatized Sophia of Hellenistic Jewish Sages, she at first tests and tries him to the limit. When he has been tested and found worthy, she returns to him in ecstasy to gladden him and reveal her secrets.

These are the important elements: 1. an epiphany of an opposite-sexed Teacher; 2. the acceptance of a sacred trust in union with the Teacher; 3. transmission of the shamanic craft; 4. practice of the shamanic vocation, with emphasis upon healing and redemptive purpose.

While the manifestation of the Teacher as opposite-sexed is not true at what seem to be the higher planes of revelation (Lao Tsu, Jesus, Moses, etc.), the parallel between Jung's Anima and Jennie's opposite-sexed male Teachers is important to preserve. Jennie has taken instruction from female guides, but her main Teachers fall into three categories of male tutors coinciding with three periods in her life.

The first is the period of her marriage to Louis Peterson, when her first Teacher made himself known and offered instruction every morning at ten o'clock for ten years. This was Omar, who had been a priest at Persepolis in ancient times and a Hindu in his last incarnation.

The second is the period of her marriage with Max Maiereder, a few years after Louis' death. The marriage was arranged by Omar and other Teachers for Jennie's protection as she approached retirement age, and was sexually ascetic (at Max's request). Now a new Teacher makes himself known: Savonarola, the martyred Christian monk and preacher of Florence. He was paramount in Jennie's further instruction for many years.

The third period is generally comprehended by the period after Max's death. At this point Omar and Savonarola seem to work more in conjunction with other colleagues, and reference is to "the Teachers" collectively, although Omar and Savonarola make their presence known strongly from time to time. It is at this point that Jennie herself assumes the status of "teacher." As I pointed out much earlier, this fact was made known to the Holy Grail Foundation in 1973 when Leona, the minister and medium, was "overshadowed" in semi-trance by the spirit of Mother Jennie and delivered a discourse in her style and philosophy. I do not know of any other instance when a medium has served as a vehicle for someone still living on the earth.

While I do not want to offer a specific interpretation of the related phenomena and parallels I have adduced, there is one other aspect of the Teachers that must be explored. The Teachers are "spirits." What, now, is a "spirit?" We speak of "spirituality" and "spiritual growth." What is the frame of reference?

Simply and plainly, "spirit" is man's most ancient religious concept. Tribal religion of modern so-called primitives is animistic, and most scholars of religion presume that animism is basic to the oldest forms of religious consciousness. Underlying the most sophisticated of Hindu philosophies is the folk-perception of all things as animate and possessing a living consciousness.

The tree must be asked its permission before it can be cut down. The deer must be thanked for its meat. Even the medieval folk-spirituality of St. Francis recognized "brother Sun, sister Moon," and "brother Ass" -- the saint's name for his own physical body, whose forgiveness he asked (in old age) for having mistreated.

There was deep awareness of the mystery of life -- killing and being killed, eating and being eaten, speaking and being spoken (for surely God has "spoken" us into existence, reasoned the ancient priests of Jerusalem). It was in the mystery of animals, totems, skins, meats and masks that the animistic consciousness of self in every perceived object was nurtured and elaborated. Thus "object" was seen as self-conscious "subject." The erotic dialectic of perceiver and perceived, I and Thou, Lover and Beloved was basic to even the most prehistoric fertility ritual. Western dualistic theologies and Eastern monistic philosophies spring from the same roots -- a mystic consciousness that all is One, everything is self-conscious, and every self-conscious being is an aspect of every other self-conscious being.

Contemporary psychological thought reduces such basic perceptions of reality to categories of unrealistic fantasy. The child's view of reality is immediately discarded in such a phrase as "omnipotence fantasy" -- a delusion in which a child believes it possible to control "external" reality by sheer force of will. The highest goals of religious aspiration are summarily dealt with by the Freudian Reality Principle, which claims to discern the Real from fantasy based on a materialistic concept of reality, and a totally inadequate theory of fantasy.

Contemporary religious scholarship reduces tribal spiritism, and indeed all theistic or mystic experience, to the common denominator of psychological "projection." Because of the presumed but elusive mentalit□," primitive, tribal persons are supposed to be prone to visions, personifications, metaphorical perception and magical operations -- all of which are projective illusions. Nothing really happened "out there." It was all an internal process projected against the screen of human perception.

The problem with our contemporary ways of understanding these phenomena is that they are reductionistic. Very well, let us understand these things as projections. But what, then, is the "within" from whence they come? We have forgotten Tao, Brahma, Eros, Logos and all other great revelations that the inner and the outer must be recognized as a single One.

We demythologize and denude gods, angels and the whole ancient realm of spirits, only to leave them clothed in the rags of an unreflective materialism. We rip the pearls from their rusted settings, but know not how to honor them with a finer art.

Why persist in talking about "spirituality?" The contemporary understanding of "reality" admits of no spirits. We speak of the essence of something as its "spirit," but Nominalism won out against Universalism many centuries ago, and we really don't consider there to be "essences" of things. Reality is in no sense unitive -- it is only quantitative. Inductive perception lost out to deduction many centuries ago, and the best models of reality which we can conceive are those built on a point-by-point calculus that doesn't even know why it works. We have cast our lot with the "realities" which in ancient times were called Maya, "illusion," or Mammon, the symbol of personal desire. We have committed our understanding to the phenomenal world of diversity, particularity and personality: the world of the mind and its images -- the world of shadows that Plato escaped when he crawled out of the Cave like a newly-born child.

No, indeed! We measure by the eyes of flesh and discount what is unseen or too subtle for the instruments of perception which we have wearied and blocked through callousness. We measure Love on a Masters and Johnson machine. We sing without knowing that we are sung, and dance without feeling that we are danced. We snatch up the daily sacrifice of raw, red meat from a Safeway butcher counter and forget the life that has been given that we might live.

Yet "spirituality" is everywhere unrecognized. It has evolved far beyond its roots in primitive animism and exercised what might be called an almost magical power in all cultures. Although the language, grammar and institutions of human religion have cast off traditional forms, they persist with their power in unrecognized ways. Being unrecognized, they assume in many cases a negative and regressive posture.

Flowing forth from the broken vessels of sacred tradition, the spirits have commingled with the profane world. They have become incarnate in political, monetary, governmental and educational systems. They reside in ethnic prejudices and the whole area of folk morality. They hold sway in such diverse realms as Hollywood, Nazi Germany and Wall Street. The gods have been imprisoned in the images of romantic love, television commercials and therapy groups.

The spirits persist apart from conscious human perception, but we have given them different names. They persist because they are part of our world and aspects of an evolving universe. Most of us simply don't know how to see them or communicate with them any more. Yet they are the spirits of our ancestors.

The Old Testament abounds in stories of human contact with angels (literally, "messengers") who impart divine revelation. The Message or Word of God was transmitted through the mouths of living prophets and preserved in the literature and poetry of ancient Israel.

The Christian Gospel (literally, "Good Message") was another production of inspired literature, rooted in the oral kerygmatic messages of early charismatics. Like the Koran, the Great Books of China, the Vedas and other transcendental literatures, the New Testament arose as a vehicle to transmit the "spirit" or essence of divine teaching. Here by "spirit" one means the non-literal sine qua non which transcends the limitations of human language and reason. It is pure meaning.

Always and everywhere there have been greater and lesser "messengers" of wise truth, whether shamans, philosophers, priests, angels, poets or other spirits. In the body or out of the body, it doesn't seem to matter.

A large part of their legacy, in the light of comparative study, reveals a universality which transcends the particularity of whatever parochial religious institution claims the Message as its own.

Mother Jennie attuned herself to the same Message. She claimed to receive it from spirit messengers, the Teachers, who have often said, "It is not the messenger but the Message that is of first importance."

How Mother Jennie perceives the messengers, I do not know. That they are real, I cannot doubt.

The mode of their existence is not easily reduced to readily known terms. Perhaps the best answer is that offered by Hermes Trismegistus to his anonymous student. Speaking through the Hermetic Father in dynamistic, regenerative discourse, he addresses himself to the student's perplexity about the communio sanctorum, the brotherhood of Hermetic saints who have attained perfection. They dwell far beyond the earth-sphere in the Ogdoad or Eighth Heaven, continually praising God, yet many of them are present with the student as unseen teachers. The student asks about the mode of their existence.

Hermes replies, "O my son, they are Pneumatics (Spirit-Beings), for they are the energies which assist other souls in growth." (Nag Hammadi Tractate 6, Codex VI.53.17-20)

Perhaps, then, it is best to understand the Teachers as noetic or intelligent energies which assist in the process of psychic evolution. By "spirit" would be meant self-conscious bio-energy which lies at the hull and helm of all existence. It can be perceived personally or as universal intelligence. It is the substance of life, the essence of light. It is omnipotent and omniscient. It is the unbegotten begetter and the begotten one -- within and without the ten-thousand things of phenomenal reality. It is the unknown knower, the source and goal of all aeons.

Personal "messengers" of Spirit, then, would be perceived according to the perceiver's power of understanding. In order to receive spiritual instruction of a progressive nature that facilitates spiritual growth, one must develop a power of understanding that reaches for a higher good and aspires to a better way of living for all, in unity. Any other form of understanding that seeks to inflate personal existence and hoard what is generally thought of as "power" perverts the aim of Spirit and brings personal danger. Used with understanding, electricity can produce light. In the hands of an ignorant person it can burn and kill. We have classified spirits as good and evil according to our understanding. In reality, we have created their valence. Like electricity, Spirit is beyond the moral categories of human mind.

In other words, the greatness of spirit that one is able to summon depends upon his strength of understanding. It is this understanding that gives meaning and value to spiritual experience.

The Hermetic student has been prepared by years of education and practice. Still he does not see nor comprehend the invisible brotherhood which stands assisting at his initiation into the Ogdoad. Finally, however, he manages to voice an intellectual insight about the invisible helpers. Hermes Trismegistus responds with this observation:
"O my son, when you genuinely understand what you have said, you will find your brothers praying with you, who are my sons." (Nag Hammadi Tractate 6, Codes VI.54.18-22)

Mother Jennie developed a genuine understanding of the truths that are glibly mouthed in so many sermons, or tacitly accepted by religious zealots. The understanding came through over half a century of practice and obedience to the Teachers, and was rooted in knowledge earned by experience.

"The Teachers can present," as Jennie so often said, "but they do not compel. They come not with grand promises of attainment and power, but in humble service. They bring a light of understanding that is not brilliant or blinding, but gentle and soft. They speak in tender and loving tones, and they are wise in their unfoldment of the Way."

***** ***** *****

Louis' work at the Moore Shipyards ran out in the fall of 1920. Having received advice from more than one spiritualist medium to go south into Santa Cruz, the Petersons packed and left. Neither Jennie nor Louis knew exactly what they would be doing, but since both had survived on the homesteads of southern Alberta with far fewer resources than were now available, they pressed on with enthusiasm. If nothing else, they could buy some property, build a temporary dwelling and find work. Jennie would accept employment as a nurse, and Louis could make his way as a carpenter.

As the train pulled into Santa Cruz there was a sudden lurch which sent Louis tumbling. His ankle was badly sprained and began to swell. Jennie removed his boot. Using some old sewing material she bound the ankle and helped Louis off the train. With Louis sitting on a bench at the station, Jennie went off quickly to find a room for rent. There was one not far from the station, and she returned for her husband. The station master helped Louis climb a flight of stairs leading to the rented room, and shortly he was able to stretch out on a bed.
Jennie was quite worried now. Louis' ankle had turned black as coal. She decided to look for a spiritualist healer, since medical doctors would be able to do no more for Louis than she already had.

After getting no response to her questions from local people, Jennie walked into the city police station and spoke to a captain. He said that there had once been a Spiritualist church, but that it no longer existed. However, there was a medium in town named Elizabeth Rose Stoddard. She resided on Cedar Street. Jennie hurried the few blocks to Mrs. Stoddard's address.

"I knocked at the door and this old lady answered. She looked me up and down and finally said, `Who is this, wrapped in the British flag? What part of England are you from?'

" `Nottingham,' I replied.

" `Hmm. What part of Nottingham?' she said. `Do you know anything about Sneinton Hollows?'

"I said, `Yes. I used to walk there as a child.'

"Then I looked at her, and something began to dawn inside me. I said, `Were you the little girl who uncovered those murders?'

" `The same,' she said with a smile.'
Thus Jennie's long association with Elizabeth Stoddard began with an astounding coincidence.

From as early as she could remember, Jennie had heard about Elizabeth Rose, the child psychic of Nottingham whose visions had solved the brutal William Saville axe murders. In those days, murder was a rare and horrible thing for a community. The story had stuck with Jennie all her life.

Mrs. Saville and her four children had been absent from the neighborhood for over a month. William, the husband, had volunteered little information except that they were visiting relatives in the east of England for an indefinite period. The local neighbors were aware that Mr. Saville was a violent man at times, and they had heard him beating his wife late at night, but this, after all, was not unusual for the lower-class community. No one thought much about the fact that Mrs. Saville had left. Perhaps there was to be a divorce, or permanent separation.

Every Sunday morning Elizabeth Rose walked home from Church with her family, passing through Sneinton Hollows. As they approached a certain meadow, Elizabeth would run merrily to the large oak tree which stood in a wooded copse, surrounded by a shallow stone wall. She appeared to be playing with make-believe friends. When asked by her father about the invisible playmates, Elizabeth was quite explicit.

"There are a mother and four children resting on the meadow under the tree. When I come along they all stand up, and the children want to play. Now they are all lying down again because we have to leave. Don't you see them?"

Elizabeth's father grew suspicious and contacted the local police. On the next Sunday, as the family walked home from Church, they were followed by policemen with shovels, who observed Elizabeth's behavior. After the family had moved on, the men began to dig at the location where Elizabeth had played with her invisible playmates. There in one large grave they found the bodies of four children, a woman and the axe with which they had been killed. The corpses were easily identified as the missing Saville family. William Saville, confronted with the evidence, admitted his guilt and was executed for the crime. Little Elizabeth Rose was celebrated in newspapers all over England. By the time Jennie was born, Elizabeth Rose had become a legend in Nottingham, both for her childhood adventure and her talent in later years as a medium.

Jennie stared incredulously at the woman, who embraced her and led her to a chair.

"I am not known by many in this country, and my married name is Stoddard. It is so good to find someone from England!"

Jennie explained the situation with Louis. Without bothering for hat or coat, Mrs. Stoddard took her by the hand and they were off. The medium was able to help the swelling of Louis' ankle with her prayers and laying on of hands.

Elizabeth Rose Stoddard was Jennie's first spiritualist teacher. She had achieved international recognition as a medium and, with Maud Lord-Drake, had established a place of retirement in Santa Cruz. The two were not only mediums, but deeply religious persons who were to exercise a profound influence upon Jennie.

One of Jennie's favorite stories about Mrs. Stoddard concerns her beautiful hair.

"She was in a disaster at sea in a little cockle shell of a boat for three days before they were picked up. She had a beautiful head of hair, and for water it was laid out on the edge of the canvas. They drank the water that had condensed and dripped from her hair until they were rescued."

Louis and Jennie bought an acre of land at the corner of Third Street and old Seventh Avenue, not far from Twin Lakes Beach. For some time they rented while readying the property for habitation. During this time they found work. Louis earned 50 cents an hour as a craftsman, and Jennie took day nursing jobs.

Summer passed, and Louis was able to get the frame of a house built on their lot. The two of them decided to move into the tar-papered shell of a house for winter, since they could no longer afford to pay rent. Mrs. Stoddard, who had become friend, advisor and teacher to both of them, began to show signs of weakening, and Jennie wondered how long it would be before Elizabeth might be needing a day nurse. The darkened evenings of that wet and cold winter were brightened from time to time as Mrs. Stoddard invited the two pioneers over for hot food and spiritual conversation.

It was deep into the night of December 13, 1921 that Jennie had her first audible contact with the Teachers. Louis was asleep, but something seemed to awaken Jennie. There was a rainstorm in progress, lashing the tar roof and pelting the exposed beams with sudden gusts. Jet Jennie was aware of an almost perfect stillness around her -- a silence somehow within all the outside chaos. It was pitch black. There seemed to be the live memory of a voice speaking to her, and the memory of the voice seemed so vivid that it was almost as though the voice were still speaking. Or was there now a voice calling? Then again, a voice was indeed speaking to her -- a voice so beautiful and tender that there could be no fear. It was delivering a poem.

"I heard the voice speaking to me, and there seemed to be a strong impression to write down what was said. But the poem was so lovely and logical -- I was sure I could remember it. The night was so cold and stormy. Why should I sit up in bed with a candle-light and no heat? I could remember what the voice had said -- or so I thought. And with that, I got down in bed and cuddled up for sleep. But in the morning all I could remember was `Come Thou, Great Light,' and something about a tomb."

Jennie realized that she had let something very important slip by. She didn't speak to Louis about the experience, but secretly chastised herself for laxity. Certainly there had been a voice. She had heard it clearly as a bell. At the time it had seemed almost normal -- so peaceful and gentle an experience. She had not heeded the strong urge to write the words down, thinking them to be so striking that she'd never forget them. But morning had come, and with it a more normal kind of reality and consciousness. The other reality had completely disappeared.

"Three nights later I again was awakened by that voice. But that was where I got my first reprimand from the Teachers. The voice said:

> " `Missed it!
> Because you did not respond to the midnight call,
> But shuffled down in bed
> And turned your face to the wall.
>
> " `So it is in life's journey,
> Where toil and care
> Blind you to the need
> Of spiritual fare.
>
>
> " `Missed it!
> O, the sad neglect
> Of failing to respond
> To the Higher Intellect.'

"And then came a silence you could feel in your very bones. You know, it stirred me very deeply to realize I had missed something that was so unusual, so out of this world. But it made me pay attention, and it was the next May, when Mrs. Stoddard was sick, that I finally got the rest of `Come Thou, Great Light.' I had just put her down to sleep when I heard that voice saying, `Come Thou, Great Light,' and I just grabbed a pen and paper and stood at attention in front of the dressing table and wrote."

Certainly by May of 1922 Jennie had been thoroughly imbued with psychism and spiritualist philosophy. Mrs. Stoddard had become terminally ill. The many friends and admirers who had once implored her for "readings" and drained her system for personal advice had better things to do than care for an old woman. Jennie assumed the responsibility and, during the long winter of care, much was imparted to her from the elderly medium.

"Child, pay attention! When you hear that voice, you just be still and write down what they give you."

Jennie had no classes in psychic development, nor did she learn the craft of a professional medium. Elizabeth Rose Stoddard was not a "professional medium," and had never exploited her gifts for money. But she was a deeply religious person, and her legacy to Jennie was an affirmation of the spiritual meaning of mediumship, with emphasis upon service to others and the revelation of divine purpose in each life. Like Maud Lord-Drake, whom Jennie was soon to meet, Elizabeth Rose was always held in reverence by Mother Jennie by reason of her religious life, more than the psychic gifts which she possessed.

Clearly, then, Jennie had experienced a period of close association with a remarkable woman before she was able to hear the voice with waking consciousness. The form and mode of Jennie's first contacts with the Teachers must have been determined by the contact with Mrs. Stoddard.

On the other hand, Jennie was not consciously seeking mediumship. She did not study psychic development. The idea had been sparked by the clairvoyant experience in Orland, in which Mrs. Saidler had been her guide. Jennie had seen evidence enough of the reality of psychism, and discovered new ways of understanding her old religious faith. But she had not fancied herself a medium, nor did she desire a vocation other than nursing. Neither had she fancied herself a poet.

The first Teacher was nameless. His voice was always the same. Jennie's first auditions had occurred in an altered state of consciousness midway between sleep and wakefulness. While the voice spoke, Jennie felt a strong urge to write down its words. Since missing the first poem about the Great Light, Jennie kept a pad and pencil within easy reach of her bed. After the reprimand, however, Jennie was given nothing for five months. During this period she nursed Elizabeth Rose and learned a great deal about mediumship and the high purposes to which it can be applied.

When Jennie finally heard the voice in May, she had just finished putting Mrs. Stoddard to bed. The dear old lady had been in considerable pain, and Jennie was glad to get her off to sleep. As she stood before the dressing table in a pensive state of mind, the voice seemed to fade into consciousness. This amazed her, for she had not been asleep.

Quickly she found a pen and paper. At long last she was able to receive the poetic revelation of which she had been unworthy. As a great invocation, with a canting and persuasive diction which seemed almost liturgical, theurgical, the voice of the Teacher spoke:

> "Come Thou, Great Light,
> Dispel the shadows and the gloom.
> Teach us of Life,
> Not beyond the tomb,
> But here and now
> While we are sore oppressed,
> That we may lift Life's shadows
> Ere we seek our rest."

And then a profound silence. She was to receive the rest of the poem several months later. What mattered now, however, was that somehow the light of spiritual understanding had penetrated into her waking consciousness. She was never to be a trance medium. Rather, she would always have possession over herself. Like Elizabeth Rose, her experiences would be visionary, auditory and in full conscious awareness.

During the twenties, American Spiritualism was developing its own style quite apart from the British movement. In many parts of the country there came to be "Mothers," or clairvoyant women called by divine voices and visions to establish new mysteries on earth. All varieties of phenomena occurred and new breeds of charismatic religion appeared, from those of the Voodoo Mothers in New Orleans to cultic offshoots of Blavatsky.

One of the most interesting of these female religious founders was Mother Clark, who became a guide for Mother Jennie and such famous mediums as the late Francis Becker.

"Mother Clark was the head seamstress at the Emporium in San Francisco, working on the trousseau for Jeremy Lee's daughter's wedding. She was suddenly overcome and fell back onto the pile of beautiful materials they were using, and she was entranced. A wonderful being of great enlightenment asked her if she would undertake an important mission to carry light and truth. But she answered that she had to earn her living. After a pause she was asked again, would she undertake this mission? And again she referred to the fact that she had to earn her living. They answered (for there was now the entire group of Hierarchs, spirit-beings of the Pleiades), `We say that you will always have provision made for you. Would you undertake this mission?' She finally consented, but said that she had to get the trousseau out on time, since it was special. They told her she would get it out on time, and assured her that she would never be in want."

The Hierarchs handed down to Mother Clark a special liturgy of initiation with other occult symbols and teachings which form the secret basis of the Orrilla Sisterhood. The mysteries were originally for women, but were later expanded to include men as the Orrilla Sisterhood and Brotherhood.

After finishing the trousseau which had been promised to Mr. Lee's daughter, Mother Clark quit her job and moved from Pleasanton into San Francisco. She established her first Center there, composed of friends who were convince of her psychism and spiritual integrity. This was the Queen Esther Center.
"It seems when she would go before the public to speak in a hall, sometimes she'd find when the trance was lifted that she had her back to the audience and she was talking to a great invisible choir. She told me this herself -- you see, she worked in trance. She was a wonderful woman, a grand character."

Mother Clark established another Center in Seabright, the Big Water Center, which was overseen by Mother Miller. Another group was begun headed by Mother Sadie, the Sun Center of Light. Finally Jennie was recognized by Mother Miller as a clairvoyant and spiritual person, and appointed Mother of a new group in Santa Cruz, the Cherokee Center.

Jennie recalls being asked by Minnie Miller to attend a small religious gathering at her home in Seabright. Everyone was given a chance to speak, and after Jennie had preached Minnie turned to her and remarked, "We need someone like you in the Sisterhood." This was Jennie's first knowledge of the secret organization.

She was invited to an open meeting of Orrilla, held once a month for interested persons nominated by members. Mother Clark was presiding, although Mother Miller had been appointed by her to normally oversee the meeting. Mother Sadie was a spirit-being who came through Mother Olson, who had also recognized psychism in Jennie.

During the meeting Mother Clark began to stare intensely at Jennie.

"There is one who stands behind you, a great being who wishes to speak through you."

Jennie was taken aback.

"Well," she replied, "what does he wish to speak?"
Mother Clark answered, "Light, love and truth."

Without hesitation Jennie again answered, "Well, if that's what he wishes to speak, that's fine with me."

The meeting then went on to other subjects, and soon it was over. Jennie decided to join Orrilla. The commitment was essentially a religious one. It was to practice the words and example of the Master Jesus Christ and to keep secret the special knowledge that would come to her as a Sister.

Jennie was affiliated with Mother Miller's group. Like all the Centers, it met on the 7th, 14th, 21st and 28th of each month. The last meeting of each month was open to candidates for initiation.

Shortly after her initiation, Rosa Lee manifested herself to Jennie. It was October 31, Halloween Eve, 1922. Jennie was in bed, midway between sleep and waking. Suddenly a childlike voice emerged, chanting simple poems in a sing-song fashion. Jennie asked her name. "Rosa Lee," was the reply. She said that she had come to help work in the Temple (a designation for the Center). She said that she believed in the Great Spirit, just like Jennie, and had been attracted to her through the bright lights of Jennie's beads.

Mother Jennie now understands that Rosa Lee came to help her lift her awareness to a "higher vibration" so that Omar, the first great Teacher, could manifest through Jennie. This was the great being which Mother Clark had seen behind Jennie. It was through clear contact with Rosa Lee on lower levels that Jennie was finally able to sense Omar.

Rosa Lee's poetry was given in stilted English at first. She would manifest at Sisterhood meetings, but in weakness. One afternoon, however, as Jennie was visiting a friend who nursed at the local hospital, a strange thing occurred.

Jennie was walking into the bedroom from Zetta's living room when she unexpectedly came in sight of collection of Indian fishing spears which Zetta's family had kept. Jennie collapsed.

When she was revived the connection with Rosa Lee had somehow been sealed. Apparently the sight of those Indian artifacts allowed Jennie's consciousness to make the final leap necessary for a strong connection with Rosa Lee.

At this point in her development Mother Jennie was able to learn more about her little Indian guide. She had been a Cherokee girl of 12 years in the last century. Her tribe had been ambushed by a warring Indian tribe of another nation, and she had been killed. She was a gay and bright spirit, and was fond of speaking on subjects like prayer, friendship and happiness. She continued with Jennie throughout her career, but with greatest frequency in the early years. Later she brought another spirit called Little Sunshine (see Appendix). After several years, Rosa Lee was well known to Sisterhood members, very fluent in Jennie's mediumistic work, and responsible for the new name, Cherokee Center.

Jennie had been quite active in the PTA, even though she had no children of her own. That fall she was to be nominated as chairman of the state PTA magazine. This was a position she hoped very much to have, since it would provide a forum for her poetry. But Omar, still nameless to her, delivered a strong message that began with these words:

> "Come ye out from among them,
> Come ye out, I say!
>
> Stand forth in the light of the morning
> And point to them the way.
>
> Stand forth in the glorious sunshine,
> The Christ Child is born within,
>
> Lay down your heavy burdens
> And turn from the pathways of sin."

Jennie was greatly dismayed. This message had come to her like the first poem, through a voice in the night. It was not what she wanted to hear. The next evening was the seventh, and Jennie went somewhat despondently to Mother Miller's meeting.

As she sat quietly during the meeting, she began to feel queer. A powerful charge seemed to radiate up her spine until her hair was standing on end.

"For the first time, Omar took control of me. He told them to keep their hands off me. He said, `Don't touch the medium!' and he put through a force that shook me from head to toe. I was like an engine running on a surplus of gas. And again I was sensitive of Mother Miller reaching forth to hold me, and he said, with a force almost like anger, `Hands off the medium!' She drew back, and I had this confounded fly settle and walk up and down my nose, but I couldn't lift a hand. After the vibration ceased, Omar said through me, `You have just witnessed a negative application of a positive power which could have killed had you interfered.' "

The energy subsided and Jennie was able to move. Several friends assisted her home, where she thought very seriously about what had happened. She realized that she had been given what she now names as the Call to Service. This might be compared to the shamanic calling or the call of St. Paul. The long poem (see Appendix) seemed to draw her out of secular life and the familiar and enjoyable social life which she had built up, and into some mysterious new vocation. Something within and without her was asking for commitment and obedience -- something fully worthy of such trust. After much thought, Jennie wrote a letter to the state headquarters of the PTA, resigning her nomination as chairman of the magazine.

At the next meeting of Orrilla, Mother Miller quietly approached Jennie.

"My dear, I must ask you to leave this Center."

"But why?" asked Jennie. This was a shock. Minnie was totally serious. Had she been offended at what the voice had said last week? Jennie tried to apologize.

"Jane, you know too much to come here any more. You must leave. I am sorry, but that is my decision."

Jennie remained for the rest of the meeting. She felt crushed. What sort of treachery had this voice brought, now that she had given up her nomination for chairman of the magazine? Was the voice something demonic, out to destroy her and every hope she had?

The same friends who had taken Jennie home after last week's experience invited her to ride in their buggy. After a long silence, one of the women looked directly at her and said, "Jane, we want to start a new Center with you as Mother."
Jennie's mouth dropped. Regaining herself, she said that this was most flattering, but that she simply wasn't qualified. She had not taken any training in mediumship and had no idea of becoming one.
Now all the other persons joined in.

"We want you to lead our group. We feel that your messages are deeply spiritual, and we want to follow that line. Don't refuse us, or you refuse God."

Jennie laughed aloud, then said, "Very well, if that is what you want, come to our home this Sunday morning at ten o'clock!"

It was that Sunday morning she learned that Minnie had nominated her to be a new Mother some time ago. Both Mothers Miller and Olson showed up at the door for the ten o'clock service, and Minnie warmly congratulated her for accepting the trust. Jane Peterson became Mother Jennie, and Cherokee Center was inaugurated at her home on Seventh Avenue. From this time forward Mother Jennie found herself able to deliver psychic messages, answer the secretly inscribed "ballots" from members of the congregation and deliver inspired discourses as the central worship of the Sisterhood and Brotherhood. Louis' interest was aroused, and he became a member of Orrilla.

Rose Stoddard had been a medium of international fame. One of her closest friends was Maud

Lord-Drake, an upper-class lady who was a personal friend of Blavatsky and Annie Besant. Before her death, Rose had introduced Jennie to Maud.

Mrs. Lord-Drake maintained a beautiful large home high above Bear Creek Road near Boulder Creek, where ladies and gentlemen of San Francisco and their European friends often met to discuss Theosophy and Spiritualism and experience different demonstrations from talented mediums. Maud's groups were scientific and made careful scrutiny of everything. They were quick to discover psychic fraud and ruthless in exposing it. But when authentic phenomena were observed they were as diligent to honor it and carry on as much investigation as the subject would allow.

I stumbled across an out-of-print book by Maud Lord-Drake entitled, *Psychic Light: Continuity of Law and Life,* published in 1904. It was presented to Dr. Jack Brofft of Santa Cruz by the author in 1934. It contains reproductions of testimonials, including several from Leland Stanford's wife. It was on the basis of Maud's psychic advice to them that they founded Stanford University. Maud had also been a psychic advisor to U.S.Presidents and other luminaries.

Jennie and Maud had become close friends. Maud's first husband had died, and she had married a Mr. Lydick, who wrote and produced Broadway plays in New York. Since he was absent much of the time, Maud looked forward to Jennie's weekly visit on Sundays, when she would bring warm food and good conversation.

Maud Lord-Drake, like Mrs. Stoddard, was a medium of international note. In her last years, however, she had lost most of her sight and was nearly paralyzed. She had to be carried or wheeled from one room to another, and had been socially disowned by her daughter because of the spiritualistic interests she insisted upon following. In spite of her many friends from San Francisco, then, Maud was a lonely and isolated woman. Jennie became deeply devoted to her.

"I never saw her in the work. I know nothing personally of her ability as a medium -- only the records in the newspapers and the like. But I do know this: between knowing her and Mrs. Stoddard, I learned a great deal about religious life. It was so terrible to see her paralyzed, and one day she asked me to take her outside. She said, `Oh, my dear, if it only did not have to be. I was just coming into the work.'

"And I said, `Dear Father, if this is the reward for labor, I do not want it. I'd rather be and continue as I am.' "

The end of Maud Lord-Drake's life was even more cruel. There was a terrible fire at her home while she was alone. She was unable to move from her chair, and was horribly burned from head to foot. She was rushed as the first patient in the Dominican Hospital, where she received intensive treatment. Jennie had been acting as Maud's day nurse for many months before the fire, but she had been in Earnest Lydick's care when the fire broke out. He had pulled her from the flames.

"She called out for me when she got to the hospital, and I was summoned. I was with her day and night for 23 days. The doctors didn't think she'd last 21 days. It was the longest anyone with all those degrees of burns had lived.

"She had two controls. The Indian control was Koala, and two of her early-day lovers who had passed on exercised the other control -- Val and someone else. Well, on the 13th night they came to me and asked if I would write, and they would give me a poem. And they wrote:

> " `The Queen of the Angels
> Is with us tonight.
>
> Her lovely dawn eyes
> Are shining and bright ...'

"And they asked me to read that long poem, which I do not remember at the present time, during her funeral.

"Ten more days and she passed out. I bought purple velvet and I clothed her body for the funeral in the casket. The President of the National Spiritualists' Association came, and he and I took the service up at Cypress Lawn where she was cremated. I read the poem, and I remember especially one verse that applied to the family and friends who had deserted her at the last part of her life:

> " `To you who have helped her,
> We pledge you our troth.
> To you who have hurt her,
> We say, not in wrath,
>
> `The harvest you planted,
> You surely shall reap,
> And that which you harvest,
> You surely shall keep.' "

After Maud's death Mother Jennie became known in Spiritualist circles, and various persons came to visit at the open meetings of the Sisterhood. Mother Miller was often in attendance, and several new members came into the Cherokee Center.

Jennie still did not have a name for the masculine being who spoke through her. She did not go into trance, and in fact made a serious point of retaining positive control of herself during sessions. Rosa Lee would give her lighter patter and simple poems at the first part of the meeting, then the Teacher would draw near for Jennie's spiritual discourse -- the central part of the service. Having been elevated into a "very high vibratory rate" for the discourse, which was presented to her consciousness in words and images, Mother Jennie would descend to the lower, psychic frequency. Once the discourse had ended and all spiritual concerns were met, the "message work" began.

Psychic phenomena were fast becoming the main preoccupation for members of Cherokee Center. The philosophy was developing that anyone, independent of spiritual understanding, should be able to develop psychic faculties and use them in daily life. Some of the members began to experiment indiscriminately with Ouija boards and automatic writing. While they were very concerned with the source of Jennie's teachings, they seemed to have no concern for the possible sources of experimental contacts.

Jennie's Teacher was yet without a name. When questioned, he simply replied that it is not the messenger but the Message that is of first importance. One evening a couple who taught at the University in Berkeley visited the group. The man pleaded to know the identity of Jennie's Teacher. After being taken into a strong trance-like state while still under her own control, the Teacher answered, "I am Omar, a High Priest of the Temple of Truth in Persepolis, and a Hindu in the last incarnation."

The gentleman said, "Very well, if you have been a Hindu, speak Sanskrit for us."

Suddenly Jennie found herself speaking Sanskrit. The professor, who was familiar enough with the language to recognize certain words and inflections, reacted in amazement. Omar then translated what he had said into English.

Phenomena like this fascinated several of the members. They now had a name for Jennie's Teacher, and they wanted more confirmation of other things. Soon that bane of all mystics, the process known as "inflation," began to spread among the group members.

Mother Clark had passed away some time ago, and she was speaking through Mother Miller. Minnie Miller had appointed Jennie as Mother of Cherokee Center by spiritual direction. This in itself was heady business. But when the members who themselves had little or no psychic ability began forming experimental contacts through the paraphernalia of seance-psychism, which depended upon physical gimmicks as the medium, problems crept into the Sisterhood. Jennie was to face her most difficult trial.

"Interferences came and jealousies arose until there came a battle between destructive, dark forces and those of light and construction. They put out one of the greatest inducements to lure them, and that was through automatic writing. They lady who did the writing was to be the Mother of the Avatar -- so said the forces of delusion. When I spoke against it, then the automatic writing attacked me as a hypocrite and anything but what I professed to be. I was selfish and thought of nobody but myself. I was a liar and deceiver. The members should ostracize me and form another group."

On May 7, the entire Sisterhood met in San Francisco. Jennie's group asked her to represent them as Scribe, so she left for two weeks. Midway through the convention her Teacher urged her to return to Santa Cruz. It was May 14, a regular meeting night. The Center was meeting at the home of the woman who was getting the automatic writing. She was sitting in the Mother's chair. There were a few strangers at the meeting who were not supposed to be there on that date. The woman asked if Jennie wanted to assume the chair, but she replied, "You sit where you have chosen. I'll sit here."

At the end of the meeting the woman tried to get messages, but to no avail. All she could do was the automatic writing. Then Jennie was asked to do the message work.
"I said, `As the Teachers will,' and began to enter the consciousness. I was shown over in that

corner a casket of a bier draped with beautiful laces in truly commemorative style. I was able to describe fine details of its surroundings and the pall that was laid over the top, and then the features of the exposed face. I was moved to turn to one of the new ladies, but before I could speak she said, `That's my husband. I've traveled all over to try making contact with him, and you are the first medium who has seen him.'

"I said, `This is probably why the Teachers sent me back, because they saw that you were searching sincerely.' "

Soon after that meeting the group broke up. The woman who had been getting automatic writing was totally convinced that her mission was to be Mother of the Avatar who was to enlighten this dispensation. The rest of the members, but for two or three, were swept up into the importance of the claim. When the woman's automatic writings spoke so condemningly of Jennie, most of the membership left to follow the woman.

For Jennie, this was in many ways a lower point in her life than the time of her divorce. Yet she knew and understood that she was being tested. She took her stand deliberately, knowing that she must suffer for it.

The pattern was beginning to emerge. She was not through with her struggles by a long shot. It would always be this way -- a period of growth and spiritual success, then one of trial and desolation. But always light came forth from darkness, and dawn from blackest night. While it seemed from a human standpoint that all things were doomed and preordained to decay and that every happiness must end in despair, somehow she had begun to feel deeply within herself, unconsciously, that in reality it was the other way around. Despair must end in happiness.

She received another significant dictation which she called Consolation. There had been many dictations and poems during the past year, but a sequence of three seemed to have special significance. The first had been Come Thou, Great Light, when the contact had been made. The second was the Call to Service (see Appendix), a poem followed by the Call to Attainment. Jennie had accomplished much, but suddenly her group was taken from her and she was in disgrace. Now she received the Consolation, a form of dictation that she was to receive at other low points in her life (see Appendix). This would be followed by three other significant poems of great length: Fulfillment; From Out the Deeps; and How to Reach It, the Holy Grail.

Four of the sequence she entitles by function, creating this experiential sequence: Call to Service (the experience of vocation); Call to Attainment (the experience of aspiration); Consolation (the experience of trial); and Fulfillment (the experience of spiritual victory).

This follows the pattern of mystic progress familiar in Christian and other religious experience. First there is a conversion, the confrontation of a divine imperative which demands a decision. Like the shaman or apostle, Jennie was summoned for service.

The next stage involves what in Christian terms might be called sanctification, the aspiration to sainthood. The first step has been a salvational decision, but this must be followed by progress on the upward Way of Christ, the imitatio Christi. The New Adam must replace the Old, and the devotee must strive for a new humanity. The goal is nothing less than rebirth or apotheosis. Salvation has been a gift, but now the devotee must compete against his lower nature to become worthy of that gift in some small way. There must be attainment, growth and its fruits.

But now a third factor enters the realm of experience. It is the test. No matter how prepared one might have been, the test comes like a thief in the night. In Christian terms, this is the Crucifixion. At precisely that place where the person is most vulnerable, the Cross appears. Like an "X" which marks the spot, the paradox strikes. The contradiction manifests. Like a surgeon's knife, the test separates flesh from flesh and bone from bone.

If the test cannot be passed, it remains. It may seem to disappear, but later it will reappear. The struggle must be met, and it must be met by, through and within the person. There can be no seconds in this duel, and no proxies can win the contest. There is no escape. There can be relief and compassionate consolation. But once the issue has presented its face, it remains until resolved.

The "trial" is a basic aspect of existence. It is, in a very true sense, an abiding reality. It is not the Reality Principle, but it is a principle of reality. It is chaos, the void, the first element of Creation. It is that which is present as an unrealized potential, and which must be made real through transformational working of the universal Logos of life.

It is not, then, that life is a series of failures -- that everything is doomed to death and decay. It is not that what goes up must come down. Rather, life is a continuing process of creation in which sequentially perceived dilemmas are resolved and made real. As each level of creation is encountered, new levels of chaos appear. But what has been ordered and made logical remains in an ever-growing trail of attainment.

Therefore, creation is ex nihilo, "out of nothing," and light does emerge out of darkness. Understanding emerges out of conflict. If the understanding existed in the first place, there would be no conflict. It is therefore conflict that brings understanding to birth. The archetypal pattern, then, is not Birth-Death, but Death-Birth. The basis for Resurrection is Crucifixion, and the basis for life is death.

The final stage for Jennie was embodied in the poem Fulfillment (see Appendix). Now with the assurance that comes only from the profundity of personal experience can she say,

> "Canst thou not see, hast thou not heard,
> Fulfillment of His promised Word?
> That they who run shall ever see
> The solving of Life's Mystery?"

Within the fourfold pattern is a basic twofold theme. The Call to Service generates a Call to Attainment, just as the Crucifixion generates the Resurrection. The sine qua non of attainment is service, and the root of fulfillment is lack. Pain precedes pleasure, and the question precedes the answer. Ignorance must be manifest before enlightenment can occur.

One must experience incarnate reality before he can look for a wider reality. The violinist must work through his exercises before he achieves the mastery for spontaneous performance. The First Coming must be in weakness, but the Second Coming is with great power.

"Verily, verily I say unto you: Except a corn of wheat fall unto the earth and die, it abideth alone. But if it die, it bringeth forth much fruit." (John 12.24)

Jennie's life of attainment in Christian service had now reached a self-conscious level. With the betrayal of her group and the false slander that was being spread and believed about her, she was made to suffer unjustly for the truth. It is at this point, of course, in Christian philosophy that the mystic is to rejoice -- when all manner of evil is spoken against him unjustly. He now becomes a martyr and follows the Via Dolorosa of Christ. "Think it not a strange thing," says the writer of the latter Petrine epistle, "when fiery trials engulf you, for this is natural and to be expected. This is integral to the Way, and is part of God's spiritual pattern for growth."

But somehow it always seems a "strange" and unnatural thing when it happens. It seems so demonically wrong and unjust. Like Job and Christ, one must see ultimately that the blame is God's. Like Job, one gags on the cup that he must drink, or like Christ one prays that it might be taken away. But there it is, the bitter draught. Might as well accept it willingly, like Socrates. Might as well fully experience the healing stripes, like Christ.

"Yet not my will, but Thine be done."

And with that death comes the dawning of a new creation, the in-breaking of a universal governance which, as Mother Jennie likes to say, is "just and equal for every soul." Through this experience and many others, Jennie learned the great Islam of acceptance. God must be trusted to bring good out of evil and order out of chaos. "Let go and let God," she likes to say. "Of myself, I can do nothing."

Acceptance is a struggle, and Jennie knew that she must make herself accept the situation.

"Well, it knocked me out, that night they sat on me good -- and they sure did make me feel worse than a worm that had been trodden on, and I fainted.

"My husband and the doctor carried me to the bed, and Louis turned to them and said, `You'd better go home. You've done enough.'

"I was practically out until Sunday morning, when the Teachers said to me, `Child, it is almost Temple time. You'd better get up and get dressed.' I did get up. It seemed silly to me. No one would be there. Why should I prepare? But I did as the Teachers directed, and when I walked into the room, there were three people I had never seen before. They had heard about my work, and came to see for themselves. So that's how the work went on, even with the others gone."

The year was now 1927. The original Cherokee Center had been Jennie's first forum as a Spiritualist leader. It was through this forum that Jennie was able to discover and organize her psychic abilities. But her prime interest had been in the spiritual dimension of reality, and she had discouraged too much fascination with psychic phenomena. This was undoubtedly why all but two members of her first group had left.

"I said, `I am a teacher. I must teach the Word of God.' But all they seemed to really want were messages from those who had passed away -- readings, ballots and phenomena. They didn't want to consider what lay behind these things."

The period had been one of spiritual instruction for Mother Jennie. Mother Clark had died in 1923, and Mother Miller a few years later. Mother Jose McClaren had succeeded Mother Clark at the Queen Esther Center in San Francisco and helped Jennie from time to time. Florence Becker had bloomed as a medium as well in San Francisco.

"The others started a class of their own. They phoned most graciously, but they wanted to save my soul. I was therefore asked to come to their class. I said, `No, I'm not going to your class.'

"Then the Teachers said to me, `Child, wouldst thou refuse an unpleasant duty to perform?'

"I thought for a moment, and I said, `No.'

" `Then you will attend,' said the Teachers.

"So that night we went, and if we had walked into a charnel house it couldn't have been more chilly. They had gathered several of their believers on this Avatar business, and we sat down. Everyone was allowed to speak except my husband and me. We were to sit and listen. As we were going home Louis says, `We're not going there any more.'

"I said, `No, I don't want.'

"Well, when it came to the next Sunday, they phoned and asked us to come. And again the Teachers said, `Wouldst thou shirk an unpleasant duty?'

"So I turned to Louis and said, `Omar says, `Would we shirk an unpleasant duty?' He shrugged his shoulders and said, `Well, I'll take you, but I don't like it.' I said, `Neither do I, but I have to be obedient.'

"So we went, and the same old charnel house feeling. We sat down, and they started in with a lesson from a book, then asking this one and that one what they thought about it. But they skipped us, and I was told to be still.
"When it got to the end, a woman sat across from us and turned to the chairlady, saying, `But Mrs. Peterson could answer this question if you'd only ask her.' The Avatar woman had no other choice but to ask me, and I answered the question. They didn't like it a bit, and when the meeting was over I knew the Teachers would make me attend no more."

Shortly afterwards the group disbanded. The woman who had received automatic writing which put her forth as the Mother of the Avatar was disgraced when predictions of the coming pregnancy failed. The actually bought baby clothes and hung them out on a clothesline in expectation, but until the day she died she never conceived a child. Many years later she apologized to Jennie for the humiliation she had caused her, when she herself had finally come to experience humiliation.

The end of the old group at Cherokee Center marked the end of a cycle in Jennie's growth. During this period Rosa Lee, Omar and several other Teachers had manifested to Jennie. They gave her prose and poetry which she received in sporadic dictation. The great poems would be given a little at a time, and no more would come until Jennie had actually learned the lesson of each verse through life experience.

Until she had come to "know" the real-life meaning of the wisdom which was given, bit by bit, she was given no more. For Jennie, then, her spiritual education was "line upon line, precept upon precept." It was not an intellectual education, but a precognitive education based upon the successful meeting of life-issues. The education was psychological and experiential, and could not progress from one stage to the next until each "lesson" was learned. These were lessons in wisdom, or the art of spiritual living. They were carried out in the crucible of daily flesh-experience, incarnated and allegorized in the "little things" of life. The key to such knowledge, then, was not the mind, but human experience.

Omar was the bridge, not only between Jennie's earlier period with the Cherokee Center and what was to come, but also between her life with Louis and the trying times that were to come after his death in 1928.

Shortly after the death of Rose Stoddard, Jennie was visited by the voice of a new Teacher. This voice was unlike the nameless one which had dictated "Come Thou, Great Light." It was far more tender and loving, and had a softness and wisdom which was impossible to miss. It was this Teacher who had infused her with the great force during Mother Miller's meeting, and who had finally identified himself as Omar.

This Teacher became Jennie's high Guide. Through a prose dictation he asked her to accept daily lessons. She considered this and agreed to undertake the responsibility. From then on, every morning at ten o'clock Jennie heard the voice and wrote down what was said.

Shortly before ten o'clock Jennie would hear the summons: "Temple time approaches, my Child." She would drop whatever she was doing and repair to the living room with pad and pencil. Sitting at the harmonium, she would say a prayer and sing a hymn. Then Omar would begin to speak to her, and she would write down what was said. The lessons would come both in prose and poetry, and she was often addressed as "Chela." The lessons continued every morning for nine years, until 1931. They covered psychic and spiritual topics and constituted the framework for Jennie's spiritual progress (see Appendix).
At the same time she was receiving the long poems like From Out the Deeps. These were larger, more profound forms of teaching which she received a bit at a time -- often taking whole years to complete.

Jennie told me that she received one of her most profound teachings during the late 40s, in the form of a vision. She saw the brilliant sun rising between two hills. That is all, and is nothing more than many people have seen on countless occasions. But people have seen it not as a vision, but in terms of everyday consciousness. Therefore it was, for them, either devoid of meaning or productive of slightly joyful awareness.

It was not until 1953 that Mother Jennie was able to express in words the meaning of that revelation, or to form a rational understanding of what had been given. When that understanding was finally brought to birth, it was deeply meaningful to her.

Meaning depends upon the awareness of the interpreter, but it exists quite happily without him. Most of us perceive the workings of universal intelligence around us and within us at every moment. But each crumb of experience must be masticated and digested before it can nourish, and how hastily we savor life's lessons! We "bracket out" most things as the product of a random universe, or excuse them from consciousness as trivialities. Before Freud took them seriously, we ignored "slips of the tongue" and other evidences of the unconscious activity which we harbor beneath the images of mundane consciousness. We consign randomness itself to the realm of meaninglessness, simply because we do not understand it. But meaning exists everywhere as an undiscovered possibility. With diligence and a willingness to take everyone and everything seriously, meaning is recognized and "re-membered" as a potentiality, and transmuted into the realm of probability. As more becomes known, it begins to exist as an actuality. Meaning does not slumber -- only the awareness of human consciousness. Only when the human mind begins to make itself supple, to respond to the subjectivity of experience and see that as a valid activity -- only when patterns, sequences and cycles of perception are taken seriously, can the human mind subject itself to the great lessons of a morning sunrise.

"When the student is ready, the Teacher appears."

For Jennie there were many Teachers in visions and auditions, but life itself was the greatest Teacher. In the names of Rosa Lee, Omar, Xitithlon, Coutumi, Moria and others of the Celestial Beings, Jennie acquired transcendental instruction.

As her reputation grew, Jennie began receiving requests from far and wide. She was wanted to serve as Spiritualist minister of several small churches. Often she would find letters asking for help by mail. People somehow understood that she was not a fortuneteller and did not embarrass her by offering money for service. But there were a few that wanted psychic readings for a price, and Jennie was quick to set them straight.
"I can give only what is given to me. It is a gift, and not for sale."

One of the large Spiritualist churches in Oakland asked Jennie to serve on Sunday evenings. She accepted, traveling each weekend by train and bus. Although the service was mainly message work by ballots, Jennie was asked to preach at times. It was after one of these sermons that she was told by a sister psychic to expect a letter in the mail when she returned home.
The letter arrived on Monday. It was from friends of Maud Lord-Drake. They had owned the property adjoining Maud's in Boulder Creek and had known of Jennie for many years. Would she be willing to take Sunday services at the new Spiritualist church in San Jose? Jennie's Teachers indicated that she should go ahead with the venture. In two weeks she and Louis made the trip.

Even though she was to be the medium, the homiletic or "teaching" part of the service was left up to male ministers. The pseudo-Pauline injunction that women were not to speak in church was still observed among Spiritualists. A talented woman psychic would be used as a medium for personal messages, but rarely as a preacher. Since spiritual teaching was her vocation, Jennie seemed a paradox to her contemporaries. It was considered acceptable for her to teach in her own home, but the majority of churchgoers considered it impious for a woman to teach in a worship service.

It was a stormy night. Mother Jennie, Louis and his brother's family arrived soaking wet at the Temple on Seventh Street in San Jose. Immediately Jennie was interrogated by one of the churchmen.

" `How do you give your messages?' he asked.

"I looked at him in amazement. He said, `Do you give them direct, or do you read?' or something or other.

"I said, `Any way that they come to me, I give them.' "

Because of the storm the speaker was unable to come. The attendance was very good, however. With some hesitation Jennie was asked to give a lecture. The Teachers agreed, and she proceeded. Afterwards came the psychic activity.
The first message was divined through a paper bead which had been sent up. Jennie gave everything she saw, but the person denied what was said. More was given, and more was denied.

"So finally Rosa Lee said to me, `Put down the bead.' I put it down and went on with others. I gave a lot of messages. By the time I was almost through, the belated speaker arrived in time to pronounce the Benediction. I asked them to come and pick up their articles for psychometry, and the woman came for the bead.

"She reached up and said, `I want to tell you that those messages you gave me are true, but I could not acknowledge them in front of the people.'

"I put up my hand and said, `Just a minute, people.' Holding up the bead I declared, `The messages that were given have been accepted as truth, and the Teachers want you to know it. Thank you, God bless you and good night. Now you may go home.'

"That was how the Teachers vindicated me that day, but I felt like going through the floor." Nothing can be more disturbing to a good medium than to be told what she is feeling is false when in fact it is accurate. Often a subject does not make a rational connection with what is given because of the nature of the message. It may concern things repressed or denied, and there can be a psychological resistance generated which actually prevents the subject from understanding the meaning of what is said. Sometimes the Teachers can bring through a key word or idea which startles the person into awareness and comes like a shock. At other times it is not until the subject has left the presence of the medium that the sudden realization comes.

Mother Jennie learned to trust her sensibilities implicitly and leave the message without attachment. Often it was years before persons bothered to tell her of a confirmed message -- undoubtedly assuming that Jennie was omniscient and didn't need emotional confirmation. Most of the time, however, the message was immediately understood and recognized.

"I will give only the truth," said Jennie. "If the Teachers give what is false, then I'm through and I'll never give another message."

But the Teachers continued to give what was true.

In 1928 Jennie was ordained as a Spiritualist minister. For her this was to serve as protection in her work from any accusations that she was a fortuneteller, and it gave validity to her full ministry as both medium and speaker. Jennie had been working in the San Francisco Bay area with Florence Becker. Florence had gained a great reputation as a medium and Spiritualist leader, and had come to depend upon Jennie's service. Others too had requested her work. It was inevitable that Mother Jennie be offered ordination.

"The Teachers requested that I would have ordination. They said that they were going to arrange for my ordination. The Teachers went through the service by speaking through me. They told me there would be two offers. I should accept the first one that came."

Florence Becker had been making arrangements with the National Committee on Ordination in the Spiritualist Church for Jennie's ordination. Normally there would be a long probationary period, with full investigation of the candidate's psychic abilities. This was to be bypassed in Jennie's case.

The day before Florence's letter came advising Jennie of these facts, however, she had received a communication from Mrs. York of the Spiritualist church in San Jose. This was the congregation to which Jennie had spoken on the stormy night when the speaker had been late. It was a large congregation, but part of a Spiritualist offshoot denomination known as the Church of Scientific Natural Law. Mrs. York's letter had come first, offering ordination, and Jennie knew she must accept.

This had been the spiritual pattern in Mother Jennie's life. She had been taken out of the "glory" spots and withheld in relatively unknown status. It would have been easy for her to rationalize things and accept the second offer from Florence Becker. This would have catapulted Mother Jennie into the spheres of international fame with notables like Becker and all the other women whom Jennie had known. Yet Jennie had her instruction. If she was to remain obedient, it was not to be. She must accept ordination in an obscure denomination (which has long since ceased to exist). She must obey the highest that was within her, and the best impulse of spirit that she could perceive.

It is perhaps interesting to note certain life patterns and motifs which seem to recur in Jennie's progress. There are parallels between the early incident at Langley Mill, where she first preached under inspiration, and the occasion of her visit to the church on Seventh Street in San Jose, where she was asked to lecture in place of the absent speaker. These each mark significant points in her greater journey as a spiritual teacher. The first incident made her aware of the ability to speak, and the second made a congregation aware of her gift. Ordination is a recognition of such calling. Jennie had received a spiritual ordination at Langley Mill, and over many years had come to a self-consciousness of this vocation. Now other persons had recognized Jennie's vocation.

But the key to her growth seems always to have consisted in a willingness to follow the prompting of spirit rather than self. The decision on ordination was simple, yet very hard. To choose the seemingly inferior and lesser part in obedience to unseen and only subtly felt spirit voices is a difficult thing. After all, shouldn't the Message go out? Should a candlestick be hidden beneath a bushel basket? How simple it would have been to give priority to self and what might have easily been perceived as public service. But no! Jennie was able to keep perspective and faith with her voices. Even though the prompting of spirit seemed unreal and easily misinterpretable, Jennie refused to be seduced by mental ideas. She chose what seemed to be the lesser part in obedience.

Jennie's years with Louis had been the happiest in her life. In this partnership, each person had accomplished rich realization of human potentiality. Together they had built a home and modest prosperity. They had found affinity in spiritual life. Jennie had been able to break free of a woman's fated role, and grown from her status as nurse of the flesh to trustee of the soul. Such joy cannot last. "If we had nothing but joy," said Jennie, "we'd become inert." Life is cyclic, and we must learn to give thanks in all conditions.

"Louis' death was perhaps the most terrible shock of my life. I was unprepared for it, and it came without warning. But all these things are necessities in each life. Light comes out of darkness, and understanding out of ignorance. The light I gained from this darkness enabled me to help others, because if you haven't experienced, you cannot know. If I'd had no conception of these domestic trials, I'd be unable to help others because I wouldn't understand."
There had been an intimation of Louis' coming death, but Jennie had not wanted to recognize it.

"In the Sunday morning meeting before Louis' accident, we had gone into the silent meditation and there was a golden wheel. A spoke radiated out to everyone, and I called upon each to give what they saw. When it came to Louis, who always sat in the big chair opposite to me, I could see that he was disturbed. He was a very sensitive man. I said, `What do you see?'

"After a little prompting he said, `Well, there is a dark, heavy shadow which settles down upon us. I see up above a soft, white mist.'

"And with considerable prompting in between his statements, which were abbreviated, he said, `And I see the Master up there, and I am with Him.'

"And I said, `Oh.'

"We went on to the others expressing themselves, and it came to mind, which was always given last. I had seen a cosmic clock, and the hands pointed to twelve. The Teacher said, `The cosmic clock, what does it mean to the children of earth? It means the hour has struck.' "

People left the meeting with a very heavy feeling in their hearts, but not really understanding why. Jennie held two and sometimes three meetings every Sunday, and that evening there was another. Everyone again was aware of a heavy and oppressive atmosphere.

"All at once I was conscious of a trumpet at the side of me, and out from the trumpet boomed a voice: `Out of the darkness shines the light. Out of the darkness shines the light!' It boomed and boomed, and I said, `I can't stand it! Take it away!'

"With that they said, `Pete, what is it?' (They used to call me Pete, short for Peterson.) I said, `I don't know, but I can't stand it. We'll close the meeting and I'll go home.' "

The next day Louis fell from a ladder while building a house. Jennie was counseling a woman from Canada when suddenly she felt a terrible crash and found herself wiping a sensation of blood away from the side of her head. The woman from Canada could not make any connection with what Jennie was sensing. Suddenly there was a rapid knocking at the front door. In an artificially casual tone a neighbor said, "They've just phoned me that Lou had an accident, and they want you out at Seabright." The woman from Canada and her friend Gladys offered to drive Jennie.

"There he lay in a pool of blood. I knelt down and asked for strength, and I touched his gentle hands that had caressed me so much. The doctor and the ambulance came. The doctor touched me on the shoulder and said, `Mrs. Peterson, you'd better come with me.'
"They put his limp body in the ambulance and me in the car, but I heard him say, `Oh, my Darling, I slipped. Take me home, take me home.' I turned to the doctor and asked if anything could be done at the hospital that couldn't be done at home. He said, `Mrs. Peterson, there's not one thing that can be done.' I said, `Then we'll take him home.'

"As we turned into the drive the neighbors came running up to see if there was anything they could do. We took Louis out of the ambulance and carried him into the house onto his bed. I took off his boots and was overcome with the sensation of sickness of the stomach, which he was feeling and I had picked up. I went into the bathroom for a moment. They said that he was conscious that brief moment I was gone. He turned his head toward the bathroom door with a moan. I got back and said, `My Darling, if it must be so, go in peace,' and that was it.

"Rosa Lee came with her strength from the Indian forces and held me up as I was collapsing."

Friends and mediums from other centers came to support Jennie that evening. Some, said Mother Jennie, had been sent by Omar and the Teachers. But the Teachers now insisted that Jennie go on without a break in her Temple services.

"The Teachers said, `The Temple work must be carried on: you must carry on.' And I remember being taken up to Pacific Grove for a service, and they left me alone for a minute to rest. Through the window I saw a beautiful daffodil -- a one-trumpet daffodil. It seemed to strain its head and want to talk to me. And it said:

"Hand in hand we'll walk together,
Side by side we'll ever stand,
Singing songs of love immortal,
Marching with the heavenly band.

"We are here to teach to mortals
Precious words of God's own truth,
Which shall help men meet all shadows,
And their saddened hearts shall soothe.

"I questioned there why this little flower was giving me poetry, and this was the answer:

"This the Teachers help me give you,
That you may know I'm ever near
To give you guidance, love and comfort,
And your drooping spirit cheer.

"We are one for aye eternal,
Rest forever in the light;
As you make sunshine for others,
Your own shadows will be bright.

"Comfort, then, the weary mortals,
Help the saddened ones be glad.
Let the light of soul shine clearly,
Through the love which you have had.

"And when you have life's course safe finished,
You will see the waters there,
Waiting, ready to come forward
And bring you to the home we'll share.

"Good bye, Darling, not thus sadly,
Au revoir, we ne'er will part;
You have but to do your duties,
And the cosmic clock will start,

"Ticking slowly off the minutes
Till the day when you will come,
Gathered in the arms of loved ones
To the bright immortal home.

"Louis and Omar, the friend, the Teacher,
Tested, found to be tried and true,
We bid you trust, and e'er endeavor
Each and every task to do.

"Farewell, dear Child, and so we leave thee
In His tender care, Who doeth all things well.
Thy loved one shall rest and soon return.
-- Omar, thy Teacher and thy friend."

On the Sunday following Louis' death, Jennie fought depression and despair. She was so deeply in grief that all she cared to do was follow the Teacher's direction. On the day Louis died she had tried to release him, and all that week she knew in her mind that she must release him.

One of the churchmen from San Jose had stopped by and, seeing her grief, had asked her why she was mourning. After all, surely by now she knew that death was not the end. She fixed the man with her eyes and said, "Jesus wept, and I'm not up to that standard. Take your hat and leave."

The meeting began with great difficulty for Jennie. She knew intellectually that all was well, but her heart was still encumbered with grief. Then one of the sisters asked the Teacher, who was speaking through Jennie, the question, "Why did Louis have to be taken away at this time?"

The answer came from Jennie's mouth with a sweetness which seemed to flow from the depths of her heart, and suddenly Jennie knew that her mindless grief had come to an end.

"The Teacher answered, `Long have they traveled abreast as a team. Now the time has come when the trail for each is so narrow and steep that one must go ahead to blaze it for the other, in single file. Jennie has a work still to do, and therefore Louis must go ahead to find the path.' "

Mother Jennie sensed Louis' closeness in many ways, and regarded him as her twin soul. She told me, "If you can experience a love like that, you will have a richness that can be neither bought nor sold."

Chapter 7

IN THE SERVICE OF THE MASTER

Mother Jennie was nearly 50 years old when Louis passed away. In a sense, her life was finished. Her personal biography had come to an end. There would be no more great loves. The anguish of growth through darkened eyes would no longer be felt. The struggle for survival with its chronicle of human activity in the outer world would no longer be evident.

At this point, biography can provide little more than names, dates and places. Jennie's "life" now becomes inaccessible because it becomes finer and more subtle. It no longer lends itself to novelistic narration any more than the daily service of a doctor or habits of a monk might.

Without doubt, Jennie's Teachers were mainly concerned for her spiritual development. It was not their purpose to make Jennie into an international medium, nor to expound their ideas to the world in a sensational fashion. Jennie had begun to realize in a full and personal way that spiritual "success" is not measured in terms of worldly success. Inner growth, in fact, is usually the product of apparent "failure" in the outer world of ideas, organizations and titles of honor.

The Teachers now began to concentrate upon Jennie herself as servant of Christ. Her period of mediumship, in which she had given "messages" of a psychic nature to the congregation, had been a preparation for delivering a greater Message. This Message was described by Mother Jennie as "the Gospel which was spoken and taught by Jesus the Christ, and which has been altered and forgotten by the sons of earth through the deception of the mind."
In a manner of speaking, the personal biography of Mother Jennie fades away in the few years following Louis' death. Certain events can be told, and a narrative of historical sequence can be offered. But the main duty of a biographer now turns to interpretation, for the real "action" from this point on is internal. It is spiritual.

The plot is essentially this: Jennie went up to Lake Lucerne after Louis had died. There she was asked to lead a congregation. She stayed, and three years later was asked by the Teachers to accept an offer of marriage by Max Maiereder. The two friends were married.

Because Max, who ran the local post office, was ill, they moved to southern California. Jennie worked as a nurse and raised money for bonds during the Second World War.

During a serious illness after the War, Jennie was first visited by her second main Teacher, the Florentine monk and reformer Savonarola. Later she and Max moved back to Santa Cruz, where Jennie was active in the local Spiritualist church.

Max died shortly after the move. Jennie lived alone in Santa Cruz, making occasional trips to various Spiritualist centers. She suffered a serious heart attack toward the end of the 1960s which kept her hospitalized for the better part of a year.

After returning to her home, she met me and through that contact the Tuesday night groups began. In 1970, one of the regular students dreamed of Jennie in her Orrilla Sisterhood robe, which motivated the re-establishment of Cherokee Center. In the framework of this information, then, I shall attempt to narrate the last 47 years of Mother Jennie's remarkable life. Since biography can never be more than a sketch, I shall follow the thread of Jennie's spiritual growth rather than trying to elaborate historical details.

******* ******* *******

The Teachers had insisted that Jennie pursue her work without a break after Louis' death. She was run around between San Jose, Salinas and Pacific Grove for several weeks of hectic activity. Now the Christmas season had come, and the San Jose people wanted her to stay with them for the duration of the holidays.

She had accepted ordination in the obscure San Jose church at the direction of the Teachers. Now Omar urged her to accept the holiday invitation. But Jennie's association with the group was to be short-lived and end in deep personal shock.

"There was to be a national convention in San Francisco, and I was scheduled to give the

Christmas Eve message. Some of the members from Oakland invited me to stay with them that weekend.

"Well, when it came to the trimming of the Christmas tree, we had to go downtown and do a little shopping. While we were down, Ethel had an opportunity to have her hair done. The husband of one of the members had driven us, so she asked us to do the shopping. She required a little more time than we had all thought. There was to be a service that night in the Brush Street Church, and it was late when we got back.

"And the wife of the man who had driven us turned around on me like a wild beast. She ordered me out of the house and called me everything you could think of. She had such a jealousy of her husband, and I was supposed to be a merry widow out for any man I could get!

"The fact is that I was still with Louis, and had no desire for any man. But she hurled every epithet at me, and I was crushed."

Jennie ran out of the room and down the stairs. Suddenly all the grief of Louis' loss seemed to come afresh. Jennie was no longer to be trusted by other women. She was a widow, and therefore a dangerous threat to all insecure married women. She sat on the stone steps and wept freely.

At that moment the minister of the Brush Street Church and her husband drove up. Mr. Maderas approached Jennie and asked if she was ready for the service. She shook her head and said "No." After some hesitation he returned to the car. The lecture had been advertised, and they were impatient to get going; so they drove off. Jennie felt terrible.

"It came to me like a flash, `What have I done?' I decided to get over to Ethel's house for a ride to the church, which I had never seen. I tried to catch the bus, but since I was unfamiliar with the procedure, the man drove off before I could board.

"Some people standing on the sidewalk came and said, `My dear, are you ill?' And I looked up at them and I said, `I'm not exactly ill, but I've had a great shock.' They asked where I was going and told me how to board a bus for my destination, and I did.

"The bus driver knew of the people, and when I finally arrived at Ethel's home she was amazed to see me. She said that I was so pale that I looked like a ghost.

"Suddenly Rosa Lee stepped in and she said, "Look at the wires; look at the wires!" We went to check the wires on the Christmas tree, and there was a frazzled edge just beginning to smoke. In the few hours they would have been gone to that service, they probably would have lost their home. So some good came out of all that."

However, as Jennie is aware, if she had not come to Ethel's house and pointed out the dangerous wires, the urging of spirit still would have operated. Ethel or her mother would have had their attention drawn to the tree, or have unplugged the wires.

"The next day I went home, and it came to me from the Teachers, `Sit down and think about what you have experienced. Think deeply. Have you been able to put yourself and your personal pride above a Message of the Master? Was that a step towards mastery of the self? Or were you subject to emotion and mind?'

"I said, `I guess I failed. But I would have gone to the church if I'd known where it was, and I didn't know Oakland.'

"They said, `Have no regrets about the past, child. But apply what you have learned to the future.' "

Nevertheless, the Teachers did not allow Jennie to go back to Oakland for three years. This was more for her protection than as a punishment for failure. Jennie had not yet learned to protect her sensitive nature from the more callous forces which could come into her field. The Teachers could inspire her and protect her to a degree, but it was up to her to stand on her own two feet.

Mother Jennie's association with the church in San Jose remained on a Sunday basis only. She was also holding a morning service at her home and evening service at a rented hall in Santa Cruz. Again, the meetings were by invitation, and she refused to accept any form of remuneration for her work.

In late October of the next year, Jennie was told by the Teachers to accept an offer that would be presented. Louis Peterson's family had come in from Wisconsin for a visit. Jennie had held Louis' ashes ever since the funeral, and the Teachers said it was now time to dispose of them.

Mother Miller offered to do the service at Twin Lakes Beach. The ashes were scattered onto the outgoing tide. But Louis spoke to Jennie in spirit and asked her to save a tiny bit of the ashes, which she preserved in a carved satinwood box. This maintained a connection so that he could help her from time to time.

Again the Teachers spoke to her. She was to be shown a new opportunity which she must gladly accept. Shortly after this Mrs. Beale, a friend of the Petersons, called Jennie. She had a daughter living up on the lake at Lucerne, and the two of them had thought it would be a good change for Mother Jennie if she could vacation up there with them.

All the Petersons urged her to accept the invitation. They would drive her up, and would lock up the house in Santa Cruz when they returned. Jennie decided to go.

When she arrived at the beautiful lake setting, the Teachers told her that she must take two weeks for rest and recuperation. This, incidentally, was always a mode of operation for the Teachers. They told Jennie in advance which invitations to accept, and regulated her physical health by apportioning times of rest and times of service. At any time she was called to serve, Jennie was obliged to respond, and the Teachers gave her the strength she needed. If an exhausting form of service was to be met, the Teachers foresaw it and had her lie down for the hours preceding. Thus for her own physical health Jennie would always respond to the urging of spirit.

At six o'clock in the morning of the 15th day of her visit, the Teachers awakened Jennie. They told her that the time had passed for rest, and now a period of greater activity must begin.

"Later that morning, the daughter of one of the promoters of Lucerne came to the place I was staying and asked if I would be willing to meet a Mrs. Olsen. She had delved a little into the psychic field, and was very bright and cute -- I remember the way she cocked her head and took full stock of me.

" `Well,' she says all at once, `do you know anything about psychic power?'

"There was a feeling of prompting from inside, so I said, `A little.'

"She said, `I think you know a good deal more than you want to say.'

"I said, `Maybe so.'

" `I'd like to come again this afternoon and bring some friends. Can we have a talk with you?' "

Jennie agreed, and in a few hours Mrs. Olsen appeared with five of the residents. They had a lively conversation. After this experience they were so interested that they wanted to return that same evening with more friends. That evening Jennie spoke to a small crowd on psychic law and spiritual matters. The congregation at Lucerne had been born.

"Mrs. Olsen brought a beautiful cream-colored rose the next evening, and when I looked at that exquisite flower with its royal fragrance, it formulated the face of one of the Masters. He had the flowing headdress moving in the wind to keep away the dust and flies. I sketched it, and it was the first sketch I made of Omar."

Jennie was requested to stay another week. After that time had elapsed, it was necessary to return home. By then, however, she had promised to return because one of the wealthier women had offered her the use of a cottage and all utilities if she would stay up there with them. The Teachers urged her to accept. Making arrangements to rent the Santa Cruz home, Jennie moved up to Lucerne. There she founded a new center of Orrilla.

Mother Jennie lived a happy and pastoral life at Lucerne. It had been a year between the time Louis died and the service in which she had cast his ashes to the waves. Now another year and the better part of a third year had passed. Jennie had no need of a man, nor any desire to remarry. Her life was fulfilling, and she had learned to find happiness in personal wholeness.

Jennie was the distant friend of a man named Max Maiereder, who managed the local post office. His wife had died, and she had requested that her funeral service not be done by an orthodox clergyman. Max sought out Jennie, who had said the rites.

The service was conducted in a new church building which had been put up by members of Jennie's congregation. At first they had requested rental of space from the local school building, but the principal wouldn't allow it to be used.

"Not for any cult or `ism,' " he had declared, so Anna Morrison donated some virgin land, Mrs. Olsen secured the cooperation of her father and the Clear Lake Beach Company, and soon many volunteers had erected a new church building. Even a large bell was donated. On the second Sunday of February, 1931, the little church was dedicated. It was February 12, Mother Jennie's 52nd birthday. She was to remain as minister of that church, serving both Nice and Lucerne, for over 13 years.

Jennie's ordination had been for a purpose after all. Although the Church of Scientific Natural Law soon passed away as a force in American Spiritualism, Jennie's ordination was recorded with the national Spiritualist headquarters in Washington, D.C. Because of the trauma at the national C.S.N.L. convention, Jennie's career in that church had waned. But now she was able to establish her own independent church as a legal institution, by virtue of that ordination.

Max's wife had been a student of the Unity movement, and he found himself interested in Jennie's work through his exposure at the funeral. He began to attend the weekly meetings. Soon he joined Orrilla.

Then a significant event occurred. Louis Peterson had always given Jennie sweet peas on their wedding anniversary. Jennie had missed this experience for two years now, and April 14 was upon her again. She sat thinking of Louis and of the happiest years she had ever known. The day passed slowly, she went to bed, and the next day came.
"Not long after the funeral for Max's wife, I was told by Omar to get out the old vase which Louis had always used for sweet peas. I did not want to do it. I said, `Why should I revive bittersweet memories?' But the Teacher insisted, and directed me to put it solitary and empty on the center of my dressing table. I was a little peeved, but I did as I was told. I thought it was ridiculous.

"Just then the doorbell rang. It was the postman with a long box. When I opened it, there were the freshest, most beautiful sweet peas you ever saw. There was no return address.

"At the next meeting, Max approached me hesitantly. He seemed very apologetic. He said, `You know, last week I was sorting the mail when suddenly I was hit with a strong urge to go into the back yard and cut some sweet peas. At first I resisted, but the feeling wouldn't go away. Finally I remembered what you said about following spiritual promptings, and I went out back rather hurriedly with a pair of scissors and cut a bunch. Then I said, "What shall I do with them?" On an impulse I dropped them into an empty box near at hand and mailed them off to you. It was a sort of present for the nice service you conducted, I guess.'

"You know, those were Max's prize sweet peas. No one else had them, and he treasured them. It must have been a strong urge that got him to cut them down."

Jennie didn't think much about the meaning of this, other than that Louis must have come to know Max's dead wife on the "other side." The two of them must have conferred, and it came out that Louis wanted to get sweet peas to Jennie this year. Max's wife (as Jennie puts it) must have thought of Max's prize sweet peas and used her spiritual closeness to Max to prompt him into cutting the flowers and sending them to Jennie. These were the lines of her interpretation.

A year passed. Max became a very good friend, and she depended on him to drive her back from the Sunday meeting at Nice. One evening as she prepared to leave the car, Max asked to see her.

"You see me at the meetings, don't you?" she replied. Nothing more was said. Max held her in great awe and esteem, and Jennie would have been happy to keep it that way.

Events conspired against her. One night on the way back from Nice, she and Max had a hair-raising experience when the steering wheel went out. Another time they had to help another motorist together. Max was becoming quite hooked on Jennie. He made an offer of marriage, and she refused.

"One morning one of my students, who was a very kind lady, said to me, "I'm going up to Max's place. Would you like to come along?'

"I liked the idea. While she went shopping, I sat on the bench outside Max's house looking at the lake. Then the Teachers came to me saying, `Would you refuse help to a worthy brother?'

"I said, `No one can ever take Louis' place.'

"Again they said, `Would you refuse help to a worthy brother?' And with all the instruction that I'd had, I couldn't say no. So they said, `Then take the step.'

"So I took the step.

"And about a year and a half later we'd been up on the Redwood Highway. When we got home, Max said, `I feel that we shouldn't come together any more.' I said, `I feel the same way.' And we didn't any more after that."

The marriage to Max was one of friendship and companionship, rather than conjugal love. For the sake of her work, it would have been better if the entire marriage had remained celibate. For such a request to come from Jennie, however, might have been destructive to the marriage. It had to come from Max, and only when he felt truly free of any need for sexual expression. He did not know that sex interfered with the delicate balance of erotic and sensitive forces which Jennie had developed. He felt, rather, that he was getting too weak to engage in sexual activity, because of his heart. But his decision made things much easier for Jennie, and she could now concentrate upon her spiritual work as a minister of Christ.

"When we were married, I went up to Nice. We started in with certain services at Nice, and some in Lucerne, and the Sunday evening in the church. At times we used to have a Sunday morning service at ten o'clock. But it was up to us to go, and as the Teachers said, `Let the chimes of the bell ring out!'

"We used to go and chime the bell to let them know it was time for service. The church was just across the road from the lake. And as the clear sound of that bell drifted out across the water, it was really like a holy day."

Jennie worked in the post office with Max. He was not entirely healthy, and at times required a great deal of care. The two of them lived happily together in Nice until 1944, when for his health he was forced to move south.

The years were filled with instruction from the Teachers and service as a gifted psychic minister. Jennie's daily instruction with Omar had run nine years to 1931. With marriage to Max, her spiritual routine was lost. Most of her work was done for other people and during services.

Shortly before marrying Max, Jennie had experienced a vision of Christ. The Master had drawn near to her in the silence of meditation. She had asked Omar who had come. Was it a master?

"Not a master," he had replied. "It is the Master."

She had fallen on her face, but Christ had raised her up and said, "Let it be unto you as your faith supplies." He had chosen her and ordained her a minister of the Gospel.

Shortly after this experience the church had been built, and she began her role as minister.

Over the years with Louis she had written innumerable dictations. A sketch would include as significant writings the following: the minor and major poems from Come Thou, Great Light through How to Reach It, the Holy Grail, all in the period of 1921-1925; Omar's Lessons from 1922-1931; The Atlanteans, The Pen, The Key, during the years 1925-1930; The Doctrine of Kandra in 1926; the service of ordination by the Teachers in 1929; the vision of Christ at the end of Omar's nine-year instruction.

The marriage ended Jennie's years of writing. Her time was consumed with ministry and helping Max in the post office.

Why had the Teachers ordered her to enter this kind of life? It seemed more of a regression than anything of progress. Most of her energy was now spent in mundane activities such as sorting mail.

One afternoon Jennie was feeling especially confused about this. Why had the Teachers directed her to marry Max, and what was the purpose of this life?

Suddenly she felt very light, and an impulse to turn around. She was alone in the mail room. As her consciousness of the surroundings began to fade, a bright vision filled her eyes. A great golden scale, with two golden pans on either side hanging from chains attached to an ornate arm balanced on a fulcrum -- and over the vision in golden letters one word: Balance.

This was the "why" of it. Jennie needed balance in her growth because the role of the medium can prove destructive. It has done so to more than one person, who has ended up an alcoholic or a fraud. Real spiritual progress can burn itself out. The seeds of truth can choke each other out if planted too closely together.

The humble sunflower can look ever upward because it is rooted in the earth. But the eagle must keep his eyes to the ground from which he has arisen and to which he must one day fall.

The medium is always in danger of the fate of Icarus. Jennie must learn balance. The time had come for a regrounding in mundane reality.

The years were happy. Trials were few. Only one event marred the years at Nice, when a jealous neighbor reported Jennie as a fortuneteller. Eventually an investigator from a state legal office arrived to check the story. Jennie was able to show him her certificate of ordination, which was also on file in the national headquarters of the Spiritualist Church. Neighbors all testified that she never accepted money for her work, and the ill-willed neighbor was disgraced.

Jennie did have the opportunity from time to time in psychic service to demonstrate its reality. The following incident is illustrative.

"I'd been in a hospital in San Francisco for two weeks, and a friend thought it was too noisy for me to come back to the post office. We lived behind a store. So she insisted that I recuperate at her house. It was a ranch out at Upper Lake, and they fixed up a cabin for me.

"One afternoon the Teachers asked me to put on my robe and go over to the big house. So I put on my Mother robe of Orrilla, although I was a bit mystified as to why. When I got to the big house, they were just coming down the steps to go out in the car, and they said, `What are you doing?'

"I said, `The Teacher told me to put on a robe and come to the big house.'

"She said, `Well, we were just going to do some shopping. Do you want to come with us?'

" `Well,' I said, `I suppose that is what the Teacher wanted.'

"So Myrtle, the daughter who always used to call me `Ita Bita Sing' because I was so small, she got some blankets and pillows and fixed up the back seat for me. We left, and they said, `Would you like to go and see Pappa Max?'

"I said, `No. I expect he'll be busy.'

"She went a bit further and asked if I was sure I wouldn't like to go. So I said, `Myrtle, you're driving. Drive where you want to go.'

"She decided we'd go see Pappa Max. So we had to come down the hill to the front of the store, and Myrtle decided to surprise him. She says, `He'll think we're customers for some gas.'

"She stopped, and in a few minutes he came out. Max was surprised to see Myrtle, and she said, `Look at what we got in the back of the car!' And there I was.

"Then he said, `Well, what a coincidence! I just got a telegram brought across from Lakeport.

You just came in time. I don't know how to answer it.' "

The telegram was for Jennie from people in Montana whom she did not know. A mutual friend had recommended writing her. The telegram's message was simple and heart-rending (see Appendix). It asked in pure faith where the body of a brother-in-law who was drowned Sunday could be found. Jennie was to wire the answer collect.

"Max said that the operator had called him over, and she couldn't make heads or tails of such a message as that. He said that neither could he, and I said neither could I.

"Then the Teachers said, `Yes, you can.' So I began to tell Max what to say in the reply. And it was that where there was a bend in the river and the willow trees grew, the body had become caught in the roots. If they watched for three days, the body would be released and come up.

"I was feeling amazed as I spoke, and my hair stood on end. Max took the message to Lakeport. When I got back to the cottage, the Teachers showed me a barbed wire fence running along a river bend, and there was a stubble field where the grain had been cut. Then there was another fence, barbed wire, and the road. I saw them take the body on an ambulance carrier and take it through the fences."

It was not for three years that Jennie heard whether her advice had been of any help. The confirmation came in this way.

"Three years later the Teachers asked me to go down to Los Angeles, but to stop off at Tulare. There was another incident there of a brother that had been in trouble, and I'd worked a lot with that and he was there. He met the bus. His son had been moved into the new Tulare General Hospital, and would I like to go and see him? I said, `Maybe that's why the Teachers asked me to stop off at Tulare.'

"So we went, and honestly I never, in all my years' experience and contacts with hospitals and sick people, saw a patient in such a mess. His hair was matted together, that if someone had taken hold it would have lifted up like a wig. His nails had grown and twisted around in circles until they were like twisted wire coils, and his toes the same. And rotting spots on his body."

Jennie went to the head nurse and gave her absolute hell, and made such a fuss that soon several aides were cleaning the poor dying boy's body. Jennie said she would be gone for a few days, and if the boy wasn't cleaned up when she got back, she would call the police and wire the Governor. The young man, Lloyd Fein, was soon spick-and-span!

It was in returning to Tulare to check on the boy and console his father, who was a member of Orrilla, that Jennie was given the confirmation of the drowning incident. The father mentioned casually to her, assuming she already knew, of his sister's gratitude for her advice by telegram three years ago. They had watched where the river made a bend in the spot described by Jennie, and the body had bobbed to the surface. It had been put onto an ambulance carrier and taken back through one fence, over a stubble field, through another fence and into the ambulance.

As usual, everyone had assumed that Jennie "knew." They had not suspected that she too needed confirmation. Yet, as Jennie said, this and many other incidents were for her personal testing. She must operate on faith without wavering, and always be instant in obedience to the prompting of spirit.

The years at Lucerne and Nice brought about a stability in Jennie's life that had been missing since Louis died. Her happiness was moderate but constant, and she was able to be active in her religious work. But as the years passed, Jennie sometimes realized that she was growing perhaps too earth-bound. Existence was too easy, too secure. She was not forced to be in contact with the vicissitudes of the world at large. The depression years had hardly affected her, since she was used to the homestead standard of living. The post-depression era passed unnoticed, and World War II approached without warning. From the mountain retreat of Lucerne, even a world war seemed distant. Jennie's associates were the old, not the young, and life continued somewhat normally even after Pearl Harbor.

One night at about three o'clock Jennie was awakened. Standing before her bed were the three Teachers from Tibet, India and Persia who had visited her on occasion over the past 20 years. They spoke to her:

"We have come to awaken you from your inertia. The time is at an end."
Jennie sank back into a fitful sleep. Suddenly she became aware of herself spinning. Around and around the bed seemed to go, just as it had in the days of her adolescence. She was being taken out of her body to travel in the astral realm. Alongside were the Teachers. Nothing was said, but Jennie realized that she was on a mission.

The atmosphere grew brighter. It appeared to be early afternoon. The sky was hazy with smoke. Looking down, she recoiled in horror. There, in the ruins of twisted metal and smoking earth, lay the bodies of dying soldiers. This place had been a village, but now it was rubble. The ground was resonating with the thumping of mortar shells nearby.

Then the Teachers led her to walk on the earth. They approached the body of a man whose leg had been severely mutilated. Jennie motioned that she could go no further. Omar looked at her with reproach. How many of the sick and wounded had she tended as a nurse? Would she now turn away from a corpse?

Looking closely, Jennie saw that the man was not dead. That is to say, he did not know that his body had died, and was clutching it miserably as a child might his stuffed animal. The teachers motioned to her, and Jennie went forward. She reached out to the man. Slowly he turned, as though in great pain. He took her hand, and suddenly pulled it back. Again, not a word was said.

Jennie extended her hand. Staring at her in confusion, the man again touched her fingers. Then he made a great effort and pulled himself up on his elbows. Jennie began to tell him that all was well, but even as she conceived the thought in her mind, the man heard it. From the right of the scene two medics appeared, and soon the man was carried away.

Most of the scene had faded from Jennie's view. Only the man himself had been visible for a time. Now the entire battle scene shifted, and on all sides there was silence. Omar spoke.

"My child, you are now ready to undertake the work of the spirit. The man you touched was what is called `dead.' He did not know he was dead. It will be your night work from now on to visit the sick, the dying, the afflicted and the newly passed-over. You will be able to communicate with their spirits, if not their minds. Some may recognize you, while others may sense you only as a welcome breath of peace and hope.

"Many times you have been taken for this work, but without your conscious awareness. Now you will be conscious and aware. We will guide and protect you. Now you must return."

From that point on, the whole quality of Jennie's dream life changed. No longer was she holding lectures or conversations with friends, or engaging in mundane activities in her sleep. Now she was on the battlefields or at the bedsides of the dying. Night after night she performed the duties of nurse and minister, and often she was satisfied to observe that she knew the next day's newspaper headlines far in advance of anyone else. All this, however, she kept to herself.

The astral experiences did not leave her tired out in a physical sense, but for the first few months Jennie was emotionally spent. Gradually she learned to accommodate it.

Max had been ill for several years, but lately his heart and lungs had given him a great deal of trouble. The doctor sternly warned Max and Jennie that if the man did not move to a warm, dry climate as soon as possible, he could become terminally ill at any time.

For the first time, Jennie regretted her marriage to Max. She considered separating from him and pondered the meaning of the move that must come. That night Omar spoke to her at great length. He told her that she must accept the circumstanced and do her best under the conditions. Things would not improve for many years, he said, and she must fortify herself for a long, hard period. The time had come for Jennie to demonstrate loyalty and perseverance. Her regrets represented the lingering forces of self and mind which must be mastered.

"Chela, long have you heard the Message and delivered It to others. But the Message is like a seed which requires careful nurture. It must grow up strong in good earth, and one day it must bear fruit like unto itself. Does a fig tree produce thorns?

"Max is a brother entrusted to your care. What vainglory would you seek in abandoning him now? It is delusion, Chela, for there is only one reality -- Love. Of all man's works, Love alone is immortal. It must be founded upon sacrificial service, and it is the self which must be sacrificed. Little do you realize that brother Max has borne your burden as much as you have his infirmities.

"Take heart, then, and try out what I have said. See if God will not open up the windows of heaven and pour you out such a blessing that you will not have room to receive it!"

Jennie realized that she must release her fears and selfish attachment to Lucerne and the church she had so carefully nurtured the past 13 years. God's service had been accomplished. Let go and let God.

In the winter of 1944, Jennie and Max drove to Ukiah. Their home in Nice had been rented, and they stayed temporarily at a shabby house which others were renting during wartime. Jennie was in terrific pain from a bad attack of arthritis, and had to be transported by car with her arms on pillows.

Once they had arrived, a telegram came advising them that many of the personal effects they had left in their garage were being claimed by the renters. Max and Jennie had to make the drive back up to Lucerne to settle this dispute. All the while Jennie was in pain and Max was weak. Because of the gas rationing, they could not get permission for enough fuel to make the trip back down South until a doctor had authorized it for the health of both.

During this period the two old people made occasional visits to the mineral baths in Palm Springs. Jennie's arthritis had cleared enough for her to serve as a Red Cross nurse. She sold over $75,000 of Liberty Bonds before they were able to move over to a better home in Banning. Finally the War came to an end.

Jennie and Max had been guided by her visions in these hard years when houses were nearly impossible to find, and rationing made survival a real task. They had been helped in every way by the Teachers, and especially by the American Indian spirits which seem to have been attracted by Jennie's homesteading aura. From the first time Jennie had seen the Indian holding the runaway horse on the homestead to the present time, many of her visions had been of Indians other than Rosa Lee. On one occasion when Louis Peterson had been lying with a fever in the tar shack in Santa Cruz, Jennie had seen several headdressed Indians approach and anoint him. Just then the fever broke and, with perspiration running down his cheeks, Louis had awakened. The Indian spirits filed out the door.

Although she no longer had her congregation, Jennie had held meetings in the homes which she and Max had rented. She also worked with a Methodist church, where she undertook pastoral visitation and was chairwoman of World Prayer Day in Banning. She showed me photographs of herself standing on a parade float two years in a row. The first year she was dressed as Liberty, and the second as Justice. As one would expect from a shamaness, Jennie loved symbolic costumes and public services. She took them very seriously, and regarded them as having a great deal more power and influence than most would like to admit. Her floats represented the religious organization to which she belonged. Orrilla, as well, had been reinstituted. Jennie was kept busy.

It was 1949, and Jennie was 70 years old. After five years of difficult trial and uncertainty, her second major Teacher appeared to her.

"I had been given antibiotics for a bad sinus infection. The specialist had given me the wrong stuff, and I had a near-fatal anaphylactic reaction. Another doctor had put me on intravenous feeding and other medications because it almost put me out.

"I was lying in bed the next morning looking out onto the balcony off the window. I saw a form build up, and I felt the sensation of burning up, being strangled and torn to pieces. I said to the spirit, who appeared in a monk's cope, `Who are you?'

"He said, `Savonarola.'
"I said, `I never heard of it. Can you stand in the Light of the Christ?'

"With his head meekly bowed and his hand over his heart, he said, `Yes. In the Light of the Blessed Master Jesus the Christ, Whom I endeavor to serve, I stand.'

"I didn't know one thing. I'd never heard the name of Savonarola. I said, `How did you pass out?'

"He said, `Seek not without. More will be added to you later.'

"I said, `Well, what is it that you want?'

"He said, `Would you take down some lessons that I would like to give you?'

"I thought a minute or two, then said, `Yes; yes.'

"He said, `Then at ten o'clock in the morning I will be here.'

"Come ten o'clock the next morning I had a pencil and a pad, just as I used to have for Omar, and he came. When he arrived he simply said, `Savonarola.' He could be as gentle and musical as any young lamb with his first cry, yet as forceful as a bull. His attitude was always one of humility."

Jennie had never heard about the medieval monk of Florence, whose reformist zeal had resulted in his martyrdom as a heretic and excommunication from the Roman Church. Her vision had occurred in May. She was promised more personal information later, when "more will be added."

On June 6, Jennie went to the library. She looked in vain for anything about Savonarola. All she could find was a brief sentence in a small encyclopedia. Then she heard Savonarola speaking.

"Look in the book which your left knee is touching."

The book, upon examination, was another encyclopedia, but without any marking on its cover. In it were nearly two pages on the saint. He had been educated as a physician, but chosen the life of a Dominican monk. At his martyrdom his body had been burned, but the faggots would not stay lighted. Then he was hanged publicly, and the body racked by being roped to horses driven in different directions. This explained the sensations Jennie had felt when he first appeared.

Always when Savonarola drew near, Jennie found that she must remove her necklace or suffer a terrific strangling consciousness. He was very powerful and spoke with great force. One of his favorite maxims was that a person can be ready and willing, but unless he has courage to act, he is of no value in service.

The day after the experience in the library, Jennie was given more information. One of the Orrilla brothers was fond of Max, and would come early to the meetings. He always brought old magazines. It was June 7.

This time he had found a photograph of Savonarola's bronze bust, which had been done centuries ago in Florence. Jennie was pleased to see that it was the spirit she had accepted as Teacher. Even the rude sketch of the new Teacher she had made in May was clearly the same person.

The teachings of Savonarola assumed the same significance in Mother Jennie's life now that those of Omar had assumed nearly 30 years before. Every morning at ten o'clock she was prepared, pencil and pad at hand. She would first play and sing a hymn on the old pump organ, then offer a prayer. Then the Teacher would appear. Over these years Jennie produced a long collection of lessons which she has called, Savonarola Speaks. In them many predictions of scientific discoveries are made, some of which have been borne out. The use of television in classrooms is one example. Another that has not yet been fulfilled is the invention of ways to harness the earth's electromagnetic field for intercontinental travel.

"One Sunday he said that this day he had not come to give me dictation, because there were other duties I had to perform. But he would see me on the coming day.

"That afternoon a group of people came in who wanted to hear me talk, and we ended up with a Sunday afternoon session.

"So you see, he had been thoughtful enough to excuse me in the morning because he knew I was going to have an afternoon session."

Jennie found herself going into a depression. She was in her late 70s, and it seemed to her that life was getting too hard. Max had been very ill lately, and between taking care of him and the move from Banning to Santa Cruz in 1957, it was getting to be too much. They had shuffled back and forth between Banning and Palm Springs the last few years, and now had moved to Santa Cruz. Why did she have to come back to Santa Cruz?

That Monday she received a package from friends at Fort Bragg. She opened it and found flowers.

"They'd been in the mail all weekend. They had been torn from their parent bed, the Mother Earth, away from the sheltering branches of the brush and the trees. They had been put into confinement until they reached me.

"And Savonarola gave me a beautiful interpretation of these things in a poem, where he said, `And yet they came smiling through. Can we not come smiling through?' "

In October, 1957, three months after having moved to Santa Cruz, Max died.

Jennie had initiated the Orrilla Sisterhood and Brotherhood at her home in Santa Cruz shortly after moving there, and Max had helped. There were 15 persons, and they met on Tuesday evenings at the Maiereder home. After Max's death and Jennie's short respite for grief, the meetings were resumed. However, attendance gradually dropped.

There had been a Spiritualist minister in Santa Cruz named Evon Shea, and he was in charge of a congregation. Jennie was his assistant. He was planning on leaving, and Jennie had the understanding that after her vacation she would be given charge of the congregation.

"Evon Shea had to get a warmer place for the winter, and he asked if I would take the church here while he was away. Then when he came back for the summer he wanted me to take the place he had established in winter. The Teachers were quite willing for that to be done. Max and I had to leave during the summer because of the heat anyway, and we were used to leaving at that time.

"When we got back, Evon had left and put Leona in charge of the church. I was very disappointed, but I didn't make a fuss about it. Leona is a fine person, and I guess they thought I was too old.

"But the Teachers said to me, `You must act ethically. If you start your own group, it might draw away from Leona. She too is a minister and has her work.'

"But I got a bit of a chip on my shoulder, and I wasn't going to attend Leona's church. That was when the Teachers said to me, `Child, if sun thou canst not be, then be a humble star. E'en the tiniest star might guide the traveler home.' "

Mother Jennie swallowed her pride and began attending Leona's church. She was given a seat of honor for the weekly meeting at Hackley Hall. As Jennie passed through her 80s and approached her 90s, it seemed as though she would never again be a teacher. She was asked only to help read the ballots and do psychic work from time to time. On a few occasions she was asked to deliver the sermon.

In the meantime a psychic in Salinas had become attracted to Jennie's Message. In her words she heard more than the usual spiritualistic sermon, and found something deeply satisfying when Jennie spoke on Christ and the Gospel. She invited Jennie to Salinas for a meeting, and soon a new group had formed around the elderly teacher. Sunday morning meetings were then organized, and Jennie would stay overnight at the Lennox home during weekends.

One afternoon while bending over to weed her garden, Mother Jennie suffered a heart attack and fell. She was unconscious for three days, and her heart stopped on the operating table.

In this unconscious state Jennie felt free. She was flying higher and higher and experiencing an ecstasy beyond words. Then the voices of her Teachers told her that she must return to Santa Cruz. She did not want to listen but, with two more repetitions of the command, she felt herself pulled downward. She awakened in a hospital bed. Around her were Catholic nuns.

Jennie was in the hospital many months. During that time she became beloved by nuns and patients. She helped cheer everyone, and elevated the general consciousness to an awareness of God and Christ.

The Christmas season was at hand, and still the doctors would not sign her release. Unless she had someone to nurse her on a full-time basis, she must live out the rest of her life in a hospital bed.

One night the Teachers told Jennie that the Temple (her home) must not be in darkness for Christmas. The next morning Jennie learned that one of the nurses was resigning. She asked her to sign a statement that she would care for Jennie, with the understanding that she would in fact only accompany her home. The woman hesitated, then agreed. Jennie was released into the nurse's care and went home. The nurse, however, insisted upon staying with her over the holidays.

Jennie's recovery was complete. Old friends came, and her little dog Cindy was returned to her. Shortly before her 90th birthday, I met Mother Jennie.

Her family had long ago passed away, and most of her old friends had died. The great portion of her spiritual labor had been done at night for many years, through prayer and in the astral.

As a consequence of her contact with me, a whole new constituency began to gravitate to the old Mother. Young people in or out of school heard about her and came to the Tuesday night meetings. Jennie was seen from a different perspective than all her old friends had developed. Instead of an old medium, the young people saw a wise teacher. They saw wisdom and all the transcendental possibilities which new directions in science and spirituality had indicated. Mother Jennie embodied something very new and mysterious for them. She became a symbol of a new kind of spiritual quest.

At first, Jennie was surprised to see the response. For once in her life, young people seemed to take great interest in her Message. They were always in danger of becoming overly fascinated with the psychic manifestations, of course. But those who were beginning to attend her discourses on a regular basis, she found, came for the exposure to spirituality. This dimension of life had become a void in contemporary society. People were now searching for a deeper meaning to life than public religion and materialistic philosophy offered.

Finally Jennie had been recognized as a teacher. At last she was ready to undertake the ministry for which she had been prepared. She had spent over 50 years under spiritual instruction. She had obeyed as best she could. She had suffered and served. She had experienced. Now the Teachers were bringing her students to whom she could pass on this legacy. She would be to them as the Teachers had been to her. Mother Jennie would become a mediator between heaven and earth, as Christ would have her.

The persons who began coming to Jennie's home for instruction were at first students from my class, then other University people who heard of the old saint by word of mouth. Soon many of the commune and street people became aware of Jennie's ministry, and they flowed in and out. This pleased Jennie, but also puzzled her. She did not like their morality or sense of values, and found herself challenging them. At the same time she withheld the impulse to condemn them for drug abuse or other kinds of dead-end behavior.

One afternoon I noticed that the lawn had been freshly cut. I asked who had done her the favor.

"Well, today a group of young people from a commune dropped in. They wanted some advice with personal problems, and I spent an hour with them. Then they asked if there was anything they could do for me. I said, `Well, yes, if you wouldn't mind getting the lawn mower out and cutting the grass.'

"They looked at each other, and the tall man said, `I'm sorry, Mother Jennie, but we believe that it is cruel to cut apart any living thing. We cannot mow your lawn.'

"Well, I saw that they had been deluded by the mind, so I said, `You believe, but do you know? Do you cut your fingernails or trim your hair? I suppose that you don't prune the grapes, thin the rose bush or discipline your own children either.

" `No, my dears. Growth and pain are all around you. Don't be fearful. You have much to learn about life and service to others.' "

Robert had come by just as the commune people were leaving, and he had mowed the lawn.

Jennie found herself in a new sphere of activity. Many of these young people hadn't grasped or even been taught the first principles of moral living. They were lost. Yet in other ways they seemed more morally acute than their parent generation. They were at least seeking. In their vacuum they had to find meaning.

But modern people were badly out of touch with the heart and center of life. Their priorities had become hopelessly jumbled. Their feelings were jaded by a callous moral environment supported by movies and the media. Avenues of perception which could not be neatly categorized were blocked up. Everyone seemed to see things in the same objectified way -- as a photographic image. Children and adults alike were in open rebellion against their own root and tradition.

At first it seemed too much for the old woman. Often she was aware of the hostile feelings directed against her from curiosity seekers who had been moved to attend a meeting. When the Teachers spoke through her on psychic realities, they were interested. But once the discourse turned to God and Christ, or to any spiritual matters, she could sense the negative thoughts in the atmosphere. The word "Christ" especially brought out aversion or hatred in many of the souls. Such experiences were severely draining.

Then on a spring morning Savonarola manifested himself to Mother Jennie in great power. He said that it was time for her to be fully protected. Surrounding her in a pure white light he declared that she was "temporized" against all negative forces. She could continue the work without fear.

Chapter 8

MOTHER JENNIE'S GARDEN

There was no doubt about it. My contact with Mother Jennie was leading me through a profound spiritual change.

I began to experience the "unseen things" of which Jennie spoke, and I came to see that the horrors of Planet Earth are conceived and nourished in the chambers of human consciousness. As a radical, I'd had to agree that man's religions, which had always advocated inner transformation as the key to social transformation, simply hadn't produced the Kingdom of God on earth. I had abandoned the inner paths for outer reform. Like Bonhoeffer, I'd decided that mankind must come of age and take responsibility as Co-Creator with God.

But that didn't seem to be working either. In fighting the World Pig, we all became little piglets, just as America, in fighting German Nazism, became "nationalist" herself.

Why was it that pacifism worked so well against the British in India, but so poorly against the rednecks in Mississippi? Civil Rights was such a beautiful movement, but it wasn't conscience that gave it power. Or so it seemed. Rather, it was the hard-nosed rioting, the tough-minded self-defense, the striking fear into racist hearts that gave some sort of victory.

I remembered the hippies up in Felton. There was a mass immigration of street people from Berkeley to the wooded areas of the Santa Cruz Mountains -- a kind of neo-pioneering movement. They were discovering what it meant to work with their hands, become skilled at a craft, grow their own food.
A group of them had settled in a Felton commune. One night the redneck who owned a gas station in town came with several of the local bullies and beat up the men while horrified women and children helplessly watched. Instead of responding with a good passive "forgiving of the enemy," however, the hippie men retaliated with a late-night attack on a meeting the rednecks had called to secretly plan more harassment. There were some black and blue local men in Felton the next morning, and that commune was never bothered again.

But as I pondered these things, I remembered more. While it is true that the commune itself survived untouched after those events, a more insidious movement of consciousness began: the vigilante groups. I recalled how Noel King, newly arrived from his work in Uganda, had been taken around to see the sights. In the Cowell Redwoods his party had run into a group of local vigilantes on horseback, carrying weapons. I remember Noel's telling me how quaint the native customers were here in darkest America!

I read letters to local editorial pages from people who had been harassed and threatened by vigilantes. My neighbor told me of overhearing a uniformed policeman casually discussing "safe" ways to murder hippies found camping on the property of a certain store-owner, with whom he was speaking. I remembered the Ben Lomond woman who put a .22 slug through the stomach of a hippie youth who was swimming nude in view of her property. I began to wonder if the whole thing weren't more complex than simple pacifism, or "an eye for an eye, a tooth for a tooth." As Jennie often said, if we exacted an eye for an eye and a tooth for a tooth, pretty soon nobody would have eyes or teeth. Yet she always emphasized the need for justice and the courage to carry it out in life.

I became aware of the never-ending battles we fight subtly within us and around us, and of the deception that our eyes and ears of flesh so facilely provide. How easy it was to believe the worst, to accept slander uncritically. How convenient our fellow human beings were to use as projection screens and targets for our own inner darkness. We no longer believed in the Devil, so we had to incarnate Him in the outer vessels of human moral perception -- the hippies, the rednecks, the commies, the niggers, the capitalist ruling class. Aha! Now I can see you, the cause of all evil! So we lay our plans to shoot him in the head, blow him to smithereens, stomp his face with our boots.

We're like a crew of rowdy kids in a car, dumping all our garbage out the window as we pass by. We think by so doing we keep our premises clean. We think that by casting blame onto the other fellow, we free ourselves of responsibility. Dump it out, throw it away. It's not mine anyway -- I disown it. I divorce it.

But we are not free of it. It comes back to us like debris on an incoming tide. It belongs to us, and we cannot throw it away. We must either transform it into something we like, or live with it.

How does one transform his own garbage? Well, he can reclaim and reuse much of it, transform it by fire into some other useful substance, or just mulch it under for life-giving compost in the garden of his own soul. But one cannot disown an act or a feeling any more than he can his own child.

Now here's the clincher, and I quote from Jennie: "You cannot recognize anything you have not experienced. Therefore, do not condemn or judge another person. In the measure that you judge, you yourself are judged."
In other words, the only way that I can perceive evil in another person or creed or political system is by recognition. I recognize something as bad or unjust because the thing I perceive matches up to a similar category in my own nature. It is the evil eye which recognizes evil, not the innocent eye. It is one thing to recognize an activity as wrong, since by experience one has found this to be so. But it is wholly wrong to label the actor, the person himself, as evil.

As Jennie put it, what we sow in the outer world, we reap in our own souls. The very act of condemning another person is a self-condemnation. We "are" the other person and, in afflicting him with the negative force we project outward, we afflict ourselves. There can be no inner peace without the practice of true forgiveness from the heart. Otherwise we are fragmented and suffering human beings, forever cut off from inner wholeness and harmony.

As the prayer of Jesus said, it is in the same measure that we forgive others that God forgives us. To the extent that we deactivate the projection/condemnation mechanism, we begin to recover innocence and personal wholeness.

But the time comes when one must take the courageous initiative to restore outer justice in the world. It is not in blissful silence that the soul progresses, but by meeting the concrete struggles of life. In the symbolism and parable of human contact, we make ourselves and the world whole. It is by right use of the stuff of life that we restore ourselves.

I thought of the primitive magical custom of healing the offender described in Frazer's Golden Bough. If a man had been cut by a knife, instead of cursing the knife he laid it in a special place of honor and anointed it with healing creams, praying for its recovery. In so doing, his own wound was healed. If he were to curse the knife, his own wound would grow worse.

Why? Because the knife, the "enemy," has pierced the personal domain of the man. It has intruded upon his sacred space in order to bring a lesson to the man, like a divine messenger. It has been the burden of the knife (or the enemy) to carry this message. If meaning is to be maintained in the human perception of reality, the messenger must be honored along with his message. Even death would be such a messenger, and certainly the activities of any "enemy." In not only forgiving, but actually honoring the wounder, the wounded one finds an inner wholeness which promotes healing and peace.

So what was going on with the hippies and the rednecks? The rednecks hated their own hippie-nature, so they violently attacked the symbols of their own self-hatred. The hippies did not respond according to script, however, but out of sheer rage and courage. They defended themselves -- a natural and realistic way to respond. This nipped the rednecks in the bud, and the commune was safe in a very specific way. But now life became miserable for all other hippies in the area. The symbols were transferred as the local folks developed respect for the local hippies. Because of the fantasy nature of local prejudices, it was only through real human conflict and a standing up for rights that hippies could be accepted as co-human. If they had responded with pacifism, the harassment would still be going on. Today, as a result of many flesh-real conflicts and resolutions, the local hippies (who are hard-working farmers or crafts people) are an accepted part of the community. The local Safeway, which adopted a policy of acceptance from the first, has now taken all their trade and has expanded into a larger store. The rival local grocery, which did all it could to keep the hippies out of its premises, fights a losing economic battle.

Cast your garbage upon the waters, and it will come floating back to you on the incoming tide.

By the same token, one must learn to give away what he has in order to receive. One has to empty the cup in order to get a refill. If all the rejected and regressive parts of human nature cannot be thrown out, but return like a boomerang, the same must be true of the beautiful and divine parts. In recognizing the beauty and goodness in others, one begins to own up his own divinity. That's why the birds liked Francis of Assisi. He had to send them out before they could return to him, as to a familiar roost.

Life, I decided, is like raising a child. You can't adopt some simple system which is dogmatically correct. You can't adopt a political line or invest in name tags and labels for the other guy "out there." There is no intellectual or mental formula for creating and maintaining justice. The literal law kills. It is only the Spirit that brings life.

In the particular case of the Felton hippies, they followed a right spirit. In beating the hell out of those rednecks, they intruded into their personal sancta and made themselves known as human beings to be respected. In this process, the rednecks learned something sacred. They learned it the hard way, but they learned it. As the God of the Old Testament says, "I gave you famine and pestilence, and still you would not return unto me." But eventually they did "return" unto the hippies with a renewed understanding. Today there is not only peace, but friendship. Instead of consigning the Felton rednecks to the flames of Hades in their own minds and moving out peacefully, the Felton hippies engaged in human struggle with them. Like Jacob, they dared to wrestle with an angel of power.

But in another case the same action might have been totally wrong. The results might have been terrible. There might have been a killing.

You simply can't say, "If that redneck attacks my commune, I'm going to pound him to a pulp." There is no hard and fast rule. If the "adversary" can receive it, often the most powerful lesson is total pacifism. And the lesson is ultimately for the doer more than the beholder.

So I began to see that life is far more complex than my simple mind could conceive, and that it takes something wiser than human mentality to bring good out of evil. I saw how all my anti-war activities could be interpreted to have simply prolonged the war in Vietnam by heightening the internal polarity in civil politics and playing into the "let's fight" mentality. I had been a player in a game of horrors, and I'd kept the game going by playing my part. "I was just following orders." It was I, and my brothers and sisters, who had ensured Nixon's political triumph by our conduct, and our suffering, at the Democratic Convention in Chicago. We pointed the finger and called them "pigs." And poof, like magic they became pigs. As Jesus said, whatsoever one asks, believing in his heart that it is so, will be granted. Poof! The police became pigs, and we became martyrs. Parents became pigs. Liberals became pigs. Black moderates became pigs. Then came Women's Lib, and all men became pigs.

This magic show was getting to be too much. I tried to change the evil in the world around me, and only ended up making it worse. Well, I was ready to start working on that old bit about "inner change" again. The monastic approach to inner change hadn't worked because it was alien to the good earth and brought forth no offspring. The secular approach to outer change had failed because it was too mental, too dogmatic, too subject to the hidden forces of the unconscious mind. Maybe some form of rapprochement could be established.

Like the surgeon, I had realized that I could cut open the flesh, remove the sickness and sew it up. But I couldn't make it heal. Like the farmer I could sow the seed and water the plant. But I could not make it grow or bring forth fruit. I could see that an activity was to be judged by its fruits rather than its mental ideals. I could see that any end was justified only by its means, and the methods which it used. In a sense, the means was the end. I had to accept authority over whatever realm was at my command, and use it rightly rather than grasping for power that was not in my realm. I had to start with what I had. I had to start with me.

*******   *******   *******

Winter term had passed and spring pushed its way up through the earth. I had begun meditating under Jennie's direction, and found it to be a rewarding experience. In the past, my first year in seminary, I had developed a habit of prayer each morning. But prayer was a duty more than a spontaneous expression: after a few years my regular practice diminished to only the authentic or heartfelt manifestations. I saw no virtue in keeping a discipline of prayer.

Now, however, I was beginning to see why monasticism had held such an attraction for so many, and what the Trismegistic mystic meant when he said, "The sleep of the body became wakefulness of the soul, the shutting of the eyes a vision of truth, and my silence pregnant with Good, and the bringing out of the Logos a birth of good things." The meditation, although at times a chore, became sweeter to me than any outer activity.

The meetings on Tuesday nights were exciting, and I had begun to realize that Mother Jennie was becoming my guru. I certainly hadn't been looking for a guru, but now I was listening to Jennie's every word with a respect and attention I'd never before paid anyone. Her words were not just part of a lecture, but living things which seemed to have a dynamistic nature, like seeds.

Seeds! I was spending a great deal of spare time working in Mother Jennie's garden. As I broke into the sun-baked earth or yanked weeds from a bed of vegetables, it seemed I was breaking through the hard layers of my own soul, weeding it and nurturing it.

Jennie taught me not to work in hope of a certain harvest, but to work for the sake of the work of that moment. When I weeded, it was for joy of weeding, not because of an attachment to possible tomatoes or squash which might be produced. Labor for the joy of labor, she would say. Leave future results to God. If tomatoes survived the weeds and bugs, one morning I'd walk out to receive a wonderful surprise. I should set my heart on "things that rust and moth cannot corrupt," as she said. "Do whatever is at your hand to do, with all your might as unto the Father. As for the rest, let go and let God." With these and other teachings she showed me the joy of non-attachment to results.

One of my first applications came soon. A young man named Robert, with his brothers Terry and Pat, had begun to take responsibility for some of Jennie's problems. I no longer had to mow the lawn and, since they were expert in organic gardening, they had begun to come into the garden work.

For some time the garden had been my own, and I coveted it. I had turned it from a jungle into a rather lovely place. For many weeks I had weeded, watered, dug and planted. It was beginning to look like a garden. In the process I had come into touch with much of my own inner garden.

In particular, I had worked for several weeks on a project Jennie wanted: a new planting bed where concreted ground and burnt lawn had stood. She had taught me that preparing the ground is like God preparing the soul. Often the heart, like the hard earth, must be broken before it can become fruitful. Like dry earth, it must be watered with tears to soften the soil for spading, then turned over completely so that the coarse growth on top is left rootless and turned under for mulch. Then the large clods must be broken and pulverized until they become fine soil, fit to receive the seeds of truth. And even then, the seeds must not be planted too closely, too thickly, lest they choke each other and prevent growth.

This, then, was the meaning in life's trial and struggle. As the ancient Desert Mother Syncletica had put it so long ago: "Sore is the toil and struggle of the unrighteous when they turn to God, and afterwards is joy ineffable. For even as with those who would kindle a fire, they first are beset with smoke, and from the pain of the smoke they weep, and so they come at what they desired. Even so, it is written, `Our God is a consuming fire,' and needs must we kindle the divine fire in us with travail and with tears."

Even the earth suffered as I tore at it, and the little weeds as I ripped them from their bed. Suffering must be an integral aspect of growth, to be interpreted and appreciated rather than feared.
Such high thoughts had come in abundance through my sweaty idyll in the garden, and I had grown attached to the soil of Jennie's yard. Like a foolish Romeo, I had thought my Juliet was a single person, rather than all humanity.
After weeks of careful and thorough preparation, the new planting bed I had created was ready for sowing. With relish I picked out the seed packets, measuring in my mind the location of each plant. I returned to the garden. I couldn't believe my eyes. My planting had been sown in my absence!

All over the dark, watered surface were little sticks with empty seed packets to show what had been sown. Several tomato plants were covered by plastic tents, and there was no room for me to plant anything. Robert had sown my planting bed!

I felt like a Viking patriarch whose daughter had just been raped. Anger mounted to my throat. This guy Robert was taking over all my duties with Mother Jennie, and now he sows my planting territory!

Just as suddenly all my lessons on non-attachment flowed into my consciousness. Well, so Robert has sown your little patch. Does that take away from the joy you had in preparing it? Does it matter who plants the garden?

I then felt an emotional catharsis, with this thought: Don't resist the flow. Let Robert and whomever else desires, begin to assume the responsibilities you have taken for Mother Jennie: cleaning the house, keeping up the garden, even caring for her when she is sick. More people can share in the experiences you've had.

How simple it was! I felt no more anger or jealousy. In place of this I was swept by a feeling of relief, as though I'd finally put down a back pack I'd been carrying for years. I discovered for myself the "joy of non-attachment."

[Robert Lynch would later co-found Harmony Foods, a major health food distributor, and become significant in establishing major organic farms and California laws governing organic farming.]

It was shortly thereafter that I witnessed my first physical "miracle" with Jennie. I had been weeding the bed of Amaryllis directly behind the Peace Roses, feeling the beauty of spring in the greenness of things around me, when a tiny flash of blue appeared in the corner of my eye. I looked up and discovered a small Amaryllis bud, perhaps a quarter of an inch long, pushing its way out of the stalk. There were a few other buds, but all of them considerably smaller and just beginning to form. All the buds were green, but this one had begun to show a tiny bit of blue as the flower began to appear. There was only about a tenth of an inch of blue showing, but I thought Jennie would like to see it as a harbinger of new life. I called her over.

She fondled it lovingly, and as I turned back to my weeding I heard her speaking to the plant, telling it what a wonderful and beautiful creature it was, caressing the stalk. After a moment I became aware that Jennie had left and was hobbling towards the house, so I looked up at the bud again.

I couldn't believe my eyes. The tiny green bud had bloomed out about three-quarters of an inch! The blue flower had increased in size by at least three times, and was protruding a distance equal to the last joint on my little finger!

"This must be a different bud that I hadn't noticed before," I said aloud. I searched the whole plant, and those around it, finding only the tiny buds I'd previously noted -- every one of them green, with no blue showing. I decided that in handling the bud, Jennie must have pulled the blue flower partly out, like a telescope. I decided to try the experiment, and opened one of the green buds. There wasn't anything to pull out. I searched the whole bed for a bud that would be similar to what I'd first seen, finding nothing until I went to the other end, some 15 feet away, where I found another larger bud with color showing. I pulled carefully on the colored part. No matter how gently I coaxed, the flower didn't telescope out. Finally I gave a yank, and the flower pulled out completely. I examined it, and found that there had been nothing to telescope out -- there was only a finite bit of matter there, no sheaths that would slide out.

I returned to the large bud and again made a search for the original bud. The large one seemed to stare at me. There was no doubt in my mind at first that the large one was the one I'd shown Jennie. It was just that I couldn't accept the transformation after her hands had caressed it. I had witnessed a "miracle," a natural transformation which had occurred in a much shorter period of time than I am used to seeing.

There was nothing "unnatural" about it. The flower would have come out anyway. There was nothing "unnatural" about the healings that occurred in Jesus' presence. It was just that they came so instantaneously and dramatically. The growth of the plant had been stimulated, not just because Jennie had some magical touch, but in order to show me something. Much more than a wonderful trick, it was a "sign" for me that reality is much more than my tiny working consciousness can comprehend. It was a demonstration that I, like the bud, would flourish in the hands of Mother Jennie and bloom like a spring Amaryllis.

Now I don't know how this miracle or illusion occurred. Perhaps there is some natural force which Jennie stimulated in the flower. It is said that when Yogananda was hospitalized, his disciples saw the flowers in a vase near the bed, which had been facing the sun, suddenly turned to face the bed of the Master. No one had moved them, and they did not see the flowers actually turn. Like me, they saw the "before" and the "after." But they considered it to be a sign and a miracle.

Perhaps it is all in our own mind and perception. Perhaps the bud I'd showed Jennie was already bloomed out to begin with, and the flowers in Yogananda's room were turned toward him at first. We, being the beholders with unconscious wonder in our beholding, suddenly made the wonderment conscious.

Then again, as our Eastern friends are so fond of pointing out, perhaps all perception is malleable, and the inner is identical with the outer, and "reality" is of our own making. Perhaps it was my "faith" that brought on the "sign," in the outer as in the inner.

The point is this: it doesn't matter. The mechanics of the miracle or illusion or transmutation are secondary to the event in consciousness itself. What is of importance is not that I may have formed some new hypothesis to match empirical data -- a mental hypothesis that is always subject to change. No indeed. The important thing is the wordless, languageless meaning which I experienced at that time. There was no theory involved. It was pure experience, and thus authentic knowledge. From the foundational reality of that experience, I can develop my interpretations and erect my mental castles. It was a mythic event, transcending and encompassing everyday consciousness. It was what Mother Jennie would call a "demonstration," a manifestation of high reality beyond what I know as "mind." I can rationalize it, but I can't deny it without losing the integrity of my personal history.

To others, of course, I "must have been mistaken." To me, it was not that I "saw things wrong." It was that I had a vision. It was my little apocalypse in the garden. Martin Luther King had a "dream," and Malcolm X had a "nightmare." But Lewis Keizer had a little apocalypse in Mother Jennie's garden. Boy, wouldn't they love that back in Berkeley!

But somehow all this pork-chop, self-indulgent inner exploration which I was experiencing didn't seem a denial of my radical social concerns. Rather it was both a development of previous experience and a new dimension of them. I noted that Sri Aurobindo had attained enlightenment while imprisoned for making bombs in the Indian resistance movement, and that it was Gandhian religious pacifism, rather than revolutionary violence, which had won India a degree of freedom from colonial rule. In that specific case, then, the workable revolutionary tactic was "spiritual." I thought of Marcuse's Essay on Liberation and his pessimism about the limited dimensionality of contemporary Protean mankind. No kind of revolution can succeed because it will automatically be co-opted. How true! Three years before, the "V" peace sign of war resistance was taboo. You could get beaten up by rednecks for giving the "V." Now it was selling Coke on television. The war still raged on, but the symbols of war resistance were selling Coke in co-optive Amerika.

Then clearly the "revolution" must cut beneath the ground of co-optation. It must exist and be brought to birth on more than just a material or mental plane. It had to be in the root of the whole plant, and the roots are within each of us.

"Now I understand why, all these years, I've been unwilling to betray my limited religious understanding," I thought. It was simple, it was easily attackable, philosophers could riddle it with paradoxes, historians could point to the evil of the Church and the opiate of the people. Admitting the truth of all this, I'd still been unwilling to dump the whole thing. Now it was beginning to make sense on a rational level.

The student and faculty strike over the bombing of Cambodia in the spring of 1970 came as a kind of impotent gesture. My course, "Gnostic and New Testament Apocrypha," had been under way for a few weeks when the strike came. The students were so interested in the material that they insisted upon meeting. In deference to the strike, we met in Noel King's apartment. Several of my students were attending Mother Jennie's Tuesday night meetings.

One of the girls, Kathy, had been raised by fundamentalist missionaries in Alaska, rebelled against that upbringing and gone all out for Eastern thought and psychedelism. She came for a while to Jennie's, and I especially remember the following experience.

Toward the end of the meeting Jennie always gave those present an opportunity to meditate on her discourse, which was inspired by her Teachers, and then offer any words which came to them in the silence. After that was over she sometimes allowed a little of the psychic work -- but only if she sensed that it was germane to the spiritual growth of the person concerned. She did not offer psychic tricks simply for their own sake. Always they were for the sake of meaning.

The meeting was nearly over, and Jennie "felt" an unanswered question "hovering around in the air." There was a young man who had a question he'd been too bashful to ask, but he wasn't speaking up.

Kathy was seated near Jennie, and apparently decided to take the opportunity to get a quick "reading," so she said, "Mother Jennie, I have a question, but I don't know how to ask it."

Jennie looked into her eyes, then spoke with great force, and as though it were a great rebuke, this one word: "Brush!" She cocked her head, eyes beaming.

There was a surprised silence, then she repeated, "I said, `Brush.' Does that mean anything to you?"

Kathy squirmed uncomfortably on the davenport and shook her head, "No."

Relaxing into a gentle, puckish smile, Mother Jennie said in a softer tone of voice, "Well, you soon will understand."

The young man was next, and when his spiritual dilemma had been touched by Jennie's words, the meeting came to a close. Kathy had asked for a lift, so I took her home. We parked outside the apartment house and talked for a while.

Suddenly Kathy's face lit up and her mouth dropped open. "Brush!" she repeated to herself. "Oh, no," she moaned.

"Please let me in on this," I begged.

"This is too embarrassing," she exclaimed, "but earlier today I was walking out in front of Book

Shop Santa Cruz when a young girl came up to me. Her hair was a mess, and she looked as though she'd been sleeping in her clothes for several days."

I knew the type: the deflowered Flower Child whose Odyssey had taken her out of the Haight-Ashbury and down to the next supposed paradise, Santa Cruz. She probably also hadn't eaten for a few days, and needed a bath.

"Well, she came up to me and asked if she could use my brush.

"It occurred to me that when everything is bad and I'm a mess, if I can just comb my hair I feel 100% better. That poor girl was probably feeling the same way.

"I took a look at her and thought, `If I give her my brush, it will be full of lice in a minute and I'll have to clean it.' The idea seemed so unappealing that I turned away and said, `No, I'm sorry. I don't have a hairbrush,' and I just walked away.

Kathy had gotten her spiritual lesson after all. She wanted a reading, and she got one -- not quite what she expected.

I thought of the religious parables of Tolstoy, the cobbler who is told he will be visited by Christ three times the next day. The day passes with only three events, in which he meets the human needs of those in misery about him. That night he feels dejected, when his eyes light upon that marvelous parable from Matthew's Gospel on the Sheep and the Goats: "Inasmuch as ye have done it to the least of these my brethren, ye have done it unto me." The cobbler saw the face of Christ, and I wept when I read the story. It still makes me weep.

The ancient Biblical admonition to be hospitable to strangers, for in so doing we "often entertain angels unawares," certainly applied to Kathy's experience, and by her psychism Mother Jennie brought out this valuable spiritual lesson. This is typical of Jennie's work and of the use she makes of her clairvoyance and clairaudience.

As Kathy put it to me later, when she had undertaken a study of yoga, "Most of what we do every day is a sort of predetermined Karma, dependent upon our language, culture and geographical location. But there are those few occasions every day when we come face to face with the transcendent freedom through right exercise of which we can transform ourselves and the reality around us."

In another meeting Jennie was asking a question about the saying of Jesus to love our neighbor. "And who is our neighbor?" she continued. Since people were too intimidated to answer, most of the group shifted around in their chairs or on the floor. One young man, however, whom I knew to be a devotee of psychedelics, offered the simple answer, "Yourself."

Mother Jennie regarded him for a moment, then said, "No, you are mistaken. Your neighbor is yourself." People became more uncomfortable. Apparently Jennie hadn't heard his answer.

She went on: "What you call `self' is not what I call `self.' For you, self is mind, and all the images and sensations of physical and mental, that is, psychic existence. You have not yet discovered anything beyond your own psyche, and so you think that ultimately you are all, and all is you. You think this is unity. It is not. Real unity is what we perceive as duality. Reality is self-conscious, and what you call `self' is only the beholder. It is an illusory projection, a gross outer medium. The reality of your being is Spirit, and it is that `self' which you must learn to love."

I was astounded. In a nutshell I had come to understand the whole basis of Western theism. It is not that "God" is out there and I am in here. God is within and without me.

The argument for Eastern monism is very convincing, but I've always thought that it was only part of the truth. Alan Watts has put it succinctly in his *Nature, Man and Woman,* where he opens the chapter on Science and Nature: "Things appear to the mind when, by conscious attention, the field is broken down into easily thinkable entities. Yet we tend to consider this an act of discovery. Studying the visual or tactile field, intelligence arrives at the conclusion that there are actually things in the external world... The thing called the human body is divided from other things in its environment by the clearly discernible surface of the skin. The point, though, is that the skin divides the body from the rest of the world as one thing from others in thought but not in nature. In nature the skin is as much a joiner as a divider, being, as it were, a bridge whereby the inner organs have contact with air, warmth and light."

Western perception has been dualistic, from the mode of its religious experience (theism) to its cultural style of relating to the environment. Monism (as the advocates of Eastern thought as superior to, not correlative to, Western thought have so vigorously claimed) is the only true universalism because it is unitative.

But is it? As Watts has said, we fragment the field of reality into "easily thinkable unities." Isn't that what the advocates of monism are doing -- abstracting the whole field of reality into one mammoth and "easily thinkable" unity?

If "mind" is unstable like the water beneath the lotus, and if all perception is Maya, *why trust to mind for an image of unity?* The truth is that Eastern philosophers have no better resources for developing a model of reality than Western thinkers. The two seemingly mutually exclusive approaches simply complement each other. They come up the mountain from different sides, in Jennie's terms.

Jennie's Message keeps returning with more foundation: "The mind has been the deluder and destroyer of the Real. You must learn to make the mind still, to become a clear, pure channel through which Spirit can flow."

As I was beginning to discover in my meditations, it works. I first wondered, "How can the mind keep the mind still?" But with effort, I soon found that there is a faculty beyond normal mental consciousness which, when exercised, can take a natural superiority to "mind." By "mind" I mean that image-making faculty which is stimulated by psychedelics and produces anxiety, fear, mental confusion and other negative effects as well as short-term positive feelings like desire and certain mundane sensory pleasures, especially transient and illusory effects like psychedelic "visions." It is hooked up to psychic faculty and seems to be coordinated to the whole apparatus of breathing. For this reason, yogic science has learned how to "kill out" the mind by using mechanistic breathing exercises.

Often I have attained to a state of "breathlessness" in my meditation, but this has been the symptom, not the cause, of the phenomenon. I can feel in myself how simple it would be to control my breath in order to attain the state. But what is important to me is the exercise of a more subtle faculty within me which I have called, after the language of the Hermetic mystics, my Nous. This "Higher Intellect" is the organ of what Jennie calls Spirit. It is superior to mental activity, and is the doorway to spiritual perception. It is what makes me weep with joy when I read the 53rd chapter of Isaiah, or tremble in pure Eucharist in the midst of a prayer. At its lowest level, it is the doorway for divine "fear and trembling," the beginning of wisdom. All these things are experiential. I cannot explain them in any other terms. Psychological explanations are probably correct, as far as they go. But they tend to be reductionistic. They tend to say "A church steeple is only a phallus" instead of "A phallus is a sacred temple." Hearing, they do not understand; and seeing, they do not comprehend.

At one of the meetings Jennie spoke on the parable of the Wise and Foolish Virgins, in which certain of the women who were part of the reception group for a bridegroom in an ancient marriage festivity were unprepared for his arrival. They wee supposed to keep the wicks of their oil lamps trimmed and a supply of oil on hand, but were lax. Jennie asked the students around her what the oil meant. There were many answers (faith, truth, hope), but finally she said, "The oil is love. By love we nourish the flame within us and light the path for those around us."

Later that evening as I was driving home, I heard a distinct voice saying to me, "What is the oil of Wisdom?" The voice was not a startling thing. It didn't seem to be outside of me, but came form inside my own consciousness. Yet it was like a sudden in-breaking of a waking dream, or like getting a communication from a radio transmitter which had been surgically placed inside my brain. The voice was very distinct, so I answered it in my mind, "Love is the oil of Wisdom." That phrase seemed to stick with me.

The next day I was making out the final exam forms for my class when I got the impulse to ask a final question as an experiment, for which no credit would be given. I would ask the question, "What is the oil of Wisdom?" and see what kind of response I got.

I handed out the exam and explained that the final question was extra. I asked them to please avoid thinking up an answer, because it was not a logical answer I wanted. Just write what first comes to your mind, no matter how frivolous, and if you wish, write out your further thoughts.

When the papers came in I made a chart on the blackboard and wrote each answer. There were 30 students and 30 answers. Nine of them were wholly separate, diverse answers (faith, blood, wine, etc.). But 20 of the students had written the word "love," and the 21st had written a long answer in which he used the word "love." Since only two of the students had been to Jennie's meeting the night before, I was impressed. When I asked these two students why they answered "love," they didn't know. I still don't know what to make of this whole experience. Only two of the students could have known what I had in mind, and they had forgotten it.

Previous to my experiences with Mother Jennie, my inner religious life was one of discipline and strange forms of suffering. They seemed to relate most closely to the ecstasies of the Old Testament prophets, and were consistently painful. Jeremiah tells it best: "My guts, my guts! I writhe in agony! Walls of my heart! My heart throbs! I cannot hold my peace!" I was subject to attacks of severe anxiety and lived with the fear of death. Yet at times I felt as though something in me were pregnant, nearly ready for birth, like a message long withheld. I actually felt about to burst with some profound emotion which I did not understand, only that it was divine. At times, when under a siege of anxiety, I felt glimmerings of euphoria, as though one day the negative perception would flip over like a coin and all that energy would become beautiful and positive.

I remember envying some of my fundamentalist Jesus-Freak students who spoke so joyously about their ecstasies with Christ and their babbling in tongues like small children. Especially I remember one young girl whose face was so sweet, and her temperament truly innocent and peaceful. How wonderful, I thought, to experience such joy.

"All you have to do is ask for joy," she would tell me. So simple. And yet I knew that somehow in the pain of my own quest I was coming into contact with a greater reality than the little ones can apprehend, and that it was not right to cop out and beg for relief. Like learning to master a musical instrument, there must be, for me, rigor and true devotion to that rigor. I thought of that statement by Jesus ben Sirach, 4.17: "At first she [Wisdom] will walk with him [the seeker] on tortuous paths; She will bring fear and cowardice upon him, and she will test him with her ordinances. Then she will come straight back to him and gladden him, and will reveal her secrets to him."

First obedience, and then freedom. First discipline and then mastery. First crucifixion, and then resurrection. That is the pattern in all paths, and the example all nature teaches. First the root, stem, branch, leaf, and then the fruit. The fruit bearing seed for new life.

"What is the reward of service?" I once asked Jennie.

"More service," she replied. "Therefore learn to find joy in service."

But under Jennie's tutelage the whole quality of my religious experience began to change. I had undertaken painting again, as Father Geiser had advised through Jennie. I took Jennie a painting of a wild iris and began doing watercolors of flowers. At Easter I painted lilies and took for Jennie's approval a painting of Christ crucified. She looked at it for a little while, then said, "No, Lewis. This is all wrong. It is far too dark and sad. Try this over again."

I began to paint again. producing a symbolic painting of a lily crucified, but straining upward with flames yearning from its face to the sun, which was a golden Star of David with interlacing sides and the Tetragrammaton written at the center in Hebrew. She was very pleased with this and kept it for three years. This, she said, showed great progress.

In that period I first began to experience the joy that had been so long coming. It began with a visionary event on the morning of March 5, exactly one month before my 29th birthday. The visual phenomenon was so important to me because of the feeling and knowledge that came with it that I painted what I saw. Ever since, my painting has been reserved for events of like nature.

I was lying in bed awake, feeling fully alert but not thinking about anything. My eyes were open. Suddenly a bright golden light seemed to appear before my eyes. It wasn't anything I could reach out and touch, but it gave the illusion of being that close. Yet it was no part of the world around me, and came by impression not from eyes of flesh but through the inner eye of Nous. My normal visual perception faded away, and my whole attention was concentrated upon that golden light.

It seemed to grow in intensity until I began to see four other lesser lights surrounding it -- above, below and on both sides. Within myself I felt an incredible alertness, and a subtle feeling of euphoria began to literally rise up my spine.

This was not the euphoria of a drug, in which the heart rate increases and respiration must be redoubled. My heart was almost silent, and I felt great inner peace. But like the effect of a most subtle amphetamine, I was stimulated with a fine euphoria which rose up from beneath my stomach through my diaphragm into my throat and higher, like a rising thermometer or water in a thin capillary.
It was like the folk tale of catching a leprechaun by looking him in the eye and getting every wish you can think of fulfilled before letting him go. I had to keep concentrating on that golden light at the center in order to keep the vision going.

As I stared at the golden center, more detail seemed to come. Around the light appeared six blue points, and soon I could see that the whole configuration was a strange flower. The central flower had a golden heart and six exquisite blue petals, as did the four others surrounding it, and I began to make out green and golden leaves in the background. They seemed to be flowers on a tree, since the almost bark-like stem from each flower led into a central joint behind the main flower upon which my attention was focused.

Suddenly the whole branch began to shake and strain toward me as though a strong wind were blowing it from behind. Yet it seemed to be the action of the flowers themselves, as though they were sending me a dynamic and powerful blessing. At that time my whole system was uplifted in such a sensation of euphoria that I could hardly bear it, and I lost my concentration on the central heart of the flower. The vision and the sensation faded away.

Perhaps "sensation" isn't the right word. It was a consciousness of well-being and a deep knowledge of blessing, yet experienced dynamically and with brilliant intensity. Later it seemed that the five flowers were like the fingers of a hand raised in blessing.

Immediately I stood up and found my oil paints. I still have the crude painting I produced, with the description of what I experienced written on the back.

My labor in Mother Jennie's garden was beginning to bring me an inner harmony which I'd been long seeking, and to generate the flowers of joy.

It occurs to me also that the flowers I saw in the vision were blue-petaled, just like the Amaryllis.

The following week during a Tuesday night meeting, another strange thing happened. At the end of her discourse, Mother Jennie stared at me and slowly put her hands to her eyes.

"Lewis, you have a serious imbalance in the eyes," she said. This was correct. My father, an ophthalmologist, had detected a mild glaucoma ten years before, and I was on medication every twelve hours to avoid the build-up of intra-ocular pressure which could destroy first my peripheral vision, then finally my entire sight. I knew that she had picked up this condition from me, but did not answer her observation.

Jennie raised herself from the chair and hobbled over to me. Standing behind me, she covered both my eyes with her palms and said in a strong, firm voice, "You will not lose your sight!" She stood there for about a minute. I felt nothing -- no "energy" coming into me from her hands. I thought to myself that I had never really been fearful of losing my sight, since my father was certain that consistent prophylactic treatment would maintain my sight. But I sat there quietly, and when she had removed her hands I confirmed that what she had said was right.
Since that time my intra-ocular pressure has remained fully controlled by the same weak dosage of medicine that was initially prescribed in 1963. It has not been necessary to increase the dosage for nearly 14 years, which in itself is remarkable, and I haven't lost any peripheral vision.

That spring my course in Early Occult Traditions of the West was coming to an end. Because there were several hundred students registered for the course and I had no teaching assistant, I had decided to substitute a series of projects for the final exam.

Actually, I was still trying to get some kind of a political consciousness out of my rather apathetic Santa Cruz students, and had decided that the best approach was to combine radical politics and spiritual consciousness. My strategy was to answer a request by the Provost of College Five to integrate the course with his annual spring fair by planning a final Occult Festival for the Exorcism and Transmutation of Porcus Mundi.

Porcus Mundi was a Latin reference to the "World Pig" or Satan. My students would each prepare demonstrations or other visible projects which would become part of the Festival in the quadrant of the College. Several of them produced a Gnostic drama. Some researched the religion of the horned god and produced an enthusiastic witches sabbath dance. Others did displays on acupuncture, astrology, palmistry, metoscopy and many other things.

But the central event, which was to occur before the procession to the sacred grove, was the exorcism of the World Pig. This followed a drama which related contemporary political events (Vietnam and Cambodia) to apocalyptic mythology in which the "Establishment" was represented by the figure of Babylon the Great Harlot. She would fall, and Satan would be bound for a thousand years.

My students hadn't liked that. They wanted Satan to be totally transformed, rather than simply "bound." This was rather unrealistic (politically speaking), but at last I relented and we changed the theme from simple "exorcism" to exorcism and transmutation. How was the World Pig to be exorcised from the World-Soul and transmuted?

That was up to my chemistry students, who were following my translation of a medieval alchemical tract. For a period of forty days they followed explicit instructions which I had translated from a Latin document loaned to me by my colleague Manly Hall.

I had earlier spent a day with the great occultist at the Philosophical Research Library in Los Angeles reading through his Coptic manuscripts on the strength of an introduction by Mother Jennie.

The student alchemists worked for six weeks and followed directions to the letter, but were unable to achieve the Philosopher's Stone. However, we decided to use whatever they came up with after the attempt -- in this case a sealed glass bulb with black material. To climax the political rally which would center on the exorcism of the World Pig, I was to invoke Porcus Mundi into the papier mache image of the Pig, then put the Philosopher's Stone into its mouth. This, supposedly, would "transmute" Satan by means of sympathetic magic.

The day arrived with everyone in costume. The events of the Festival came off beautifully. Finally everyone gathered around the papier mache idol of Porcus, which was sitting on a large metal barbecue pit. I led a "power to the people" rally, hacking off an ear or arm of the beast in tribute to the Chicago Seven and other revolutionary figures. Porcus was assumed to be within his "image," by the principle of sympatheia. I had "invoked" his presence.

Now the time came for the exorcism and transmutation. I stuffed the alchemical glass bulb into his mouth, commanded him to be exorcised from the Psyche of the Kosmos, declared the Aeon of the Water-Bearer to have officially begun, and set the Pig on fire! That inaugurated the celebration, and we undertook the sacred procession to a grassy hillside across the campus, where I lifted my trumpet and began to play with the jazz band I had asked to come. Everyone danced and celebrated.

For all these priestly functions I had worn a pure white macrame-like vest that Ann had knitted for the occasion.

At the end of the affair one of my "alchemy" students approached me nervously. He was holding the glass bulb, which he had retrieved from the fire. It hadn't burned, and he felt something ominous about it. What should he do with it? I told him to give it to me and we'd ask Mother Jennie about it that evening during the meeting. Suddenly I realized that Mother Jennie would take a very dim view of my invoking Satan into a papier-mache pig covered with swastikas, Monopoly money, names of people high in government, and other symbols of radical protest. I did not look forward to that Tuesday night meeting!

At the beginning of the meeting the same student asked Mother Jennie what he should do with "this," he said, holding up the glass bulb which I had given back to him.

Jennie took one look at it and said, "That is the most negative thing I have ever seen. It must be burned in a very hot fire!"

At the end of the meeting, Jennie looked at me and made this interesting statement:

"Lewis, I see the Teachers coming around behind you. They are putting a white knitted vest upon your shoulders for your protection. It is a vest of great honor, and will protect you from all adverse influences. It also represents the attainment of an important step."

What she had described was a spiritual version of the kind of vest I had asked Ann to make me for the Festival. This gave me comfort about the whole situation. I took the glass bulb and tucked it into my pocket, covered with a white napkin. The student's mind was relieved.

As I began to drive home, the thought occurred to me that I should throw the bulb into the ocean. Then I thought of the story of the monkey's paw, and realized that would be a stupid solution. Jennie had directed that it be burned in a very hot fire. Where was I to find such a fire? I looked at the small gas flame burning next to the Taco Bell stand as I went by. That would not be hot enough.

Finally I arrived home. To my surprise, Ann had put a candle on the kitchen table, which I could see burning through the window. "Aha!" I thought. "This is a sign that I can burn this thing in my own fireplace."

Ann and the kids were already in bed. I kindled a fire in the large stone fireplace and built it up until it was very hot. Then I bent a coat hanger in such a way as to hold the glass bulb tightly while I jammed it up the fireplace into the highest and hottest part of the flame. I held it there for a few seconds, then "Boom!" There was an explosion that rocked our entire house!

The impact was so great that I was blown backwards almost five feet. Ann and the kids were literally thrown out of bed!

"My God!" I exclaimed to myself. "Those students must have put more mercury and gold in this thing than I had realized!"
For the next two weeks, everything Ann put on the gas stove burned or boiled over. No matter how carefully she watched the pot or pan, it inevitably boiled over.

I also noticed that whenever I looked at the stove I could see the mixing bowl reflected in such a way as to form the perfect image of a pig's face. It looked just like the papier mache Porcus we used in the Festival.

Chapter 9
A CHRONICLE OF FURTHER EVENTS

In the early part of my relationship with Mother Jennie there were two occasions on which she became terribly ill. She refused to be taken to a hospital, partly because she'd had such a difficult time getting out after her last illness, and mainly because she knew that God would take care of her.

On both occasions she became so weak and exhausted that she couldn't speak. I found her in this condition one afternoon that I'd had an urge to stop by. She was lying on the couch white as a sheet, and I thought she had died. As I approached she groaned, still unconscious of my entrance. She barely recognized me, but took my hands. I had decided to call a doctor when she said, "Lewis, please read to me from the Bible." I read to her, and at her request prepared a Eucharist, which she partook. In less than an hour she was sitting up and talking animatedly. I'd never seen such a quick recovery.

A month later Ann was doing some errands in Santa Cruz and felt a strong urge to visit Jennie. She obeyed and found the old woman as I had found her before -- in a state of sheer exhaustion. Jennie asked Ann to take her hands in a special way, right to right and left to left. As Jennie held her hands, Ann closed her eyes and felt as though she were spinning counterclockwise. How long this went on she could not tell. Then the direction reversed, and she was conscious of a clockwise spinning for some time. Suddenly she was aware that Jennie was speaking to her, thanking her for being a channel to "recharge her battery." As before, Mother Jennie was dramatically improved, and able to get up for tea. In talking with Ann recently about this, she told of a similar experience she had with her sister, and of having the same sensations during certain meditations.
As Mother Jennie went on in her teachings, she made me aware of many subtle forces and of their use and abuse. I do not wish to divulge these things. But I will give some examples of how I first became aware of the powerful but little-known energies which surround all living things.

Jennie always had me sit directly across from her in the Tuesday meetings, as her husband Louis Peterson had done many years before. She said that there were "lines" of force which extended between us when she delivered the discourse, and that no one should stand up or walk between us during "the Work." On the two occasions when a person who was ignorant of her wish did break the line, she became angry in a strong, judicial sort of way, and told us that if the Teachers had not quickly raised the lines, she could have received a shock to her system that would have killed her.

The importance of my position across from Jennie as some sort of anchor and energy funnel began to dawn on me. I thought that perhaps psychically Jennie had some ability to draw energy from people, as a bee takes nectar from the flower. So one evening when Jennie was quite tired I concentrated my attention on giving her my strength as she spoke. What a mistake! In less than two minutes I felt like a shriveled old man, or as though I'd been up for three days living on cigarettes and black coffee. It was an awful feeling, like bleeding to death but being unable to stop the bleeding. In a moment I was going to pass out.

"Mother Jennie," I gasped. At just that moment there was an interruption, and Jennie turned away to greet people coming through the door. It was like a reprieve. I realized that Jennie was not a psychic vampire. She did not take her energy from me, but through me, as through a straw. I had made the mistake of thinking her energy came from me, and offering it to her instead of simply serving as a channel. With this realization my strength returned. As the discourse went on, my energy was replenished and increased even beyond its original state.

I learned something very important from that experience. It is not so much what we do to help others, or what mumbo-jumbo we use to heal the sick. What is important is that we do it ourselves, with our own bodies. Something much more primary to healing than drugs or antibiotics comes to the sick from the concern of those who minister to them, and it cannot be bought or sold. Whether it is a doctor at the Mayo Clinic or a desert Indian shaman sucking the "evil spirits" out of one who is afflicted, the important thing is the human contact. Deep belief and trust in the system of healing, modern or primitive, is the vehicle. But the person himself is the channel.

Mother Jennie often told us that even though she was weak or tired before the Tuesday night meeting, she was able to "draw energy" from the people who came and cared for her. She called it "recharging the battery," and taught us to use the "tremendous force for healing" that can be generated by a group of people "all of one accord."

I began to understand Jennie, and indeed all sainthood and mastery, in terms of a basic primitive religious institution: Shamanism. The great historian of religions, Mircea Eliade, in his Myths, Dreams and Mysteries, page 87, introduces the issue:

We now touch upon a problem of the greatest importance, one which cannot be altogether avoided although it exceeds the range of the present study -- that is, the question of the reality of the extrasensory capacities and paranormal powers ascribed to the shamans and medicine men. Although research into this question is still at its beginning, a fairly large number of ethnographic documents has already put the authenticity of such phenomena beyond doubt.

According to the classical studies of shamanism done by such eminent scholars as Eliade, Evans-Pritchard, Lopatin, Malinowski and a host of others, there are several themes which characterize the shamanic experience. Clairvoyance and clairaudience are common, faith healing is basic. The old shamans are typically virile and mentally acute, able to perform feats of physical strength which younger men cannot -- such as Elijah's legendary run before the chariot to Jezreel. Spirit voices and teachers are common, especially those of the opposite sex, such as the Ayami. It was out of shamanic rigor that the yogic techniques of the East developed, and still the parallels can be found: the ascent of Kundalini during meditation as a spiritualization of the liturgical ascent to heaven by a ladder or pole aligned with the "center of the earth;" ability to walk on burning coals as a refinement of the "mystical control of body heat," by which the Adept could survive in frigid water or heat up a tub of water to well over normal human body temperature.

Aside from the obvious parallels in Jennie's mysticism, the shaman likes to wear costumes and act out symbolic liturgies with his body. Jennie had photographs of herself dressed as Liberty one year and Justice the next, being towed in a float in a parade. Her white gown with blue trim comes to mind.

The shaman's drum is the vehicle for his "magical flight," or ascent in consciousness to the Other World above. For Jennie her piano and organ, and most especially her writing pen and paper, have paralleled this function.

Primarily a healer and servant of his tribe, the shaman works for the benefit of all in his sphere of consciousness. To Jennie, the whole world was her tribe, and even more. One example: On a winter afternoon I had stopped by to see Mother Jennie. She looked very tired and told me that she had been out "in the astral" all night lifting up the fallen spirits of thousands of people who'd experienced a terrible tragedy "down South." She said that many had lost their homes, and whole families had been buried alive in mud slides.

Later that evening, radio and television broadcast the first public news of the mammoth Peruvian earthquake which had killed tens of thousands.

This sort of thing happened more than once. Whenever I'd walk in to find Jennie shaken and wan, I'd know there had been a calamity in some part of the world. She had been called to minister in spirit to the victims while she was sleeping. A great deal of her work was done "in spirit" during the night. There was no way Jennie could have known about these catastrophes through any media but her own soul. The information had not yet gone out on the news-service teletypes.

She has told me of the agony of being a "supersensitive." For many years she felt a shock in her body whenever there was an automobile accident on the coast or mountain highways. As traffic became so much heavier in recent years, her Teachers gave her a technique for selectively closing off her sensitivity. This, however, was a mechanism of only the conscious mind, and she was vulnerable to any influences which she has no conscious way of circumventing.

She traveled "in the astral" without remembering what she had done, at times. One good example was described to me by Leona Richards, minister of the Church of the Holy Grail in Santa Cruz. Leona is a trance medium, although she remains in control or at least aware of what she says in her discourses. She is overshadowed by several teachers, including a Catholic priest who speaks in a strong Irish brogue. The Church was founded by revelation from its patroness, St. Teresa, who also overshadows Leona. I have witnessed demonstrations of Leona's ability, and she is an excellent medium.

At the time of this particular incident, Jennie had mentioned to me that it seemed the Church never called her to come and speak. I believe that what occurred subsequently was Jennie's unconscious way of getting their attention, with the full cooperation of the Teachers.

At the Wednesday night meeting of the Church of the Holy Grail, Leona prepared to be overshadowed by her teachers. A hymn was sung, prayers were asked, and she began to speak. But this time the voice was not of the Irish priest or other teachers. It was the familiar voice of Mother Jennie, delivering her discourse in her own inimitable way. Leona tells me she still has the tape recording of this incident.

To me this was highly significant. It was much more than Jennie's way of getting to speak at the Church, for she had no conscious remembrance of having tried to project herself there, nor felt any impulse to try. I believe that this phenomenon demonstrated that Jennie must no longer be thought of as just a medium. She had assumed spiritual status as a teacher herself, on a par with the spirit entities who speak through Leona. She was allowed to speak through Leona as a sign of this fact, and as a debut.

As I continued my apprenticeship with Jennie, I saw many strange things which I will not attempt to interpret for the reader. It became a practice for me to bring persons who were in need of spiritual help -- the bereaved, those who had suffered some form of shock or loss, or those who were deeply depressed or confused -- to Mother Jennie for counsel. I learned more from sitting in on these highly intimate sessions than from all my work in psychological counseling. I was able to see how Jennie used all the insights of contemporary psychologies and therapies without ever having read them, and went far beyond the techniques of the time in Gestalt or T.A. But hers was not a dogmatically "psychological" style. It was dynamistic and almost magical. She was truly a shamaness of the soul.

For example, she could use her hands as a channel for relieving grief. Even the most hard-boiled persons, when Jennie took their hands, right to right, left to left, would melt into tears. This, said Jennie, relieved "the pressure on the heart," which let healing begin. I remember especially the time she took the hands of Marky, one of my sister's old friends who had undergone a divorce from which she still suffered. Marky is a strong woman, not given to tears. When Jennie took her hands I saw what appeared to be black, vibrating snakes generated like flowing water from a ground-spring. They danced tensely down Marky's arms onto Jennie's wrists, and the young woman simply burst into tears. Jennie got up and washed her hands under running water clear up to the elbows, returned, and the healing words began.

My old friend Craig had been staying with me. His father had recently died of a heart attack after suffering paralysis on his left side from a stroke which came a few years back. Craig had many problems, but was a fine jazz bass player. He'd come to stay with me after a term in a drug rehabilitation hospital, and still had a few more years of wavering before he would be able to establish himself firmly.

We came in and sat down. Jennie prayed for a moment, then with closed eyes sat in silence. Her sensitive fingers moved back and forth like fine antennae.

"There is someone who comes in with you. I feel him on the heart-side. He must be very close to you -- a father or a grandfather. I feel a blow to the head, and my left side is paralyzed. No, it's not a blow to the head, it's more of a popping inside the head. Blood. Now the heart. He went out with a heart condition. Can you place him?" She arched her eyebrows, with compassion in her eyes.

Craig was deeply moved and tears came to his eyes. Always in these profoundly intimate sessions I found myself moved with the same emotions that my friends under counseling were feeling, and I felt a tug at my heart and a lump in my throat. Sometimes I'd feel this way without seeing visible evidence of this response on the other person's face, but I'd know they had been moved.

"Yes," he said huskily. "My father."

"I feel dancing and rhythm and a warm fatherly concern for your well-being. Yes, rhythm and a bouncing, dancing feeling. Your father had some connection with music."

Craig broke down. His father had been a well-known dancer and dance instructor. This was the connection between him and his father -- music and dance. Craig had followed music. Certain intimate things ensued that cannot be revealed publicly, and then the following interesting sequence:

"You are riding a horse. The horse throws you, but you continue to mount it. Now you come to a fence. You cross to a greener pasture and learn to gain balance."

Often what Jennie said to people had meaning only for them. She did not want any information about them or their background when she undertook "the Work." This would only distort her perceptions with in-breakings of mental ideas. She usually refused to let a person say anything at all about his problem. Very often, however, I have known much of the situation and could interpret what was being said. In this case, the "horse" was a common name for heroin. Craig had been an addict, kicked several times, and was now in Santa Cruz, the "greener pasture" where he'd learn to get some balance.

The literal meaning of many things was hidden from Jennie. They would have shocked her and made it difficult to deliver counsel with an undisturbed mind.

On another occasion I'd met a friend named Howard. His wife, whom he loved very much, had suffered for a year and died of cancer, leaving him with two adopted children who were the same ages as my children. I was in the process of a divorce and had my two children with me. Howard and I had become friends, and he wanted to meet Mother Jennie.

For this particular session I had invited my brother. Joel taught chemistry at U.C. Davis, and was somewhat skeptical about religious phenomena. He wanted to come, so I asked Howard's permission.

We sat with Howard facing Jennie, and Joel and I on either side facing each other. I wanted Joel to furnish me with his ideas on how mediumship worked. Just as we got seated, Jennie closed her eyes and said to Howard, "You play violin." She opened her eyes and smiled.

I did not know that Howard played violin, and fount it hard to believe until he actually showed me his fiddle and played a few notes for me later that week. This became the first point of departure for the conversations that Joel and I had on the subject on later occasions. How did she know Howard played violin? Joel proposed the Sherlock Holmes theory -- from a thousand subtle clues such as the way he held his fingers, Jennie deduced that he played violin. The problem with this approach was that I, who had worked as a professional symphonic musician, am unable to deduce such a thing in anyone, let alone Howard. Another problem was that Jennie always closed her eyes when she made such discoveries. How could she deduce without visual evidence?

In fact, she said that she saw an "image" of whatever was in question. It might be a motion, an allegory or a simple metaphor. The images came from Jennie's own personal perception, like Craig's "horse," and had no archetypal significance. Often it was left for the hearer to interpret what she gave, so that I missed large portions of the "meaning" even though the subject found each word or phrase deeply meaningful.

In Howard's case Jennie "saw" the image of a violin with her inner eye. To her this meant that he had something to do with a violin, so she said, "You play violin." Her interpretation was correct.

How did she get her images? "They are brought to me by the Teachers when I make my mind a clear, pure channel through which spirit can flow," she said.

Mother Jennie's inner eye saw father ahead and behind than normal eyes. A person sees a flock of geese on the horizon and he knows that soon they will be directly overhead. Mother Jennie saw things "coming" to a person weeks, months and years ahead because what we call "time" was more like what we call "space." She could look down from a great height upon one person's journey and see where he had been, where he was going, and what he would meet.

For example, she would close her eyes, sense a time period of perhaps two weeks, feel something in her hands. She would rub the thing in her palm and realize it to be a bundle of money. She told Craig's friend (who was staying with us) to expect a small fortune within two weeks.

Less than two weeks later a cashier's check arrived for a little over $2,000. The woman had finally been located by the trustee of her uncle's estate. (She was open-mouthed!)

For me, "now" is a brief moment between the past and the future. My consciousness is limited. I can follow out cause and effect for only a few moves ahead on the checkerboard of possibility. Mother Jennie's "vision" transcended my tiny comprehension. Her "now" was a much broader area. To the ancient philosophers her vision was known as pronoia, inadequately translated as "foresight." It was a virtue of the true philosopher, like Epictetus, and functioned through the organ of Nous or "understanding." Normal human vision through the eyes of flesh is myopic in comparison.

In the long session with Howard, beautiful and incredible things occurred which I cannot describe because of their intimacy. The deceased wife was brought to him on a bed, where she was still being nursed for recovery from her long illness -- illness is psychic as well as physical. Things were communicated to Howard which neither Joel nor I could understand, but which touched the man beyond all words. He had quit his job to care for his wife during the last year of her life, and there was great love between them.

The materialist or logical positivist could argue that Jennie had simply duped Howard into believing that he was in communication with his wife, and then skillfully played on his tender feelings to evoke all the sensations and highly private understandings that he'd known with her. Perhaps it is just like looking into a mirror. I cannot say. But however his wife was invoked or evoked, powerful feelings were settled in Howard and resolutions given to secret grief and emotional pressure through the experience. Any psychologist would have been impressed.

One afternoon I was browsing through an occult bookstore which a friend of mind managed, and found the autobiography of an English medium who was under the "control" of an American Indian named Red Cloud. This surprised me, since I'd noticed a portrait of an Indian spirit Jennie called Red Cloud hanging above the clock in her living room. I turned some pages and found a series of photographs. One of them was the very image of Red Cloud as I'd seen him in Jennie's sketch. The photograph was supposed to be a "spirit picture" of Chief Red Cloud taken by exposing a photographic plate at a seance.

"Well," I thought. "Red Cloud really gets around."

Jennie had mentioned him several times. He was not one of her Teachers, but made his presence known from time to time. The portrait she had was done by a traveling male medium who was talented at oil and pastel chalks. His name was Stan Matrunick, and the Church of the Holy Grail hosted his yearly visit.

I bought the book and took it to Jennie. She was pleased to see the "spirit photograph" and to note the strong likeness to her portrait.

It occurred to me that perhaps Matrunick had read this book and used the photograph as a conscious or unconscious model for what he gave to Mother Jennie. I'd heard that he was coming to town, so I made an appointment to see him and get a feeling for his integrity.

He was a sort of "fundamentalist" spiritualist, having come out of the evangelical Christian style and still using much of that approach in his communication. I found him quite likable and genuine, so paid $10 for a sitting. I thought, "Well, if this man can see the spirits by painting them, I'd like to get a likeness of Father Geiser." That, I decided, would settle the question for me.

I sat in a chair while Stan rattled off a constant stream of talk designed to keep himself open and the client quiet. As he talked, he worked with his chalks on the portrait without even looking at what he was doing. "Very Muse-like," I observed.

His patter was quite accurate at times, but when he was finished and showed me the portrait I'd asked of Father Geiser, I was truly amazed. It was a very good likeness -- the ears, the shock of white hair, the eyebrows, the chin. I could see that I'd have to find more answers. Could the "spirits" really be "real," whatever that means?

Jennie always stressed, "I am not reading your mind. I do not look at the palms or soles of the feet. I do not read the minds. If I were to enter in by any but the open gate, I'd be a thief and a robber."

"Perhaps," I thought, "this all works unconsciously, and our minds exist as fields all around us, giving impressions even of information hidden from what we know as the unconscious mind." This theory of "mind" was my last attempt to keep a strictly mental and seemingly "monistic" view of reality. It was on the verge of collapse. I was going to have to start using all that language about "spirits" in order to progress any further in this epic journey. I had seen beyond "mind," and beyond the illusion which the mind creates of "monism." I began to understand what Jennie meant when she said, "Real unity is what we perceive as duality."

Real sanity is often perceived as madness. True courage is often seen as cowardice. The disciples of Jesus accepted this paradox when their eyes and minds told them that the Master had been destroyed and defeated, and yet the eyes of spirit saw him as the Christ, reigning in splendor and victory even on the cross.

Perhaps real unity was to be found in the duality of discourse and struggle, and true healing in the recognition of brokenness.

The evidence kept accumulating. One evening I had been all day translating Tractate 6 of the Nag Hammadi Codex VI before rushing off to Jennie's meeting. She looked at me as I arrived and said, "There is an Egyptian man who comes in with you. I cannot understand his language." The language was Coptic, the last form of spoken Egyptian in the ancient world.

On another occasion a young man, who had studied Indian religions at Bombay and spent several years in a little-known Tibetan monastery under the tutelage of a now-deceased guru, had become my friend. I took him to Mother Jennie's. As we walked in the door she stood up and saluted the man, saying, "Your teacher says this," and then recited five words in Sanskrit. The fellow was taken aback, but returned the salute and repeated the greeting. Later I asked him what it was all about. He said that his teacher used to greet him with a mantra to remind him of fidelity to his monastic labor. No one else knew that mantra, and it was not used by anyone else. It was not difficult for him to accept the reality of the situation, however, since he was familiar with phenomena like this in India. It was not the phenomenon that surprised him, but the fact of finding it occurring in the setting of a home-grown American Western mystical tradition. He didn't know that spiritual light existed in the West, and was amazed to see it in action. He attended many more meetings and often remarked on the meaningfulness of Jennie's words for him. Although his true Master was a Sikh, he took time to learn from Jennie as well.

One of my favorite students was a woman named Debbie. She graduated in Religious Studies in 1972. For her senior thesis she did a translation and interpretation of the gnostical "round dance" of Jesus and the disciples described in the apocryphal Acts of John. We had developed a lasting friendship and, from time to time after graduating, she dropped in to talk. She was also quite close to Mother Jennie, and initiated into the Orrilla Sisterhood and Brotherhood, which Jennie reinstituted after one of her students dreamed of her in the Sisterhood gown.

I believe it was late Sunday afternoon when another student, John Zinner, called me. Frantically he said that Debbie had been swimming up at Big Basin and dived headfirst into a hidden rock. She was paralyzed from the neck down, and was being held in intensive care at Dominican Hospital. She wanted to see me. I was there in a flash. The nurses were adamant about keeping me out of the room, since Debbie was asleep.

I returned at the next visiting period wearing my clerical collar. They let me in. I recoiled at what I saw. Debbie was suspended between two giant circular hoops in a bed that was for total paralytics. She greeted me with tears in her eyes. I took her hand and stroked her forehead, looking deeply into her eyes. She was terribly afraid. We talked, and she described what had happened, what treatment she was getting and how she was feeling. I asked her if she would like to pray, and she said yes. We prayed together in silence.

She asked if it were at all possible to see Mother Jennie, and I promised to try to get her up for a visit as soon as possible.

I was in to see Debbie every day.

Jennie was shocked at the news. She went into deep silence, and then said, "Lewis, I want you to take Debbie this handkerchief and touch it to her neck. Tell her this: `Hope thou in God, and thou wilt yet praise Him, Who is thy counselor and thy Redeemer.' Then let us talk to Debbie by telephone." It was a major event whenever Jennie left her house, and we tried on several occasions to get her up to Dominican. She had, after all, come up to the University for lectures on several occasions. But her health wasn't up to the trip this time, and she was never able to visit Debbie in the flesh.

The situation at the hospital had changed. Debbie was put into a room of her own and had many visitors. They would file in and make small talk, trying to be cheery and overcome the sickly sensation in the pit of the stomach which comes at seeing someone you love so badly hurt. Debbie lay there with shaven head and metal supports driven into her skull, like a Frankenstein monster. Her complexion was mottled and pale, but her indomitable spirit smiled bravely through.

Jennie had told me with great emphasis that I was not to listen to anything the doctors had to say about Debbie's not recovering. She had been told most definitely by her Teachers that Debbie would have a full recovery. It was important for me to instill and nurture that faith in Debbie.

Debbie's parents told me differently. The doctors had said that no hope should be given because, in a case like this, the patient would get her hopes raised and then be crushed later if therapy was unsuccessful. The damage was severe, although it was being treated with a new experimental drug that was supposed to help stop spinal bleeding. The best psychological approach was not to give any hope. She was totally paralyzed from the neck down.

I don't know how to explain this, but I knew with a firm assurance that Debbie would recover. I simply never doubted Jennie's prophecy. Her Teachers had always been right, and as she used to say, "If they don't give me truth, then I'm through with all this. I'll give nothing but truth."

I had spent many days with Debbie, not as the other visitors making small talk, but concentrating upon reaching her faith and helping to keep it alive. We sometimes prayed together, and other times I stroked her forehead and helped her to find meaning in what had happened, and resolution to go ahead in strength.
The day before Jennie had given me the message for Debbie and her handkerchief to act as her personal emissary, I had held Debbie's hand and told her that I strongly felt she would be using her hand again soon, even to play the guitar she so dearly loved. I asked her to squeeze her fingers, and I thought I detected a slight motion. But it was elusive and perhaps illusory. I wanted so much to be able to say, "Debbie, you can move your hand," and see her move it. But I couldn't quite believe in that sort of miracle.

The next day I came with the message and the handkerchief. The nurses wouldn't leave us alone, and I wasn't certain how I was going to be able to touch Debbie's neck with it anyway. She was flat on her back, and the metal head supporter interfered with any attempt to touch the neck. Besides, what do you say? "Hi, there. I'm going to touch Debbie's neck with a magical faith-healing prayer cloth that some old lady gave me!"

My opportunity came the next day. I managed to get the cloth in contact with Debbie's neck, and I gave her Jennie's message. By then they were installing a telephone for her in the room, and she was able to speak directly with Jennie while someone held the phone.

The next day Debbie told me of a beautiful dream in which she found herself asleep on her hospital bed. Mother Jennie came to her, like Asclepius in his ancient temples of incubation, and touched her right hand. Immediately it was free and she could stretch out her fingers. She awakened with a feeling of joy, but now she was depressed because it was just a dream, and she couldn't move her fingers.

I rejoiced in my inner being. I knew that if Debbie had been able to receive healing at the unconscious level, it was sure to manifest later in the physical body. I took her hand and told her to squeeze. I felt a slight pressure. Debbie said, no, it is just the wrist movement, which never was completely gone. But I knew differently. As usual, I strongly urged her to search within, to pray and trust.

Shortly thereafter, Debbie Kaplan began to manifest a recovery that was startling to everyone, especially her doctors. If there had been any doubt that she would make a total recovery, it soon vanished. She made such fast progress that she soon was taking it for granted. Neurologists called a special conference on Debbie's case at Dominican, and Debbie dropped in to see Mother Jennie. She was in a wheelchair, but she was able to use her waist, feet and arm muscles. She was so elated at being free that she went out carousing with her friends and worried her parents to death.

Another month and Debbie came back to visit. This time she had moved to a hospital in San Jose, and was able to walk in a walker with wrist supports. A little more time elapsed and Debbie was walking on her own feet, driving her own car and accepted as a law student at Berkeley. At this writing her recovery is still in progress, but I still don't doubt that it will be total.

At the time of her great spiritual need, while she lay helpless at Dominican Hospital. she was able to muster a strong faith. Doctors gave her little hope, but Jennie knew that all would be well. If it was not to be, Jennie would have told her and helped her to accept the condition. But Jennie saw the recovery and urged me to reinforce hope in Debbie.

I don't know how much Debbie herself attributes her recovery to Jennie's faith and strength, and to what it stimulated in her. But I am certain that without Jennie's firm certainty Debbie might have blocked any path to freedom by imprisoning herself in the despair of empirical medical methods. The doctor can treat, but he cannot heal. The mental attitude is extremely important in cases like this, and if there is any hope it must be emphasized above all things. Otherwise acceptance of the situation must be encouraged. Debbie was able to do both things. She accepted her present situation, but she learned to aspire to a future situation that would be much improved. That, I believe, is realistic.

The mind can build a prison. We let our minds "set" every day in different ways -- with prejudices, one-sided ways of seeing things, the closing off of possibilities to give the illusion of impossibility. Sometimes it takes a great blow to jar the mind back into the flexible, impressionable and receptive vehicle it must be.

We "set" our minds with labels and names: Debbie still insisted on calling herself a "quad," and then as she healed a "para." Even in jest, these labels imply that she "is" something, namely a paralytic. This was not good for her progress, and did not promote healing. She overcame this.

One morning we look in the mirror and seem ugly. Another day we are surprised to see a handsome person in the mirror. If we think of ourselves as inferior or ugly, we take that on and manifest it to others. If we see ourselves as full of hope and optimistic, life "works" for us in amazing ways.

If we "know" that things are going to turn out okay no matter what, then we can bear our burdens with patience. I believe that Jennie's faith provided Debbie with that "knowledge" and enabled her to labor in hope of recovery. I do not think that she could have recovered with such speed, or possibly even at all, given the attitudes of those around her, without Mother Jennie's gift of hope.

Chapter 10

THE FINAL YEARS

In his Autobiography of a Yogi, Yogananda tells of meeting Giri Bala, the old saint of Northern Bengal who neither ate nor drank. He was overjoyed that she was willing to receive him, since one never knows how true yogins and yoginis will respond to publicity. True saints are often hidden until they have reached the full flowering of sanctity. In many cases it is not until they have entered the final years of their lives that they are brought forward and made known.

As Yogananda says, "An inner sanction comes to them when the proper time arrives to display their lives openly for the benefit of seeking minds."

The same process was at work in the life of Mother Jennie. At every critical point when she might have become famous, she was directed to remain obscure. This broke her heart, but hers was to be a hidden labor.

When I came to know her, Jennie was like a brilliant moon eclipsed by the shadows of earth. To most people she was a sweet old lady and nothing more. Those who recognized her were very few. One was Mary Oliverio, her closest student and spiritual heir. Another was Alice Cole, who nursed her during times of crisis. Terry, Stacy and especially Lucy Lynch devoted themselves to her care, providing regular Sunday "family" meals and other kinds of support too numerous to recount. Five or six other members of the Sisterhood also contributed greatly to Jennie's care during the final year of failing health. Many of us took turns sleeping on her lumpy couch all night when she was too ill to be by herself.

But my meeting with Mother Jennie was fateful because it was through me that all the "young people" were brought in. Not that I had planned things that way! But circumstances made me her "scout," as she liked to call me. I had taken her to the University, and this had started the Tuesday night meetings. It was I who understood the importance of writing her biography, and had been trained and prepared as a scholar of religions to interpret her life to others.

As time went on I brought all my friends and students to hear Mother Jennie, and they in turn brought theirs. The meetings grew like topsy.

Next I began to bring Mother Jennie persons in need of counsel and other help. She set aside her usual rule of confidentiality and always insisted that I stay to experience the sessions. I was a trained psychological counselor who ran Gestalt, TA and various personal-growth groups, yet I learned more from these sessions than any training seminar had offered. Here I began to discover the "flaws" in current theories.

Soon the people I had brought to Jennie were giving my telephone number to others in need, and I became a kind of general secretary for her. Finally the numbers of people seeking advice became so great that I had to refuse all those who were simply curious to get a psychic reading, admitting only those in real need. After another year Jennie opened herself to everyone and made her own appointments, giving me permission to have people telephone her directly. She kept a date pad and pen next to the telephone. Whenever the doorbell or telephone rang, she stopped whatever she was doing. She said that human need always took precedence over prayer, solitude, rest or any other personal activity. She would never take the phone off the hook to give herself relief from its constant ringing, for then she would be violating the "trust" she had been given by Christ to "do the Work."

First Mother Jennie became known by the Santa Cruz youth culture -- students, hippies, commune people. Then I began to lecture on her life in my adult education classes, and this brought an older generation to her. Next I brought her to St. John the Baptist Episcopal Church. This was the first "orthodox" church that had ever allowed her to preach! I submitted a news release for her guest sermon, and this attracted Margaret Koch, a feature writer with the Sentinel Newspaper. Soon she had done her own article on Mother Jennie.

The meetings attracted a young man named Steve who was doing media work at Cabrillo College. Soon he had videotaped an interview and parts of a discussion for community television. Another person did a radio interview which was released in small segments between rock music selections on a local "pop" station.

In 1974 I presented a paper on Mother Jennie to the national convention of the Society for the Scientific Study of Religion. I was deluged with requests for more information or photocopies of her autobiography, but was unable to fulfill them due to lack of funds. Soon after this I nominated and elected Mother Jennie to the honorary founding faculty of a new liberal arts college which I was helping develop on the Monterey Peninsula.

During the spring of 1975 I brought in an independent Bishop to hear her discourses. He was so deeply impressed by her sanctity that he asked if he could transmit the Episcopal or Apostolic Succession to her as a recognition of her Apostolic calling. She assented, and in a ceremony on the spring equinox witnessed by the entire Sisterhood and Brotherhood, Mother Jennie was made the first woman Bishop in the United States, through all 16 lines of succession. She was titled a full and independent *Episcopa Vagana.*

By this time Mother Jennie had become a local legend. She no longer needed me as her "scout" because people were coming in droves. Her living room rug was worn through by the great multitudes who crowded the Tuesday night meetings and the many who came every day for help.

Robert, Terry and several other able-bodied young men and women had taken it upon themselves to keep up her yard, clean the house and provide healthy food for her refrigerator. Jennie had no choice but to accept these love-gifts because she was no longer in good enough health to go to the grocery store or the drug store or do the kind of housecleaning made necessary by so many visitors.

Although her mind was sharp as ever, Jennie's health began to fade. Most noticeably, her hearing grew worse. I finally decided to buy her a hearing aid. She agreed that it was necessary, so we made the trip downtown to see an otiologist or hearing aid specialist.

After giving the old woman a series of tests, the otiologist confessed to me that he was puzzled.

"Normally," he said, "a person of this age has the acuity problems she manifests in the lower octaves and decibels, which explains her inability to distinguish the `m' from the `n' sound, for example. But when I take her into the higher octaves or vibrations of sound, her acuity increases remarkably. This old gal can hear high-vibration frequencies far above the human range, and what's more, she hears them at low-decibel intensities I've never seen before! She is a most unusual case!"

This was very intriguing because Mother Jennie had always maintained that she heard the Teachers by being elevated to a very high "vibratory rate." She said on many occasions that she heard clairaudiently by sensing "higher vibrations" than the normal ear.

Because of her extreme sensitivity to high-frequency sound, even of the softest intensity, the otiologist had to make shift for a special kind of filter to block out these frequencies when she wore the hearing aid. Actually, she tried valiantly to use the gadget, but the filter didn't help and it was agony for her to wear it. I begged her not to use it if it was uncomfortable, even though it had been expensive. After trying to adjust the hearing aid for several months, she stopped using it. No one minded if she had trouble hearing every word spoken to her, and the people learned to speak loudly and distinctly in her presence.

Mother Jennie's final trials began two years before her passing, when the City of Santa Cruz finally began construction to widen Delaware Avenue. Her little house had been built almost flush with the place that a sidewalk would have been, but all the other homes were set back from the road. With Robert representing Jennie's interests, a contract had been worked out with the City which took some of her property in exchange for building a fence (to keep Cindy off the road) and a small approach from her front door to the new sidewalk, which would be just a few feet from the front of the house. They had originally wanted to actually tear down and rebuild the front of the house.

Because of the construction there were quantities of dust and pollen in the air. A normal person would not be bothered, but for a "sensitive" like Jennie it was much different. Soon her skin was broken out, a terrible-looking infection was running from the thumb of one hand, and the second hand was threatened.
At two or three different times over a period of several months people took her to doctors. None of the medications worked, and soon Jennie lost the use of her right hand. She was in misery night and day with an itching that never ceased. This kind of condition may not be such a severe problem to a physical yogi, who uses mental control to block pain from his consciousness. But Jennie's path was that of the "sensitive." She was not the stoic Socrates, who could quaff the bitter dregs without flinching. She was more like the Nazarene who wept over the suffering of others and fully experienced its horrors during the agony of Gethsemane. Like Jesus, she would have died very quickly on the cross, and there would have been no need to "break her legs."

The worst possible torture for a "sensitive" is the kind that grates the senses. The skin in particular develops from the same germ layer as the human nervous system, and often reflects inner nervous problems in its complexion. Conversely, it can be used to torture the nervous system -- and that was its effect with Jennie. Her suffering was greater than anyone knew, other than those who attended her.

For six hours she had only a few fitful hours of sleep each night. She did her best to avoid scratching at her open sores, and we applied witch hazel and all kinds of pioneer herbal remedies which she suggested when the doctor's medications proved ineffective. Life became a terrible irritation to her, yet she held her temper and did "the Work" as God presented it for her. She never missed a meeting or turned down a person seeking help.

After more than a half-year of this agony I could no longer stand to see her suffer, and I cried out in tears for help. Someone had suggested seeing an allergy specialist named Dr. Israel. I made an appointment and took her there. At this time none of us really knew whether it was an allergy or an infection, and most of the medical advice we had received was designed to soothe the pain rather than actively investigate the causes.

Dr. Israel pulled back Mother Jennie's blouse and noted that the irritation existed almost like a sunburn, wherever the skin was exposed to the air. How logical! None of us had made that simple observation before! He asked if there was any reason for Jennie to be exposed to air which was dusty or laden with pollen. I told him about the construction. He then prescribed a simple cortico-steroid to promote healing and told me to clean her house of dust, top to bottom.

I went over every part of that house with the vacuum cleaner. Then Mary Oliverio brought an air purifier which worked on an electrostatic principle to take all kinds of impurities out of the air. I made certain Jennie applied her medicine regularly. Within three days the sores were healing and the itching had nearly stopped. In a week she was able to begin using her right hand, although the thumb nail had grotesquely warped and the digit itself bent like the joint of a rheumatoid arthritic. The rest cleared up in a few weeks, and we all rejoiced.

But what had happened? In retrospect it is clear that Mother Jennie suffered directly because of her visitors. It was they who brought in the dust and pollution which, when ground into the carpets and chairs, caused such a severe reaction in the old saint. It was not the dust and pollen of the construction which had irritated Jennie, for the construction continued several months after her recovery. Rather, it was the physical and psychic pollution of the multitudes that caused her such agony. People left more than physical dust behind them when they said good night to Mother Jennie. Over the long run it took its toll on her nervous system, and this came out on the epidermal surfaces.

The final year of the old woman's life was undoubtedly the most difficult in many ways. First she became dependent upon others for food and most other necessities. This was totally against her pioneer spirit, and brought her self-esteem very low at times. Robert Lynch came in often twice daily to feed her, and more than anyone else truly understood the depth of her suffering.

For another thing, her health began to fail even more seriously than before. From 1970 to 1975 I watched the old woman draw her frail body from the bedroom when she was utterly exhausted in order to hold a meeting. People didn't want her to go on, but any suggestion that she should quit was sharply rebuked.

"The Master ordained me with His blessing to go forth and preach the Gospel. The medical doctor takes an oath too. Shall he back down on it? No, my dears. God will supply all my needs, and He will supply me with strength for the meeting."

And indeed Jennie was supplied with strength for the meetings. The transformation that she underwent during the initial silence of a meeting was incredible. Drawing through me and the people gathered, Mother Jennie was "recharged," as she put it, "like a battery." She did not take energy from us, but through us. Her voice became strong, her posture erect, and soon she would be delivering a brilliant discourse. When the meeting was over she was often still vibrant with energy, so that we came to understand an important principle of divine service. As Jennie said, "All your needs will be supplied if you will submit to God's will in service."

But her physical vehicle was failing. She had lost half her weight over the past 15 years. Her shrunken body looked like an old tent that had collapsed on its moorings. Her arms were black and blue with veins, and she walked with a cane or by feeling her way from chair to table. Her digestive system had been in terrible shape ever since the breachy cow had crushed her liver and gall bladder over 60 years before, and she could eat only a bit at a time. If she ate any kind of bran, fat, grease or other hard-to-digest food she would be in pain for days, yet her grateful students plied her with garbage food like fried meats, sickly pastries and even pizza! Robert did his best to guard her food supply, but inevitably she would become ill.

For the first time her memory began to fail. Although she was fully aware and sharp as a whip to the very end, during the last year on rare occasions she remembered things differently than had actually happened. This failure precipitated Jennie's final trial, which I will not describe in detail. Let it suffice to say that through a serious misunderstanding, one of the oldest members of the Sisterhood went at loggerheads with Mother Jennie.

The member had fallen under the influence of a self-proclaimed Cherokee Indian guru. Jennie became concerned and made a remark which caused her friend to take offense and leave the Sisterhood unless the old woman apologized. Jennie refused, insisting that she had said no such thing. She was deeply hurt by her friend's offense, and honestly did not remember saying anything offensive.

In this final hour it had become necessary for Mother Jennie to undergo a fiery trial of the soul. Like Job, she would be sifted by Satan, as wheat from the chaff. And, as Jennie herself often remarked, "Who is the Devil? There is no Devil. He is the evil of our own nature."

Perhaps Mother Jennie had become slightly inflated during this latter period, now that she had finally achieved recognition. Public adulation, after all, had been the one soul-trial she had never experienced. In any case, this final infection of personal pride had to be brought to a head like a boil.

The process took five months, and her physical health radically declined. She was bedridden from late June through November. Meetings became erratic, and she was often too weak to answer a cry for help from someone else. She couldn't understand what was happening, and poured out her self-doubts and misery to me. She felt as though she had a venomous poison deep within her that was making her ill, but she didn't know how to expel it. She told me that sometimes an anger would well up inside her breast so great that she knew it could make her kill someone with a blow of her tiny fist. She was bothered by nightmares. Psychic and physical phenomena occurred which I cannot reveal, but graphically illustrated the true depths of the horrors she experienced. She nearly died at least three times.

I finally understood what Maud Lord-Drake had meant when she said to Jennie, "Oh, my dear, if only it didn't have to be," and Jennie had replied, "If this is the reward of service, dear God, I do not want it." Maud died a month after receiving third-degree burns all over her crippled body. She too had a final trial of "fire." With Jesus also it was at the last hour that he experienced his greatest agony.

Perhaps the one greatest lesson that Jennie taught was her own humanity. She saw herself not as a bloodless plaster saint, but a living, fallible human seeker. She tried to recognize her mistakes and rectify them. She said that her worst fault was her temper, although I never saw it displayed. She was very candid about this fact and often joked about it.

"If we were perfect," she said with a twinkle in her eye, "we would have no need of flesh and blood!"

Mother Jennie was already weakened by serious health problems. She suffered a constant battery of arthritic and digestive pains, and even more was continually vulnerable, as a "sensitive," to experience the agony and sinfulness of the world around her. Remember, this was a woman who felt the pain of earthquake victims in Peru many hours before the reports had hit the news wires!

Savonarola had "temporized" a protective shield around her to spare her the effects of hostility directed against her by random members of the open meetings. But there could be no protection against the betrayal of a beloved friend. Those who were closest to Jennie had a "hot line" to her heart, and therefore the power to hurt her deeply. Betrayal of this trust, like the decision of Judas, left her defenseless. She was forced to receive and respond to a barrage of critical and vicious thoughts directed against her by one of her oldest and most trusted friends. The pain of this betrayal paralyzed her ability to forgive and forget. Until she could finally do so, she would suffer unspeakable agonies.

Slowly the venom was released. Reconciliation began to take effect. There had been disaster on both sides, and when I telephoned the friend in August she was ready for reconciliation. She promised to come visit Jennie, but never fulfilled the promise. Yet Jennie's recovery was in process.

Two months later Jennie had a dream in which the Teachers were reprimanding her. They were all seated in a large classroom filled with many people. She was told that because of her stubbornness and refusal to give "messages," and because she had overstepped her authority as a "teacher," she had been put down into a lower "grade" or classroom of experience. Now, however, she had served her time there and could begin to progress again. But she must return to giving "messages" in order to keep on the path.

Meekly she set about the work. Her health dramatically improved, and soon there was no need for the many shifts of helpers to stay with her every day. She was up and around on her own again. The meetings were held regularly, and her discourses returned to their original atmosphere of inspiration and truth.

By Christmas, 1975, Mother Jennie had overcome her last and greatest trial. Jennie had triumphed victorious over the evil of her own nature, and how we celebrated that year! How beautiful she was, how warm and loving, as she sat surrounded by young people with the winter sun glistening from her pure white hair! The babies cooed at their mothers' breasts in the circle of friends as the beloved old woman delivered the joyous Message of Christmas.

The period of victory was like a long celebration lasting through the Christmas season and until sometime after the Feast of the Epiphany. People dropped in from all quarters, many of whom had been out of touch for years. There was an atmosphere of gaiety and festivity for all concerned.

In late January Jennie suddenly lost her strength, and by February we had put together a 24-hour shift of volunteers to care for her at home. Again her suffering was intense, but now it was not determined or conditioned by inner contradictions. It was instead a pure physical suffering, the consequence of old age and a failing bodily vehicle.

Sharing duties with five other persons, I chose Tuesday and Friday nights to wrestle with the lumpy old couch. As I lay in light slumber monitoring Jennie's every agonized breath, there would come a sensation of many beings present in the tiny living room. During the last period Mother Jennie was rarely fully awake, and she was barely able to speak above a hoarse whisper. She had to be carried like a baby, and was light as kindling -- little more than skin and bone.

Friday afternoon, February 27, I was sitting with her in the living room. I had brought her out to the couch, where she was sleeping. One of my University students had just arrived for a consultation with me and was standing outside the screen door saying "Hello."

Before I could stand up to let him in, Mother Jennie shot up into a sitting position, and in a firm, deep and almost masculine voice commanded, "Lewis, take your pen and write!"

I couldn't believe my eyes and ears. One moment she was dead to the world, unable to speak above a whisper, and the next she was speaking with the voice of the Teachers. She had been weak as a ruptured balloon, and now she was sitting up without effort, commanding me to take some kind of dictation from the Teachers!

Clearly this was something very important, and it was from the Teachers rather than Jennie. I told the student to sit for a while on the outside lounge. Grabbing my pen, I reached for the nearest thing to write on, which happened to be my paperback copy of the New English Bible. Mother Jennie began to dictate in clear, measured tones.

The message was a concise set of symbolic directions for me to meditate upon. I was to reveal the message to no one at the present time, and to avoid even discussing it with anyone. After meditating upon it and understanding it, I would receive and be able to use Mother Jennie's gifts of psychism. "Study this well in the Silence, and you will have something on which to build the present unknown. Do not discuss it at the present time, but meditate upon it and give thanks." I noted the time: 4:00 p.m.

Friday night passed fitfully. Mother had a bad night. I woke the next morning with a potent and foreboding pain in my throat, the sort that indicates the onset of a serious illness. Beverly arrived early, so I went home to bed. During the day I grew feverish and by Saturday evening was running 102⬚ø", which for me is very serious. My brains were scrambled and I couldn't get to the bathroom without clinging to a wall. I couldn't see straight, and my head was throbbing with pain. What is worse, Tess (my wife of three years) was coming down sick too.

Late that evening the telephone rang. It was the person staying with Jennie. She was slightly hysterical because the old woman was vomiting and asking to be taken to the hospital. Taken to the hospital! Jennie would never request such a thing unless she knew she were dying.

Since I couldn't get out of bed, let alone drive a car, I gave the woman who had telephoned another number where she could contact a Sister with a car. Speaking clearly and calmly, I gave her explicit directions on how to get Mother Jennie into Dominican Hospital as quickly as possible.

Mother went into the hospital and was hooked up to all kinds of life-sustaining equipment. Lucy, Mary and others were able to visit her the next morning while I lay in bed. A telephone call to the head nurse of Jennie's ward assured me that she was "stable," but I knew she was dying. At the same time my own illness had gotten even worse, and Tess had begun to run a high fever.

As the day passed my strength slipped away, and I felt the same way I had that night I'd "sent" Mother Jennie my own energy instead of letting her draw through me. My heart was weak and lapsing into fibrillation, and I couldn't move. The whole history of my relationship with Jennie seemed to pass through my fitful consciousness. I remembered the recurring dreams: always Jennie was in some kind of trouble and I'd be there to help her. She might be falling from a wall, and I would catch her. In other dreams she would be instructing me, but most of the time I dreamed of situations in which I was called upon to help the old woman.

Then I realized that somehow my illness was causally connected to her dying, and that if the causal connection weren't broken, I would be pulled into death with her. Was she somehow drawing from me in an unconscious way as her body fought to preserve its life? Or was I somehow "giving" the last of my strength to keep Jennie alive? I prayed to God and called upon the Great Ones of Orrilla to sever the connection between us so that God's strength would suffice for each of us. Immediately the fibrillation ceased and I lapsed into sleep.

Sometime before midnight Sunday, February 29, Robert called to tell me that Jennie had passed away peacefully. She had "died" at about 9:40 p.m., 30 minutes after I had prayed for release from the psychic bond that connected us.

Mother had given explicit directions that the executrix of her will wait for a period of three full days before cremating her body. She felt that the soul may retain an attachment to the body for as long as 72 hours after medical "death" has occurred. Mother had also left instructions for her funeral, which Mary Oliverio did her best to carry out.

I had recovered enough by Wednesday to drag myself out of bed and offer the benediction at Jennie's funeral. But after an hour my headache became severe and I was too weak to walk. Tess was too ill to attend, and her fever had reached 105□ø" on Monday evening. We were both bedridden until the end of March, and did not fully recover until the week of Passover and Easter in mid-April.

Tess was psychically sensitive. When I met her in 1972, a year after my separation from Ann, she was already extremely psychometric. She didn't know much about the phenomenology of psychism and was in an open, vulnerable state with no real control of her sensitivity. With guidance from Jennie and suggestions from me, she had gained excellent control of her talent. During her five years with Mother Jennie, Tess had forged a psychic bond with the old saint. When we were married in 1973, that bond became much stronger, since I was very close to Jennie. It was this psychic bond with Jennie we shared that had caused Tess to share my reaction to Mother Jennie's death struggle.

In retrospect, our mutual illness was a kind of initiation. During the Easter season we conceived the child we had wanted for three years. At that time I felt it right to share Jennie's last "message" to me with Tess, since I had been meditating upon it and begun to understand it. By the end of summer we were both able to put what we had learned into practice. Seven months after Jennie's passing I shared the "message" with Mary Oliverio, whom Mother had designated as her spiritual successor in the Sisterhood.

There are many more things that could be said, but let the future reveal them.

Mother Jennie was much more than a psychic medium. She was a prophetess of Christ. Like Elijah being fed by the ravens, she was cared for by the people around her. The final phase of her sanctified life was devoted to passing the precious Message on to the younger generation.

******* ******* *******

"I have been ordained by the Master Jesus to preach the Gospel which he taught and exemplified.

"It does not exclude the scriptural teachings of other ages, for in all times and places there have been enlightened ones to lighten the world and proclaim a degree of the Truth."

APPENDIX

The following poems and lessons represent only a small, random selection. Mother Jennie had reams of poetry and lessons from Omar and Savonarola. I have not been able to read even ten percent of that material.

The few major poems that appeared in my text of Jennie's life will not be reproduced here, Generally, what I have been able to collect for this Appendix reflects the earliest period with Omar. At Jennie's request, the selections represent biographical rather than poetic considerations.

CONTENTS

Major Poems:

A Call to Service

From Out the Deeps

How to Reach It, The Holy Grail

Fulfillment

Minor Poems:

Stoop But To Rise

Prayer

Poppies

Look Forward

In the Garden

Little Sunshine

Peace

Prose and Poetry From the Lessons of Omar:

A Meditation

A Vision

Meditation on the Unseen Guest

Omar's Lessons on the Psychic Work
(Selections)

Telegram Requesting Jennie's Clairvoyant Aid in Finding Body of Drowned Man

MAJOR POEMS

A CALL TO SERVICE
Spring, 1922

Come ye out from among them,
Come ye out, I say!
Stand forth in the light of the morning
And point out to them the Way;

Stand forth in the glorious sunshine,
The Christ Child is born within;
Lay down your heavy burdens
And turn from the pathways of sin.

The shadows are heavy around you,
The storm clouds heavy and dark.
But hark! What is that in the distance,
In the storm's fitful light -- a bark?

Yes, out in the tempest-tossed waters,
Alone -- a wreck in the waves?
Who dares to go to the rescue;
Who dares that frail bark to save?

149

Up springs the brave lighthouse keeper,
His lamps all shining and clear.
"I, through the waters of trouble
To rescue that bark will dare!

"In the height of that storm he struggles
His lifeboat to launch in the sea;
Will he -- ah! -- will he make it,
Or will efforts all futile be?

With a call to the angels above him
For strength in the time of his need,
He bravely bends oar to his struggle,
Guided truly by those who achieve!

At last, at last! he has made it;
He has reached that rudderless bark.
The rays from his lamps are now guiding
His Way -- and piercing the dark.

The storm-tossed weary traveler,
'Most swamped by the storms of night,
Looks up to see the bright radiance
Of a soul lit by heavenly Light.

He is breathing words of contrition
For the willfulness which brought him to err;
Now in the dim light of morning
He faintly hears songs of cheer.

They are coming nearer and nearer
To that safe shelter from storm,
Where Love Universal is clearer,
And new understanding is born.

For the rays from the lights trimmed and burning
Have traveled far out in the storm,
And guided a wanderer safely
To shelter and rest at home.

"Safe home, safe home!" said the Master,
"Beloved, thy task is well done.
Thou hast saved at least one of my children,
And thou now to me art a son

Of Righteousness and great splendor,
Tested and found to be true.
He who is faithful in small things,
A great task will faithfully do.

"Keep thyself one with the Father;
From the pleasures of life keep apart,
And thou shalt build mansions above thee,
And many shalt thou lead to start

Building bright homes for the future,
Who long have been living in sin,
And Peace, Love and Wisdom we'll give thee,
For thou has the Christ born within!"

FROM OUT THE DEEPS
(before 1925)

Wouldst find the Path that leads to the Holy Grail?
Follow the Light, that leads thee to the Trail.
Know thou thyself! Thou art then secure
To stand and, trembling, knock at the fast barred door.

Who knocketh at the door?" thou hear'st Him say,
"Stand and make known thy desires of this day!
Art ready, as this door shall be unbarred
To follow Him, and to obey His Word?"

Yea, follow Him I will, where'er He go,
On pathways high, or if He leads to low
Lands or valleys, or to mountains high,
I know He'll lead me up unto the sky

Where dwell in glorious splendor the great, vast throngs
Who thunder forth His melodies in sweetest songs;
Where all who truly know Him shall meet in bright array,
Clothed in their robes of spotless white, made pure along the Way.

For the road which leads to the Holy Grail
Is ofttimes steep and rough,
And many a weary traveler wails:
"My God! This is enough!

"Take from my shoulder the burdens, drear
Is my path, and hard to bear
The shadows heavy along the Way;
Take from me now the burdens, I pray!

"The answer comes in loving tones:
"Did'st choose the Way and then with moans
Cry out in terror on the Way
Along which thou must travel many a day?

"Know, travelers all who would step into Light:
The path thou must follow is only so bright
As the light in thy soul just so surely shines,
To brighten the shadows so oft in thy minds;

And as thou dost follow along the Way
Just where He hath led thee thou standest each day;
And as thou art willing to follow Him, so
In safety thou'lt travel from dark depths below,

Into the heights to which thou'lt aspire,
As thou travelest afar each day reaching higher,
Until thou shalt come to His own vast dominion
And find that within is the Kingdom of Heaven.

The Kingdom of Heaven, where dwelleth thy God,
Who chasteneth in Love, with rigid rod,
All who thus unto Him do sincerely aspire;
And thus are all souls brought safely up higher.

To rule there in Wisdom their own vast dominion,
To know that of such is the Kingdom of Heaven.
For all must unto Him as little ones come,
That He may thus lead them in safety home.

And with burdens heavy now laid at His feet,
They'll strive in the pathway all shadows to meet;
And seeing Him there shall know face to face
All who hath entered life's greatest race,

And seeing the Love Light shine in His eyes
Shall know He is watching, as all He doth prize;

For unto the Father, so unto the Son,
All who would enter must read and then run
The gauntlet of rear, doubt, trouble and pain,

And stumbling ofttimes must put effort again

Forth, to gain the great goal which in far distance awaits
All who will struggle and through greater Faith
Shall receive strength and knowledge, and so greater power
To enable them reach and hold the great Dower

Which is given to all who drink of the Cup,
Which he in His Love gives them to sup.
And so as ye follow the pathway, so dark
Seems the Way that the soul it doth hark

For the voice of him Who is leading the Way,
And listening will hear Him in tender voice say:
"All who would follow, in safety may go
Down in the valleys where the dark waters flow,
For He is leading, he knows well the Way,
And His Holy Purpose He'll show you some day.

"Just simply trust Him, and follow Him on
Through shadows so dark, until rising sun
Shall swallow up fast all shadows drear,
And, looking, you'll see that the Master is near,

Safe guiding his flock, who thus in strange lands
Know not the pattern of His divine plans,
To bring closer to Him the Children of the Earth,
That thus they may enter the Kingdom of Mirth.

For all who dwell thus safe in Heaven
Is joy, peace and plenty thus unto them given;
And as they have followed in safety they may
Look back and thus see many more on the Way.

And knowing the struggles in the quagmires of doubt,
May send forth the Word in a glorious shout
To encourage the travelers along the Way:
"Look up, and you'll see the Master today!

"For all who would reach to the Holy Grail
Must follow His Light along the Trail;
And as He hath thus bid them come
As little children, to follow home;

So through the darkened desert drear
Must they follow Him truly full many a year,

Until they shall hear: "The Goal is Won!
Step forth and share the glad Welcome Home!"

HOW TO REACH IT, THE HOLY GRAIL
[A continuation of From Out the Deeps]

Go -- ride thee on!
Thou hast the fight nigh won!
Press forward towards the Goal,
And there thou'lt find the Holy Grail.

What? Doubtest thou the battle's done?
Press onward in the day begun
At one with Him;Thyself and He
Shall soon make plain the Victory.

Would'st sing the song of the Holy Grail?
The effort of soul should never fail
To lead thee up on paths of Love,
Until thou hast reached the Realms above.

What matters it now, if on thy brow
Were drops of blood from soul's agony?
To find The Grail each soul must know
The darkness of its Gethsemane.

For through the drops upon thy brow
Thy soul is purged from sin's dark stain;
And as the Love Divine thou'lt know,
So too thou'lt know that loss is gain.

For who would dare to reach the Goal
Must cleansed be from every stain,
And purified in mind and soul
If on the pathway would remain.

Oh! -- go thou on from sorrow's cup
And drink the wine that lifts thee up
To realms divine, so bright and fair,
Which thou wilt see when thou art near

To the Great Goal of every soul,
Along the Pathway so long foretold,
Which must be followed by all who'd see
The Holy Grail in its Mystery.

FULFILLMENT
(February 2, 1928)

Canst thou not see? Hast thou not heard --
 Fulfillment of His promised Word?
That they who run shall ever see
The solving of Life's mystery?

What is this mystery to thee?
A wave so great upon Life's sea,
That rising in the sight of man
Shall give him glimpse of Life's great plan,

Bringing to Him each child of earth
As they rejoice in a new birth
To spirit realms so pure and free,
Where they may solve Life's mystery.

And coming 'pon the greater plan
Where God reveals the soul to man,
Each one who to Him doth aspire
Must tested be -- to reach up higher.

Where in those realms divinely fair
They too shall learn to do and dare:
E'en losing all of earth's estate,
That thus they may from dark and hate
Come into glorious Light supreme,
And see the realm where late hath been
Enacted in the bowers of earth
A play so great -- it hath been worth

Far more than man in his estate
Can gather -- in this dark world's hate
As he enfolded -- thus hath been
Enveloped -- from the greater sheen

So blinded by the world's great light,
He hath been dazzled by the sight,
And turned from Love to path of hate
Where he hath wandered, and where late

He hath thus seen his brother man

Fulfilling this life's greater plan,
Where all who look and do and dare
May with their brothers fully share

All that is gained by soul within,
Gathered in travail from paths of sin,
Into the Light, where souls who aspire
May see the Way, which leads up higher

Into the realms so vast and fair
Where they may see as they enter there;
And coming at last to their own dominion
Shall find that it is the Kingdom of Heaven.

The Kingdom of Heaven where dwelleth Thy God,
Who chasteneth all with rigid rod;
For His Law is unbending, all souls to save,
Who see the wave, and then will brave
The wrath of Life's angry stormy sea
To succor a brother whom they may see
In peril and danger great -- so dire
The need of a hand to lift up higher;

And so in the angry sea is cast
The anchor strong which shall make fast
And hold in the harbor -- the ship to save
Which is tossed and tried in the foaming wave,

And coming at last to the harbor true
Shall know that the Light which e'er shines blue
Is the symbol of Truth from spirit fair
Which endeavors to do and thus will dare

All -- for the sake of Truth -- to keep
The pastures safely, wherein His sheep
May in shelter safe enabled to stand
And shine forth His Light to every land.

This then we say: Canst thou not see?
Hast thou not solved this great mystery?
Canst thou not learn from lessons given
The way to know His servants from Heaven?

Canst thou not see the souls who brave
The anger of the threatening wave,
To throw out the lifeline upon the dark see

To brothers -- thus solving Life's mystery?

Oh, thou who art blind, restore thy sight,
That thou mayest receive in sorrow's dark night
The comfort of Spirit, freeing from pain,
That thou mayest see thy brother again,

And standing together to do and to dare,
Shall know no more sorrow, as all then will share
In the Light of the Morning,, in risen sun
Shall step forth and know His work is begun,

As souls once in Unity shall now again see
The solving of one of Life's mysteries.
Go thou within and then compare
The incidents many of yesteryear;

Look then without, and there thou wilt find
That which doth hold thee and shadow the mind,Withholding the Power to which ye aspire,
Traveling after each day to reach higher,

And as we see the endeavor to do
That which is right and just to a few,
So do ye know that time will outlast,
And in making amends for errors long past,

The souls will be freed, gaining greater Light
Which shall enable them step from night;
And all looking up shall once again see,
'T'is Love which solveth Life's mystery.

Thou'rt writing a book! -- the pages are turned.
What of the past? Thou thinkest it's burned?
Nay! The book which thou thinkest thou'rt writing anew
Is but a page forward, on which thou wilt strew

The Message so great which is given to thee,
Helping to solve Life's mystery
And so -- as thou'lt know that daybreak is past,
Thy soul it shall see and know then at last.'

T'was bathed in the glare of Mara's great light,
Which blinded thy vision and wounded thy sight;
And turned from the pathway which thou hadst gained,

Has led thee through swamps, where thou hast feigned

The Pathway of Light to follow afar
Bringing thee out to where the shadows are,
Made by the Light Illusive, and glare
Shows not the danger awaiting thee there.

But thy soul's reaching upward hath brought to thine aid
Messengers heavenly, endeavoring to save
Each child from the sorrow and want and care
Which comes unto all who tarry there.

And so, as ye write in the page of the book,
Pause -- look -- and listen, for Voice which will brook
Of no interference, and which on the Way
will lead each child to a more perfect day;

And bringing them out and up and on,
They shall see the work which hath nobly been done,
And through understanding shall gain greater sight
Of paths leading souls from darkness of night

Into the Light, to which souls aspire
Traveling afar, each day reaching higher,
Until they shall come to their own vast dominion,
And find that within in the Kingdom of Heaven;

Thus knowing He works all souls to save
Shall make taut the ropes, enfolding the sails,
And ships coming in from the travel of night
Shall rest in the harbor, glittering, bright.

And looking out on the stormy sea
Shall say: "O Father, we give unto Thee
Thanksgiving and praise that thus have we learned
Our books in the past have not now been burned!

"But enabled to turn to a page of the past
May see there the sorrow, from which at last
A lesson of life hath been fully learned,
And to a new page we now gladly have turned.

Enable us pray, in letters of Fire
To write there the message: O souls looking higher,
Wait! 'til the glamor of new things hath burned,

And then in the crucible the dross will be turned

Into pure gold of living fire
As each one will see, and never will tire
In standing, waiting, for storm at sea
To pass -- thus solving a mystery.

And taut and trim, with sails unfurled,
Thou shalt put forth to a waiting world;
And guided safe by Voice above
Shall know thou'rt folded in His great Love.

And coming thus to do His Will,
Shall say to them, just: "Peace! Be still!
"And waiting 'til the glamor's passed
Shall know He doeth well. At last

The Light will break, and in day ye'll stand
Working together -- a stronger band.
For souls in freedom thus shall see
'T'was but one more great mystery.

"According to Hoyle it is not done!"
That is conception of minds, but one!
But traitors e'er their price will pay
To lead souls seeking Light astray.

And thus, "The heavenly helpers," we
Inscribe their names, that each may see
In message for self a greater power
Than they had known until this hour.

Again thou wilt say: "It is not done!"
A still, small voice has but begun
To be heard from a servant true
Who thus in danger, was led to do

Their will, in the plan which is at last
FULFILLED, an the darkness is almost passed.
Betrayers all, their prices paid,
In things done, felt and said.

And so we say: As thou dost see
In the Way of Life's great mystery,
The Price is paid -- ambition's curse

Fills the heart, mind and purse.

So the Betrayer's work is done
And soul from the Light is surely won.
Canst thou not see? Thus hast thou heard
This which we give thee now in word.

The Teacher whom we brought to thee
In Mara's light thou couldst not see.
And one who endeavored to reach up higher
Thou -- in thy blindness -- trod in the mire.

And so when the journey is fully run
We say unto thee: In duty well done
Strength is thus gained, the Goal to reach,
And words are given with which to teach

The Gospel of Love; Brothers true
Shall strive in the Path all tasks to do,
Guided aright by the Brothers who gave
Their lives, from the earth the many to save,

And souls who are tried and thus found true
Are given the strength and power to do
His Will, as He leads them in perfect Way;
And now we will say a glad Good-day!

And as we leave thee this great day,
Once more we reiterate what men shall say:
"According to Hoyle it is not done!"
But they must pay their PriceTo the Betrayer -- Nobly won!

At soul's great Sacrifice!

MINOR POEMS

STOOP BUT TO RISE
(October 30, 1925)

Stoop but to rise,
And yet again to conquer
All thou hast been or seen
In days gone by;

The Light is come,
The shadows flee before it,
And Love shall sing to thee
Sweet lullaby.

Fear not, dear child,
For duty now awaits thee,
The duties for which
Thou hast been prepared:

Step forward bravely,
Climb to heights supernal,
And Joy shall come
To take the place of tears.

We come to tell thee
That we're standing near thee,
New hope, new courage
To inspire thee we bring;

Ope up thy soul,
The Light is shining for thee,
And let the praise
In joyful anthems ring.

Ring out the Truth!
A weary world is waiting
For Light and power
Which sets the captives free!

Go forward bravely
To the tasks awaiting,
We will sustain

And hand in hand shall be.

PRAYER
(September 16, 1924)

From day to day
Lord, teach us how to pray
"Thy will be done."

It may not seem to us 't'is best,
But help us to pray,
And then to rest
Securely in Thy Love.

For Thou dost know each soul's great need,
And Thou wilt give what's best indeed
In this our daily bread.

And as we come thus nearer to
The Father in Heaven and Mother true,
No matter what there may betide,
He will for each soul, full provide.

And giving daily without stint,
Will let no word, or thought or hint
Turn any soul aside,
From the pathway Light
Which will make more bright
The shadows of the way
Which leads from day to night,
In which we're sheltered from heat of sun,

And as we see each day's begun
With aspiration sweet,
O give us grace and power to see:
"Thy Will is done on earth, through me,
As it is done in Heaven;"
And Light shall shine of risen Son.

POPPIES
(March 30, 1922)

Beautiful poppies with colors of gold,
Showing more beauty as their petals unfold.
Each evening they close as the sun's day is run,

Each morning unfolding as the day is begun.

So quietly opening each petal so wide,
Their sheen as of silk is a glory beside
The leaves of soft green, so lacy and rare,
A beauty so great no tongue can compare.

Their hearts pale and slender are deeply enshrined
In the cups of gold, which a simple mind
May liken to thorns 'neath a crown of gold,
Which a Savior bore in the years of old.

Beneath all this radiance is a touch of black
Which brings one's thoughts to the end of life's track.
To the time of the harvest when the seeds shall bear,
In apparent death, life's germ so dear.

Under all is the cup, with its delicate rim,
As though their life's blood were held within,
Supporting the blossoms on its slender stem
To hold their beauties to the eyes of men.

Oh, the lessons we may learn from the poppies of gold,
As each day their beauty to the world they unfold!
So quietly their tasks are performed each day,
Until death gently shakes each petal away.

LOOK FORWARD
(November 23, 1921)

Let the past be buried
With all its shadows and strife;
Set your eyes to the future,
Towards everlasting life.

This life is full of sorrow,
And trials and despair,
But there is a bright tomorrow
Awaiting us -- over there.

So while we travel this pathway,
Look up towards the Light;
It will help you carry your burdens
As day passes on to the night.

And when this life's path is ended,
And its shadows are passing away,
We can give to the world our lessons,
That brought us from night into day.

IN THE GARDEN
(September 20, 1921)

The sun shone o'er the hilltop
On the house so dull and gray,
As I walked in the garden
On a bright summer's day.

The roses were all blooming,
The phlox and daisies too;
The violets so humble,
The lilies wet with dew.

The hollyhocks in their beauty
Sedately standing by,
Like sentinels doing duty
With a bright and faithful eye.

Thus it is in Life's garden --
The shadows, storm and rain
But bring us to the flowers,
And the harvest of golden grain.

LITTLE SUNSHINE
(November 16, 1925. Dictated in trance at a meeting. Little Sunshine was an Indian girlfriend of Rosa Lee, one of Jennie's Teachers.)

I'm just a little sunshine,
I come to spread the Light,
To chase away the shadows
And make all things seem bright.

I come so bright and early
That you may know 't'is I

Who brings the greater Sunshine
To make sore bright your eye.

I draw so closely to you
At early dawn of day,
And when the shadows leave you
I'm shining on your way.

You welcome Little Sunshine
And the darling Rosa Lee,
Who gladly brought me to you
Where I will always be.

So when the shadows hover
Around you on your way,
Why, call for Little Sunshine
And 't'will be bright as day!

For together we are watching
And waiting to help you,
And so we greet you gladly --
We'll help your dreams come true,

To brighten up the pathway
And lead them into Light,
And souls shall shine with radiance
And many hearts be light.

For days are coming nearer
When many more shall see
The Truth which you do carry,
And weary souls shall be

Liften from darkest shadow,
Into the Light of day;
This we promise to you,
So now we are on our way.

We'll always help you truly,
So bravely strive to win,
And Rosa Lee and Sunshine
Will always enter in

To help you in the Temple,
To brighten up the home;

But more than all, the others
Will gladly bid us come.

To the Doctor Lady:

Our blessing comes to you, Dear,
And soon the shadows flee,
As nearer comes our Sunshine
And darling Rosa Lee.

PEACE

(November 24, 1922, C. 1970, Jennie Hopkins Peterson Maiereder)

Stay! Stay! thou maddened empires, stay!
Stay thy hands,
Which doth relentlessly cast away
Earth's glories grand
In these and other lands.

What wouldst thou have in this benighted day?
Earth's glories fade,
Its beauties soon will pass away.
Anger and fight,
Doth but pass on to night;
Each day, bringing a new way
To teach us RIGHT.
And so to lead our foes
From hate and darkness
Into that most glorious LIGHT

Of LOVE DIVINE and PERFECT UNDERSTANDING,
Which doth give us Sight
To see the folly of our puerile struggle
To overcome and sway the wills of others,
Who from that Soul within
Must cast out all of sin

And stand alone for the fiercest of all fights --
Self to conquer, and so to see
That man's first duty is to that Soul within:
And there to kindle in a flame so bright
The TRUTH that shall make him live aright,

And shall bring PEACE -- where even all was strife!
And LOVE -- shall still those ravening hordes
Who late were thirsting for their fellows' blood.

PROSE AND POETRY
FROM THE LESSONS OF OMAR

Received in the silent hour of meditation from 9 a.m. to 10 a.m., September 20, 1927. -- J.H.P.

This shall be called CONSOLATION, inscribed to all those weary souls who, while struggling through the darkness of the way to find the brighter Way, seem to be enveloped in a dark morass of doubt and fear; and yet still knowing that The Way is near -- struggle still onward with greater hope -- letting the Light they have shine forth to others they may meet upon the way. And so we say to all such weary travelers on The Way -- read, mark, learn -- and inwardly digest this MYSTIC TRUTH.

O.X. and Others of the Celestial Way.

Sit down, O child, and write as we will give unto thee -- TRUTH!!!

This day thou shalt see that we -- thy Teachers -- are around thee in power and strength to do His Will -- and to build a mighty monument to Him -- from realms of Living Fire -- for as each soul shall study life anew -- so shalt there come a revelation true of that which now they are and that from which they may obtain -- all -- that will help them reach and gain the TRUTH which makes men free.

And as this life shall still seem more of a mystery, we strive to give thee true, the message which from Heaven's own blue shall penetrate within and there thus coming to the soul of Him -- Who dwells in secret shrine -- shall open wide the door and let thus shine The Light of His Beloved Son -- Whom thou shalt then hear say -- "Well done, thou good and faithful servant true -- enter and partake of Living Waters too," and then thou'lt forward go, on the pathway here below, leading thee to greater height, as thou shalt travel forward in the Light --

 The Light of understanding great -- which brings thee from the realm of dark and hate -- where souls who true aspire -- to reach and climb to realms up higher, receive from Soul of Him -- the daily Bread which thus shall nourish them: and give them strength so great -- to overcome the weakness which late hath bound soul of them ...

[The poem continues for 20 more single-spaced typewritten pages.]

A VISION

[On July 17, 1928, Mother Jennie had a vision: "There was a glorious light, and these white-robed figures with their hands upraised. And in that vibrant tone of joy and accomplishment, these were the words I heard:"]

It is, it is
God's greatest gift to man,
The concept given to mortals
Fulfilling His great Plan.

MEDITATION ON THE UNSEEN GUEST

[No date given. Jennie explains that people used to have a little sampler over the dining room table saying that Christ is the Head of this household. He is also the Unseen Guest at every meal:"]

[Omar:] Dost realize what this might mean in its greater fullness, by understanding the working of a mighty Law to absolve each soul of errors from the forgotten past? Go thou into the Silence and we will there reveal unto thee that which shall teach thee of all that is within thyself. Go thou into Peace, and Silence shall reveal unto thee thy Soul, in the essence of which is emanating that Power of the Life Divine, bringing thee unto greater Light, and enabling thee to radiate a greater light unto men.

Be thou then satisfied to fortify thyself against the unseen enemy, to build well around thee an outer wall through which nought can penetrate but that which thy Soul accepts and welcomes in its advance upon the Citadel where Christ should reign in regal splendor upon his throne, which thou hast made by sincere endeavor to win over self a victory. Be thou on thy guard that no enemy lurking near may find entrance, and we assure thee that in the Feast Which awaits thee, thy senses unchained, thy vision clear, thou wilt see the radiant Light of the Divine Son, the Sun in Truth of a brighter morning Who shall be at the Head of the Household -- the Unseen Guest at every meal.

And for this we have prepared thee that thou mayest go forth unto men a Power in His Might to send forth a greater light in the knowledge of the Truth Eternal.

Be at peace. We speak unto thee. Know that all is well. All thy needs shall be supplied. This we pledge thee with right hand upraised and extended forth as evidence and emblem of our troth. Peace be unto all men. Fare thee well.

Omar, thy Teacher and thy friend.

OMAR'S LESSONS ON PSYCHIC WORK
CHAPTER ONE, MAY 2, 1929

Now we will write another book showing that we can come to others who are channels and given through them our Message.

We come now to the early stages of scientific study of the afterlife. There are many laws governing the communication between the two worlds. First the Law of Transmission, then the Law of Reception, and again the Law of Translation. This means a preparation of our forces, and in order to direct there must be concentration, for scattered forces have not much power, being like an army disorganized by the loss of common order, so that we must necessarily obey the Law to concentrate, centralize and consolidate our forces, when we may then consciously direct or utilize them in the manner which seems best.

How many people on earth are there who fully recognize this necessity in their daily lives? Not many, or there would be more accomplished in the ordinary life than there is today, with less hurry and confusion, and consequently less error. This is a never-ending source of loss, and when recognized will be converted into steady gain.

So we consolidate our force and bring it to bear upon an individual who is sensitive enough to respond to it, and intelligent enough to write what we direct by that breathing forth through the power of the mind and its reception by them. At times it becomes a necessity to direct and exert a tremendous force in and through the arm, as explained in the last book, in order that the instrument may realize that an entity or person (individual would be better) desires them to use the hand and write. This is a different method from the automatic writing, where one directs the force into the hand and arm, consciously directing the writing of the words by the actual motion of the hand. But in this instance the impression is made upon the hand only, while in the present case it is made upon the mind.

So we see distinction and difference between the two methods, but both are good, excepting that a greater amount of concentration is necessary by the latter method, both by the recipient and the giver -- making it a conscious effort or task. This, then, is accomplished, as at this present time, by the Laws referred to in the beginning: Concentration, Centralization, Consolidation. So the message is given forth in apparent ease, and yet not without the cost of effort.

Try it, in giving but your own messages to the world, and watch results. We are eager to help you carry the message of Truth to a waiting world. See what greater results are secured by this method.

I am permitted by the Teacher to give you this instruction, that you might be awakened to the greater possibilities which are within your soul, and as you go out upon your new tasks, you may rest assured that we are with you to give of the help that we can bring, enabling you to give the Message more fully to mankind.

So we leave with you our message and our love in the scientific rendering of messages.

CHAPTER TWO, MAY 2, 10:15 P.M.

We will proceed to receiving a message. Concentrate upon the individual, centralizing the attention upon the facts presented. Consolidate them all together, and then you will have identity of the communicator, with sufficient data to convince the one communicated with, or at least to give them deep thought and desire for further search.

Simple as this may seem to be, the power is attained only by constant remembrance to practice what is here outlined. Concentrate your energy. Centralize your thought upon the individual, and then Consolidate the facts presented, letting neither doubt nor fear intrude upon you. Then bravely state what you have received, quietly but firmly reassuring your hearer of its truth. For such you will find it to be.

A quiet waiting until all the facts are presented will furnish a medium whereby you will receive more -- in many instances it being necessary to collect and collate the data to be given, and this means time, where impatience or a straining at the gates breaks the necessary conditions, bringing ofttimes failure or incompleteness of a message, which otherwise would have been fully rendered, bringing hope and radiating its cheer to those who wait unceasingly for that which will give to them the final proof of continued life of their loved ones, and the power to return and communicate with knowledge and understanding of their problems and with sketches of their lives beyond the veil, with a description of their surroundings.

This is all for tonight. Thank you. 10:45 p.m.

TELEGRAM REQUESTING JENNIE'S CLAIRVOYANT AID IN FINDING BODY OF DROWNED MAN

Kalispell, Montana, June 1, 1936

Mrs. Peterson Macreder, Nice, California

WHERE CAN FIND BODY OF BROTHER-IN-LAW stop DROWNED IN RIVER YESTERDAY stop WIRE ANSWER COLLECT

Mrs. Pearl Giebe Roos   12 p.m.

[Jennie's vision led them to find the body, which had snagged under a submerged tree several miles from the site of the drowning.]

XXX
XXX

17327931R00099

Printed in Great Britain
by Amazon